THE WHOLE TRUTH
AND NOTHING BUT

Other Books by Hedda Hopper

FROM UNDER MY HAT

The Whole Truth and Nothing But

HEDDA HOPPER
and
JAMES BROUGH

1963

DOUBLEDAY & COMPANY, INC.
GARDEN CITY, NEW YORK

DEDICATION

To my son, Bill, who never took
any sass from his mother
and never gave her any.

I'm told that when you write a book with a title like this, you must let your readers know something about your life. Well, I was born into the home of David and Margaret Furry, one of nine children. Seven of us grew up. Three of us are still here, including my sister Margaret and brother Edgar, who played a good game of football when he attended Lafayette quite a while back.

I first saw the light of day in Hollidaysburg, Pennsylvania, a beautiful suburb of Altoona, which used to live off the Pennsylvania Railroad and its affiliates. Since railroads have fallen on lean and hungry years, I don't know what's feeding the place today.

My mother, an angel on earth whom I worshiped, named me Elda, from a story she was reading at the time. Years later, after I'd married DeWolf Hopper, a numerologist changed Elda to Hedda. My husband, Wolfie, was much older than my father and had been married four times before. The wives' names all sounded pretty much the same: Ella, Ida, Edna, and Nella. His memory wasn't as sharp as it had been, and he couldn't always remember that I was Elda.

As time went on, this started to irk me, so the numerologist came up with *Hedda* Hopper. I asked how much. "Ten dollars." That's exactly how it happened; it changed my whole life. It was the best bargain I ever made. Wolfie never forgot it, and I've never regretted it.

My sister Margaret was my father's pet. He and I didn't get on well. He thought women should be the workers; I believed my brothers should share the burden. Mother was ill for six years after Margaret's birth, and I took on her duties as well as my own, since my older sister Dora had married. I had to catch a brother by the scruff of the neck to get any help, but they all helped themselves three times a day to the meals I prepared. I also did the washing, ironing, cleaning, and helped Dad in his butcher shop.

When I couldn't take it any more, I ran away—to an uncle in New York. I found a stage door that was open, walked in, and got a job in a chorus, which started a career.

My family now consists of my son Bill, who plays Paul Drake on the "Perry Mason" TV show without any help from me. When he went off to war, he'd already attained stature as an actor. On his return—with a medal for valor which I've never seen—not one soul in the motion-picture industry offered him a job. Hell would have frozen over before I'd have asked anyone for help for a member of my family.

So Bill went to work selling automobiles for "Madman" Muntz. One day he woke up to the fact that he was an actor, got himself a part with director Bill Wellman in *The High and the Mighty*—and asked Wellman not to tell anybody who his mother was. Bill has a beautiful daughter, Joan, who'll be sixteen next birthday.

I don't like to dwell on death, but when you reach my age (and I'm still not telling) you realize it's inevitable. I've left instructions for cremation—no ceremony—with my ashes sent to an undertaking cousin, Kenton R. Miller, of Martinsburg, Pennsylvania. I'd wanted a friend to scatter them over the Pacific from a plane, but California law forbids that. You have to buy a plot.

A salesman from Forest Lawn told me they'd opened a new section and I could rest in peace next to Mary Pickford for a mere $42,000. "What do I get for that?" I asked.

"Well, a grave, picket fence, and a golden key for the gate."

"How do you figure I could use it?"

"Oh, Miss Hopper, that's for the loved ones who will mourn you."

That's when I decided on my cousin.

One

I knew Elizabeth Taylor was about to dump Eddie Fisher in favor of Richard Burton soon after *Cleopatra* started filming in Rome. Because in forty years in Hollywood I've told the truth—though sometimes only in part for the sake of shielding someone or other—I wrote the story. This was in February 1962, one week before the news burst like a bomb on the world's front pages.

But Elizabeth, Burton, and I have something in common: Martin Gang, a top-notch attorney, has us as clients. He saw my column, as usual, before it appeared, and came on the telephone in a hurry. "Oh, you couldn't print that," he said. "It would be very embarrassing for me to sue you, since I represent all three."

I was in Hollywood at the time, not in Rome, so I was wanting the firsthand information, the personal testimony, which would be important in self-defense. I deferred to his judgment—and kicked myself for doing it when the news from the Appian Way began to sizzle.

I've known Elizabeth since she was nine years old, innocent and lovely as a day in spring. I liked, and pitied, her from the start, when her mother, bursting with ambition, brought her to my house one day to have her sing for me. Mrs. Sara Taylor was an actress from Iowa who had appeared just twice on Broadway before she married Francis Taylor, who worked for his uncle, Howard Young, as a manager of art galleries on both sides of the Atlantic. When World War II came along, she was in raptures to find herself with a beautiful young daughter, living right next door to Hollywood—her husband came to manage the gallery in the Beverly Hills Hotel.

Sara Taylor had never gotten over Broadway. She wanted

9

to have a glamorous life again through her child. She had the idea at first that Elizabeth could be turned into another Deanna Durbin, who had a glittering name in those days. "Now sing for Miss Hopper," she commanded her daughter as soon as our introductions were over and we were sitting by the baby grand in my living room.

"Do you play the accompaniment?" I asked. "I can't."

"No, but she can sing without any. Elizabeth!"

It struck me as a terrifying thing to ask a little child to do for a stranger. But in a quivering voice, half swooning with fright, this lovely, shy creature with enormous violet eyes piped her way through her song. It was one of the most painful ordeals I've ever witnessed.

I remembered seeing the four-room cottage—simple to the point where water had to be heated on the kitchen stove—in which Elizabeth was born. Little Swallows was its name, and it sat in the woods of her godfather, Victor Cazelet; his English estate, Great Swifts, was in Kent. She had a pony there and grew to love animals like her chipmunk, "Nibbles," which ran up my bare arm when she brought it around on a visit one day. I screamed like a banshee, but Elizabeth was as patronizing as only a schoolgirl can be.

"It's only a chipmunk; it won't hurt you," she promised scornfully.

You couldn't have wished for a sweeter child. She would certainly have been happier leading that simple life close to woods and wild things to be tamed, maybe through all her years. But her mother had been bitten by the Broadway bug, and few women recover from that.

Once the family was settled in Hollywood, Mrs. Taylor maneuvered the support of J. Cheaver Cowden, a big stockholder in Universal Pictures, to get a contract for her daughter at that studio. Elizabeth was there for one year, but studio chieftains always resent anybody who's brought in over their heads through front-office influence. They made sure the girl got nowhere fast. Her mother tried everything to find her another job, but it was her father who happened to land her at

MGM through a chance remark he made to producer Sam Marx when they were patrolling their beat together as fellow air raid wardens. She was given a bit in *Lassie Come Home*, then blossomed in *National Velvet* with Mickey Rooney.

I remember the day she cinched in her belt, which showed her charms to perfection, and Mickey turned to me and said: "Why, she is a woman."

"She is fourteen," I replied. He started toward her. I caught him by the seat of the pants. "Lay a hand on her, and you will have to answer to me. She is a child."

He looked hard at me and said, "I believe you would beat me up."

"I sure would."

Victor Cazelet, on a wartime mission for the British Government to New York, wanted desperately to get to California to see the godchild he adored. Though he was a millionaire in his homeland, strict currency controls meant that he hadn't any dollars to pay the fare. He was staying as a house guest of Mrs. Ogden Reid, owner of the New York *Herald Tribune* in those days, but he had qualms about borrowing from her.

When he telephoned me, I had what I thought was a brain wave: "What about Victor Sassoon? He's rich as Croesus, and he's holed up through the war at the Garden of Allah." I wanted to call him at that exotic sanctuary on the Sunset Strip, where the likes of Scott Fitzgerald, Robert Benchley, and Humphrey Bogart used to frolic before it was demolished to make way for Bart Lytton's bank.

"He doesn't do anything for anybody," Victor warned me, but I couldn't be convinced until I spoke to Sassoon myself. Lend Cazelet dollars just to visit his godchild? "Certainly not," growled the old tightwad. "He's got plenty of money of his own."

So I booked Victor into the Ebell Theatre in Los Angeles to give a lecture to earn his passage money west. He stayed with the Taylors for a week, which was the last he saw of Elizabeth. Several months later the Nazis shot down the plane he was in, believing that Winston Churchill was aboard. They were halfway right. Victor was on a mission for his friend Winston Churchill.

I remember Elizabeth visiting my house with Jean Simmons when she was on her way back from the South Seas and the filming there of *Blue Lagoon*. They sat together on the long settee in the den, bright as birds and chattering nineteen to the dozen. I thought I had never seen two more beautiful young girls.

As the years went by, I saw Elizabeth through many romances and four marriages, starting with Nicky Hilton. He was a boy, and I don't believe he'd had too much experience. On their European honeymoon he left her too much alone, though everyone wanted to meet his beautiful bride. When she came home, she took a second-story apartment in Westwood with a back entrance on an alley. Before she had a chance to sort out what had happened to her, the parade of suitors began—married men, stars. Did any of them love her and try to help? No. They used her. I'm making no excuses for her, but I'm trying to be objective.

Then she was put into another picture. She was exhausted from working too hard and too fast in the rat race on the sound stages. She was swamped with advice from everybody. She couldn't tell true from false. Thus it went from one man to another, one picture to another, until she fell in love with Michael Wilding, who was twenty years older than she. Was she unconsciously looking for a strong father? She loved her own, but he didn't stand up to his wife.

Mike and Stewart Granger were pals and playmates; had been for years. Each married beautiful young girls—Stewart had his eyes on Jean Simmons when she was fifteen. Elizabeth sat on my settee again the night she came in with Michael Wilding. Stewart and I had exchanged some words over the telephone before Michael and Liz arrived.

"You're not coming here with them," I said flatly, "and if you do, you won't be let in. I have nothing to say to you. I want to talk to her." That was that. So two, not three of them, knocked at the front door.

What was to be said was for their ears only. "Elizabeth, I don't think you know what you're getting into. In the first place, he's too old for you. And the rumor around town is that Michael Wilding and Stewart Granger are very, very close."

She blushed deep red. "It couldn't be!"

There was one fair question to ask, and I asked it. "Are you denying it, Michael?" He sat there with eyes downcast.

I turned to Liz. "Are you going to marry a man like that? Do you know what kind of life you'll have?" He should have got up and hit me, but he sat still.

"I love him," she exclaimed.

"You don't know what love is. You don't know what you're talking about. He's sophisticated, he's gracious, but I beg you not to marry him."

She didn't listen then or later. She drove Wilding into marriage. "I *am* too old for you," he'd argue. "It will never last, Elizabeth."

"I love you, and you're going to marry me, that's all," she would say.

The Wildings and the Grangers lived together in Hollywood for a few months. British men like to drink—it's part of their daily diet—and the girls learned how. Then Mike left for England and Liz followed him. From that marriage came two sons, Michael and Christopher. After each birth she had to go to work too soon. Before she could face the cameras, she had to take off pounds in a hurry, just as Judy Garland did, and it weakened her health.

Mike was given a contract at Metro, her studio, but when it ran out it wasn't renewed. During this time she bought two homes, the second because the first wasn't big enough for two children, a nurse, and Mike's eighty-six-year-old father, whom she brought over from England to stay with them. The studio paid for both houses, deducting the money from her salary, which was standard practice.

I knew the marriage was over when Mike started to criticize her in public—before strangers, before anyone. She never stopped working. She was a lady, America's queen of queens, who loved her children and was a good mother to them.

She played in *Giant* with Jimmy Dean, whom she respected and loved like a brother. His senseless death shattered her nerves. Her director, George Stevens, was mad about her and had been since she made *A Place in the Sun* for him.

I saw her on her good days and bad. In *Raintree County* and *Suddenly, Last Summer*, she got to know Montgomery Clift and admired him. Then he raced his car down the hill from her home after a drinking bout with Wilding there, ran into a telegraph pole, and nearly died. Elizabeth sped after him, crawled into the wrecked car, and held his head in her lap until the ambulance arrived. Soaked with blood, she rode to the hospital with him and stayed long enough to know that he'd live.

Then along came Michael Todd, who taught her an awful lot about love and living. He was one of the most sophisticated and ruthless men in show business. He had gone through the jungle of Broadway and come out with many scars.

After Mike had made *Around the World in Eighty Days*, he wanted someone to help sell it. Who else but the queen of the movies? I don't think he needed her more than she needed him, but they fell in love, and he taught her everything he knew about sex, good and bad. He proposed to her in the office MGM gave him at the studio when he was shooting *Around the World*. He said: "Elizabeth, I love you, and I'm going to marry you, and from now on you'll know nobody but me." Only he didn't say "know."

They were married in Mexico, and they started one of the craziest, fightingest, most passionate love matches recorded in modern times. She appeared in the newspapers and magazines every day, every issue. Every facet of their lives was exploited for the benefit of love-starved fans. Gold poured into the box office for her pictures and his *Around the World*.

He bought her the world, or as much of it as he could lay hands on: a new jewel or a half dozen of them every Satur-

14

day; a plane; a villa in France; dresses by the hundred. Whatever she wanted, she got. He knew he was spoiling her rotten, but he loved to see her face light up when she saw his presents. For the Academy Award show where he expected her to collect an Oscar for *Raintree County*, he bought her a diamond tiara. "Hasn't every girl got one?" he asked blandly. He gave her a Rolls-Royce and a $92,000 diamond ring.

"Don't spoil her," I told him time and again. "She's impossible enough already."

In return she gave him a daughter. Her pregnancy was heralded like Queen Elizabeth's or Princess Margaret's. She had an operation that almost took her life. She has two vertebrae in her back that came from a bone bank. I didn't know about that until she told me. The baby arrived, Liza, a dark-eyed witch who at three months could read your mind.

Mike used to say: "If you want to be a millionaire, live like one." For the London opening of his picture, Elizabeth was draped in a ruby-and-diamond necklace, with bracelet and earrings to match. It was an occasion straight out of the Arabian Nights.

In London for all the high jinks, I watched Eddie Fisher's maneuvers to pay court to Elizabeth in the enormous suite at the Dorchester where Mr. and Mrs. Michael Todd were registered. Debbie lingered in the Fisher suite several floors below. I had missed Elizabeth and Mike like the dickens when they left Hollywood in advance. They made me promise I'd be in London with them for the *Around the World* hullabaloo.

When I checked into the hotel, there was a message from Mike inviting me to see them. I unpacked, changed, then went on up to the top floor, which was taken up entirely by their double suite. I happened to walk first into Liz's half. There she sat, bulgingly pregnant in a white lace robe, with her bare feet on a coffee table, drinking Pimm's No. 1 from a pitcher at her side, with the diamond tiara hanging out of a pasteboard box.

I left Elizabeth and went into Mike's suite. He was talking

to four of the most prominent newspaper publishers in London about the opening of the picture, and they were laying out the seating of the theater, since royalty would attend. Crawling around the floor were Elizabeth's two sons, picking caviar sandwiches off a low table and stuffing themselves. I gathered the children up, took them back to Liz, and closed the door firmly. Just then Eddie Fisher came in to pay his respects to Liz. He was in and out all the time.

Mike was frantically busy with two spectacular shows to put on, on the screen for his premiere and at Battersea Festival Gardens, where he threw a champagne-and-fun-fair shindig for two thousand people to celebrate his picture, scoring a triumph that gave him every front page in London, except *The Times.*

He gave us plastic raincoats, to save us from the pelting rain, but we didn't use them. We slithered in mud and scooped coins by the fistful from ash cans he'd had filled to provide fares for all the rides. The Duke of Marlborough stood patiently in the rain with Jock Whitney, waiting to climb on a carrousel. I rode around on my painted charger with Ali Khan and Bettina ahead of me and, in back, a gaitered bishop with his wife. Liz wore a Christian Dior gown in ruby red chiffon. The Doug Fairbankses were there, Deborah Kerr, financier Charles Glore. Debbie and Eddie showed up together. And the Duchess of Argyll, classically understating it, observed as the fun began: "I hear that this is going to be just an intimate little gathering for a few friends." The Gilbert Millers, with Cecil Beaton, left before the fireworks. It was too damp for them.

It was one of the few times I saw Mr. and Mrs. Fisher side by side. Every time Mike asked me to the top floor, Eddie would be there but never Debbie; she might just as well have been sitting home in Hollywood.

The pitcher of Pimm's, the white lace robe, bare feet on a coffee table—and Eddie. That was the pattern. Eddie had latched onto Mike. "You're just like a son to me," Mike used to say, sincerely attached to the hero from Philadelphia, happy that Liz had company during her pregnancy.

The first time I'd ever seen Eddie he'd come sauntering into Romanoff's, Beverly Hills, for luncheon surrounded by ten characters who seemed more familiar with punching bags than pianos. "Who in the name of God is that?" I asked my table mate. "And who are those terrible-looking men with him?"

"That's Eddie Fisher; they're his handlers."

"Handlers?" said I. "Is he a prize fighter? I'd heard he was a singer."

I took him to the Fourth of July garden party at the United States Embassy in London a few days after Mike's opening. Jock Whitney, our ambassador then, sent the invitation, and I invited Mike. But he was too busy and suggested his protégé, who was standing by, as usual. We were offered a glass of champagne before leaving, but Eddie declined. "You know I never drink," he told Mike blandly. "Nothing but Coca-Cola."

In my rented Rolls we drove to the embassy. Making our way through the crowds, I introduced Eddie to Jock and Betsy Whitney, who was looking very frail after a recent operation. She and I sat for a few minutes chatting, while Eddie hung around. As we walked away he asked: "Who'd you say those people were?"

"I introduced you to Mr. and Mrs. Jock Whitney."

"Who are they?"

"He just happens to be our Ambassador to the Court of St. James's."

"Oh," said Eddie, "*oh.*"

In one of the marquees put up for the occasion I was offered some bourbon and water. "I'd like some champagne," Eddie told the waiter.

"Sorry, sir, but we're not serving champagne."

"Then I'll take a dry martini."

"I'm afraid we can't mix drinks—too many people here today, sir. We can offer you whisky, gin, vodka, or bourbon."

"Well, then, I'll have a scotch and soda," said my non-drinking companion.

As we left he walked over to the U. S. Air Force Band, which was playing there, borrowed the baton, and conducted the orchestra. What some of the London newspapers said the next morning about that bit of ham-handed showmanship would have driven a more sensitive man into a knothole.

Back in Hollywood, Liz started on another picture, *Cat on a Hot Tin Roof*. Then came the spring day when the plane, *Lucky Liz*, dived into the desert in New Mexico; the end of Mike Todd was almost the end of her.

She finished the picture like a trouper only weeks later. The following July I flew with her to New York. We sat up aboard the airliner until 3 A.M. talking about the happiness she had known with Mike. She showed me his wedding ring, taken from his finger after death. "I'll wear it always," she said. "They'll have to cut it off my finger before they'll get it off my hand."

I took her to the first party she went to after Mike's death. Though Arthur Loew, Jr., the producer, had her children in his home, she then had a suite at the Beverly Hills Hotel. When I went in, it looked as though a cyclone had hit her bedroom. Every dress she owned had been pulled out of the closets and thrown onto tables, chairs, bed or floor. She was wailing, "What shall I wear?" as soon as I opened the door.

I picked up a red dress. "This."

"But it's the first time I've been out. I can't wear red."

"Wear it," I said. On the bathroom window sill, by an open window with no screen on it, I saw the big diamond ring Mike had given her, left there unnoticed. I took it in to her. "Did you miss this?"

She glanced at her fingers. "Oh yes. My ring. Thanks."

"You've got to watch things like this, Elizabeth."

There was not much else to be said then and there to do her any good. We rolled down to Romanoff's in her Rolls an hour and a half late. Everybody clustered around her as though she were a queen. I am sure she believed she was.

That night she'd taken me up to see Liza, who was quartered in a crib in a room of Arthur Loew's house no bigger than a closet, with its only ventilation provided by a skylight that could be pulled open by a thin chain. The room was sizzling. "Good Lord, Liz," I cried. "She can't get enough air in here."

"Oh, she's all right," her mother said, turning on the light to wake her. The baby woke silently—I have never heard her cry. She opened her eyes wide and looked straight into mine. It was impossible to believe she didn't know what I was thinking. My own eyes lowered in self-protection.

Liz spread the word that she was getting ready to go off on a long vacation in Europe with Mike's long-time Japanese secretary, Midori Tsuji. Eddie talked about having business to attend to that kept him in New York. Debbie Reynolds believed both of them. Through the closeness of Mike Todd and Eddie Fisher, Elizabeth and Debbie had become what Hollywood called "best friends." Liz, in fact, looked down her nose at Debbie and usually referred to her as "that little Girl Scout."

Debbie and I went together to an "all young" party at Arthur Loew's home in a new car Eddie had bought her. Elizabeth was away in New York, restless, without the remotest idea of what she really wanted. One thing she was sure of—she didn't want Arthur Loew much longer, though she knew he was deeply in love with her.

The only guests at that party who would acknowledge to being middle-aged without a battle were Milton Berle and myself. The house rocked to the blare of records by Sammy Davis, Jr. There was nothing else to play. He had sneaked in early and hidden every other album. Most of the girls had squeezed themselves into Capri pants as tight as their skins and a hundred times more brilliant.

"Wonder if they can sit down without splitting 'em back and front?" said Milton.

"Doubt it," said I—whoever invented Capri pants had his mind on rape.

I left early with Debbie. "What's keeping Eddie so long in New York?" I asked, suspicious nature showing.

"Oh, he'll be back here tomorrow," she answered dutifully. Of course he wasn't. He took a detour by way of Grossinger's, that Catskill haven of rest and romance, where he had married and honeymooned with Debbie. There, he and Liz had arranged a rendezvous.

Then Liz arrived back in town, and every newspaperman was combing the thickets trying to find her. Eddie, too, was back home with his wife and two children, though reporters camping outside their house could safely assume that the marriage was breaking up, if the shouts they heard through the walls were any clue. Newsmen looked in vain for Liz after she whisked into the Beverly Hills Hotel, then ducked out through the Polo Lounge into a waiting car. I had an idea she would be hiding out in the house of Kurt Frings. He is her agent, and can take credit for finishing off the revolution begun by Myron Selznick, a pioneer in the business of squeezing producers dry and making the stars today's rulers of Hollywood. I'd put an earlier call in to her, which she returned.

"Elizabeth," I said, "this is Hedda. Level with me, because I shall find out anyhow. What's this Eddie Fisher business all about? You're being blamed for taking Eddie away from Debbie. What have you got to say?"

I flapped a hand furiously for Pat, one of my secretaries, who had picked up the extension, to start taking shorthand fast. Elizabeth's voice was innocent as a schoolgirl's. "It's a lot of bull. I don't go about breaking up marriages. Besides, you can't break up a happy marriage. Debbie's and Eddie's never has been."

"I hear you even went to Grossinger's with him."

"Sure. We had a divine time."

"What about Arthur Loew, Jr.? You've known he's been in love with you for the past six months, and your kids are still living in his house."

"I can't help how he feels about me."

I sighed—I sometimes do. "Well, you can't hurt Debbie like

this without hurting yourself more, because she loves him."

"He's not in love with her and never has been."

"What do you think Mike would say to this?"

"He and Eddie loved each other," she said.

"No, you're wrong. Mike loved Eddie. Eddie never loved anybody but himself."

"Well," she said calmly, "Mike's dead and I'm alive."

My voice was rising with my temper. "Let me tell you, my girl, this is going to hurt you much more than it will Debbie Reynolds. People love her more than they love you or Eddie Fisher."

"What am I supposed to do? Ask him to go back to her and try? He can't. Now if he did, they'd destroy each other. Well, good luck to her if she can get him. I'm not taking away anything from her because she never really had it."

We went at each other for a minute or two longer before we hung up. By then, she had said something that sent my anger soaring like a rocket. I didn't include that quote in the story I snapped out in five minutes flat and got it out on the news wires before I could start to simmer down. I had been very fond of Mike Todd, who had been dead not quite six months. This is what Elizabeth Taylor had to say that set me alight: "What do you expect me to do? Sleep alone?"

The story ran front page in the Los Angeles *Times* and many more newspapers that syndicate Hopper. The Hearst papers, at least in Los Angeles and San Francisco, paraphrased my scoop and lifted the quotes without giving me as much as a nod by way of credit.

One of the first people to read it was Elizabeth. She called the next day, naturally furious, storming over a portrait in print which she believed pictured her as being as cruel and heartless as a black-widow spider. I must say I had no regret. If she'd been my own daughter, I'd have done it. Without a sense of integrity you can't sleep nights.

"Of course, I didn't think you'd print it," she said. "You betrayed me."

"You didn't say it was off the record," I answered. "And it had to be printed."

That was the last time we spoke to each other for a year. At the office the mail started arriving in stacks, all in Debbie's favor.

Another call came that day from Debbie. She hadn't seen a newspaper, she said. "You can't stick your head in the sand," said I.

Debbie, who is as shrewd as she is pretty, knew she had been cheated. She needed no prodding to be frank. "Obviously, the man loved me. We had lots of problems the first year and a half we were married. We went to a marriage counselor for advice. We both wanted to make it work. When he left for New York, he kissed me good-by and we were very close. It didn't mean anything that my husband had to go to New York on a business trip. I had no reason to be suspicious."

It wasn't the moment to tell her once again that Eddie had never wanted to marry her. In my book, the little baritone from Philadelphia wanted a reputation as a great lover. He preened in the publicity that marrying her brought him, but I believe she forced that marriage. His Svengali, Milton Blackstone, didn't want it—the men who steer any entertainer's career always scheme to keep him single because a wife is an interfering nuisance in their plans. After Debbie had received an engagement ring, plus barrel loads of publicity, Eddie answered a call to Grossinger's. A friend advised Debbie: "Pack your wedding gown and trousseau. Get on a plane quietly and go after him, then he'll marry you." She accepted the advice, and Eddie accepted her. At least she got what she wanted, then.

The storms continued to blow for months. Liz complained to one reporter, Joe Hyams, that I had "betrayed" her, and swore for the dozenth time that she wanted to quit Hollywood, though work for the time being was "therapeutic"— and her pay was rocketing up toward a million dollars a picture. Debbie applied for a divorce, but that wasn't fast enough for Eddie. He got a quick end to their marriage in Las Vegas.

Liz and he were married in that paradise of syndicates and slot machines on May 12, 1959, after she had embraced his religion and dragged her parents out of the background to lend a look of dignity to the proceedings.

Elizabeth's hatred lasted for a year. But when she had packed to leave for England and the first disastrous attempt to make *Cleopatra,* she called. "Hedda, don't you think we ought to be friends again?"

"Yes, I should like that."

"So should I. Let's get together as soon as I'm back."

Before she returned, she had nearly died in London with the lining of her brain inflamed by an infected tooth. The first of the millions that Twentieth Century-Fox was going to pour down the drain had vanished in *Cleopatra.* But the women of America, who'd been ready to all but stone her, forgave everything because of her illness. She had been back in town forty-eight hours when the telephone rang: "Will you come over, Hedda?"

"I'd love to. Will Liza be there? I'm anxious to see her."

Before I left, I wrapped a gift Mike had given me one Christmas along with other things—a music box that played the theme of *Around the World.* I took a present for each of the two boys, too. Liz and her sons were drawing pictures for each other when I arrived. The children accepted their gifts graciously, then Liza wound her box, the first she'd ever seen.

After she had played the tinkling little tune over and over, she gravely allowed each brother one turn apiece. Then she wound it again and danced with each of them around the room. At last it was my turn. We held hands tight and waltzed until everyone but Liza was completely exhausted. But she still went on winding and winding the key to play the tune again.

Liz looked pale, quite different from the woman I'd last seen. "You won't know me," she said. "I came so near death I'm just thankful to be alive. I lie out in the sun, listen to the birds sing, look at the blue sky, and say: 'Thank God for letting me live.'"

I believed her. She felt in that mood that day. Later, inevitably, we talked about the telephone call she had made one shattering September morning in 1958 and how she was "betrayed."

"I considered you my second mother," she said. "As a matter of fact, I loved you better than I loved my mother. You were kinder to me than she was. That you could do what you did nearly killed me."

"That one line you spoke did it, Liz. I couldn't take it. That was why it was done."

We had several visits after that, before I went on a visit to New York and she whirled off on a trip to Moscow. When we were both back in Hollywood again, she was another creature entirely, out most nights instead of resting and restoring herself to health for her next stab at *Cleopatra*, in Rome this time.

Champagne was ruled out during her convalescence, so she drank beer. She'd send her chauffeur down to Dave Chasen's restaurant to pick up two quarts of chile, which she'd eat to accompany the beer. When she left for Italy, she was too fat to fit any of her costumes. Her doctor had to be flown out from Hollywood to put her on a crash diet so she could be photographed as the Serpent of the Nile in the most balled-up motion-picture production of all time.

She won her Academy Award not for *Butterfield* 8 but for nearly dying. And her studio joined in by putting on a terrific public-relations campaign against Debbie—with planted stories in fan magazines and loaded interviews for the newspapers—to clinch sympathy for Liz.

She has become Cleopatra to the life now, and the world is her oyster. What she wants, she takes, come hell or high water—and this includes Richard Burton. In the huge Roman villa which she made her home during *Cleopatra's* making, she reigned like an empress, reclining on a chaise, summoning Eddie to bring guests up to her for an audience. The honored guest would sit on one side of her and on the other side

24

Eddie, delicately placing a hand on her breast before she spoke a regal word of greeting.

In the old days the scandal of the past four years would have killed her professionally. In these changed times it seems only to help her reputation. The million dollars and more which her *Cleopatra* contract gave her was doled out, at her insistence, in installments on every morning of shooting. She consented to work only after the day's check for $9000, drawn on a United States bank, lay snugly in her hand. While he lasted, Eddie drew $1500 a week for getting his wife to the set on time. Yet she spends money faster than she makes it. If Twentieth Century-Fox had gotten ruined, putting more than $35,000,000 into the picture before there was any hope of completing it, she didn't give a damn.

At Liz's say-so, Eddie had adopted Liza Todd, though Michael Wilding wouldn't let him take over the two boys. Even after he knew what was going on in Rome, Eddie hung on. Allegedly, he's the one who told Richard Burton's wife, Sybil, the truth and drew the Welshman's question: "Now why did you have to go and spoil everything?"

Eddie wasn't his smiling self when he flew to Rome to try to quash the news of the romance. Liz was in the hospital again; the newspapers said "food poisoning," but the real diagnosis was too many sleeping pills. Even after he landed back in New York, he was still declaring the marriage to be a happy one—until Liz spelled it out for him in three words over the telephone.

At last she finished the picture and gave herself the asp, and I predict that Burton will turn his back on her, after every woman in the world blamed her once again for taking somebody else's husband. But Burton didn't have to submit in the first place.

Can you picture him passing up Liz and simultaneously collecting more publicity than ever Mark Antony and Caesar combined received in their prime? He started the romance with Liz just as Eddie did in his day, when he was sitting at her feet before Mike Todd was dead.

Men are supposed to be the stronger sex. I do not condone what Liz has done. I do condemn these fellows who followed her around like puppy dogs. They took her favors as long as she'd give, then each and every one of them wanted more.

What's left for Liz but to go on repeating her mistakes? What's to become of her? I'm not a prophet, but I have a terrible suspicion.

Two

Right from the beginning, when Hollywood was a sleepy, neighborly village of white frame bungalows and dusty roads cutting through the orange groves, every top-rank woman star has been fated to regard herself as Queen of the Movies in person. It's as invariable and inevitable as the law of gravity or income taxes, so you can't blame them for it. When an irresistible force, which is flattery, meets a readily movable object, which is any pretty girl who finds she's clicked, then she starts to behave as though draped permanently in sable with a crown perched on her head.

She is mobbed by crowds, wooed by the world, and flattered without shame or mercy from the time she puts her dainty feet in the front gates of the studio in the morning to the time she leaves at night. She's surrounded by her own special set of courtiers, all busy lubricating her ego—hairdresser, make-up man, script girl, wardrobe girl, still photographer, press agent, drama coach, and interviewers.

Liz Taylor is only one more deluded figure in the scintillating succession that stretches back to Pola Negri, who liked to go walking with a leopard on a golden chain, and Gloria Swanson, who rode from her dressing room to the set in a wheelchair pushed by a Negro boy. But I once discovered that while movie queens aim to live like royalty, there was one young and adorable princess who enjoyed living it up, at least for a day, like the movie stars.

In London soon after V-E day I received an invitation to go down to Elstree to meet Queen Elizabeth, as she is now known, and Princess Margaret. They were going to watch the filming of Charles Dickens' *Nicholas Nickleby*, which starred Cedric Hardwicke. I looked forward to seeing the princesses, but I admitted to a slight bewilderment about what

27

I was supposed to do and how I was supposed to do it. But there were daily columns I had to write, and the day before the visit I was having tea in the Savoy Hotel with Jean Simmons and her mother.

Jean, a schoolgirl of sixteen, had heard that day that she'd been given the role of a seductive native girl in *Black Narcissus*, with Deborah Kerr, and her head was spinning like a top. "I simply can't believe it," she was gasping. "I simply don't believe it's true," when Noël Coward came in. Noël, a friend for years, was reassuring. "I know the part," he told her, "and you'll be darling in it."

"Oh, I wonder," she persisted. "I don't think I'm old enough."

Noël turned blandly firm. "My dear, if they chose you, they know you can do it. So do it. You're going to be absolutely wonderful, so please don't say another word."

I needed some of his confidence for my own venture next day. I told him about the invitation. "What do I do when I meet the princesses?"

"You say 'ma'am' and you curtsy," said Noël with all the authority of a prince of royal blood.

" 'Ma'am'? I'm old enough to be their grandmother, and I've never curtsied in my life."

"It's time to learn then," he said. "Here, I'll show you. Watch me, and then you try." He got up and, with Jean and her mother watching goggle-eyed, proceeded to stick back his left foot, flex his knees, and bow his head as gracefully as a dowager duchess. The next day when I was introduced, I remembered the "ma'am" but decided that maybe I hadn't had as much practice as Noël, so I'd better not risk the curtsy.

Strict and stringent food rationing was in force in Britain, yet everybody on the set had contributed ration coupons for butter, meat, eggs, and every conceivable delicacy so that the young visitors—Elizabeth was nineteen, Margaret fifteen—could be served high tea.

I have never seen two girls dig into food the way they did. You could swear they hadn't had a decent meal in years.

There was cold lobster with mayonnaise, white-meat sandwiches of chicken, little French pastries, strawberries big as golf balls. The princesses tucked into the lot.

Elizabeth was already very regal and dignified, but Margaret was not that way at all. Through the windows, we could see a mob of people waiting outside the studio's big iron entrance gates. "Just look at those people out there," I said. "Don't you get tired of crowds?"

"Oh, you've no idea," Margaret said. "This goes on every day. You know, because people have to be able to see us, we can wear only white, pink, or baby blue. And I'm so sick of baby blue and pink. I can never put on anything like black, for instance." She was obviously itching to try dressing like a *femme fatale*.

"It's exactly like being a movie star," I said.

"Do movie stars have to go through this in the same way?"

"Every day. They have mobs around them wherever they go."

She babbled on like a brook, ignoring the icy looks her sister flashed her across the table. "We've never been to a motion-picture studio before, and I think it's fascinating. I do hope we'll be allowed to come again." She helped herself to another strawberry. "And this tea—delicious! Do they have food like this in the studio every day?"

I explained as tactfully as possible that everyone had donated ration cards. "They did?" exclaimed the princess. "Well, I don't care. It was wonderful, and I'm glad I ate everything."

The day I'd arrived in London for my first trip stays fixed in my memory because every church bell in town was pealing. Like the ham actress I was then—and still am—I wondered if they were ringing for me. I wasn't quite correct. It happened to be the day Queen Elizabeth was born. I thought about it when I went back to London again as a newspaperwoman covering her coronation. Seeing the standards emblazoned with "E.R.," for Elizabeth Regina, that covered London, an American acquaintance of mine, a Democrat to the hilt, re-

29

marked appreciatively: "I didn't realize they were so fond of Eleanor Roosevelt over here."

At the Savoy that coronation evening I got a telephone call from Reuter's. The New York *Daily News* was asking for a special story on my reactions to the gilt and glamour of London town. "Certainly," said I. "Get your typewriter ready."

"Don't you want to think about it?"

"No, I don't have to think. I just want to tell it as I saw it." So I talked about the crowds who had slept in the streets, about the pomp and pageantry of the greatest show since P. T. Barnum. "It makes President Eisenhower's inauguration," I judged—and I'd been there—"seem like sending off your impoverished relations to the poorhouse."

Hollywood's own candidate for ermine, Her Serene Highness Princess Grace, was much more stiff and starchy than Her Royal Highness Princess Margaret, at least for the first five years after marriage to Prince Rainier. Her husband was struck well-nigh speechless by all the publicity that went with the wedding. He took a back seat while the daughter of a millionaire bricklayer from Philadelphia reigned as regally as Queen Victoria in the comic-opera palace at Monaco, with its toy-soldier guards parading solemnly outside like bit players in an old Mack Sennet movie. Any moment I expected a fat tenor to come out on the balcony and start singing.

In Monaco I saw Grace succeed in cooling off in one cold spell Noël Coward, Somerset Maugham, and an assorted press corps from England, Europe, and the United States. We were all there to mark the Monte Carlo premiere of *Kings Go Forth* with Frank Sinatra, Tony Curtis, and Natalie Wood, which its producers had decided needed every line of publicity it could get, since it was no great shakes as a picture.

Frank leveled the toy kingdom like a Kansas tornado. At the movie opening, Grace, in a simple pale pink dress, couldn't pull her eyes off him, while he tore up "The Road to Mandalay" and laid it down again. A champagne supper was served

30

afterward with the Serenities in attendance. At the top table, where they sat among a gaggle of celebrities, there were three empty places. Noël Coward had come from the Riviera with Somerset Maugham, whom he'd been visiting. But Coward and Maugham found themselves consigned to sit alone at a side table, out of Her Serenity's range.

Grace and Rainier danced until three in the morning. While I was taking a turn around the floor with Jim Bacon of the Associated Press, the prince and I felt our bumpers collide, and he promptly marched off the floor. *Lèse majesté*, no doubt.

Newsmen who'd been flown in for the opening fared worse than Noël. Not a one was asked into the palace for as much as a cup of tea or a handshake. Little starlets you never heard of were nervously practicing curtsies in the hotel lobby, but they didn't get close enough to Grace to try them out.

A word or two about the peculiar hospitality you could expect in Monaco, which is a beautiful spot but with its old glamour lost forever, appeared in my column some days later.

The next time around, three years afterward, Grace made amends, proving that a little of the column medicine can do a lot of good. I was amazed to be invited by Rainier and his princess to attend the opening of a new hotel, the Son Vida, nestled on a hilltop outside of Palma de Mallorca. This time, she couldn't have exercised more charm. She arrived off Aristotle Onassis' yacht dressed in white, carrying a lavender parasol, looking like a billion, though I detected a bit of restlessness in her, as if the gilt on the gingerbread was losing its luster.

Rainier was a different man, too, outgoing and chatty where he'd been withdrawn and shy. He had some money invested in the place, along with Charles (*Seventh Heaven*) Farrell, of the Palm Springs Racquet Club. I told the prince what I'd heard from Howell Conant, the New York photographer who had been taking pictures of the Serenities since they were engaged: "A lot of people around the palace like Rainier almost more than Grace now." The prince loved it. We had a high old time chuckling over that.

He told me about their children, who were entertained aboard the train from Monaco by Winston Churchill, whom four-year-old Caroline insisted on calling "Mussolini," which Britain's grand old man took as an enormous joke.

In return I passed along Bob Considine's account of how he covered the wedding of Grace and Rainier in Monte Carlo. Each group of reporters was assigned a spot to work in; Bob's crowd drew a showroom for bathroom equipment. "I found it difficult," he told me, "to peer across a bidet at Dorothy Kilgallen and write romantically of love and marriage."

Grace badly wanted to latch onto some favorable publicity again. Throughout her engagement to Rainier she'd had her own publicity agent to advise her. Rupert Allen, who had taste plus tact, had done the same job for her while she was at MGM. He left the studio for the engagement, sailed with her when she went to Monaco, and stayed on at the palace. Last spring her purpose, which may have stuck in the back of her mind all along, showed itself: She signed to work for Alfred Hitchcock, then canceled out because the people of Monaco didn't like the idea. I guess when you've been a queen, if only in Hollywood, you find it hard to believe it's promotion to play a princess, even in Monaco.

Thanks to her own shrewd sense, or to sound advice from outside, Grace's timing was good. The people who go to movies still wanted to see her. So on top of satisfying her own ego, she could command so much money from Hitchcock that she finally couldn't turn him down. She has inherited some of her father's respect for a dollar.

I believe Grace caught the movie-making bug again after Jacqueline Kennedy went off without John F. on her triumphant trip to India and Pakistan. After all, if a great lady who can't match Grace for beauty can score a hit, why shouldn't Grace get back into the limelight? I'd bet that if Jackie had the chance to star in a picture, she'd take it. Wouldn't you if you were in her shoes?

With one possible exception, there's been a streak of exhibitionism a mile wide in every actress I've known, starting with Ethel Barrymore, who set my soul and ambition on fire when I saw her play in *Captain Jinks of the Horse Marines*. The possible exception is Garbo, who laid down an iron rule that she would work only on a closely screened set, and she'd freeze in her tracks the moment her privacy was invaded, especially if her boss at MGM, Louis B. Mayer, dared intrude with bankers or visitors from New York.

A movie queen has to be a born show-off before she wants to act, and when she finds she can get paid for it too, her joy is unconfined. Most of the breed don't hesitate for a second if today's producers of soiled sex on celluloid call on them to do a Bardot, without benefit of bath towel. I'm sure Liz enjoyed doing her bathe-in-the-nude sequence for *Cleopatra*. Jean Simmons didn't object to playing stripped to the waist in one *Spartacus* scene that Kirk Douglas ordered to be shot in a spiced-up version for European distribution. And those calendar poses didn't bother Marilyn Monroe. "I was hungry," she explained, wide-eyed, when I asked her once why she'd sat for them.

Even Garbo had some odd quirks when the cameras stopped rolling. She used to go regularly to the house of some friends who had a big, secluded pool. Before she arrived, all the servants would be dismissed, and her host and hostess would take themselves off for an hour or so, too. Then Garbo undressed and, naked as a jay bird except for a floppy hat, swam gravely round and round in the water. Katharine Hepburn is another home nudist, presumably finding it better than air conditioning for keeping cool in summer. After all, it's nature's way. Didn't we all come into the world stripped to the pelt?

Under stress, the deep-down desire to show themselves to an audience can take strange turns. Once in front of the crowded long bar of the Knickerbocker Hotel, an actress whose career had run into trouble—she was happily remarried in 1958—began to strip. This was Hollywood, remember, so hot-eyed stares were the only help she got from anybody in the room. When she was down to her shoes and stockings, and the rest of her clothes lay discarded on the barroom floor, she gave a shriek and ran down the front steps out onto Ivar Avenue. Then at last somebody remembered to telephone the police.

More recently an agent from one of the big television studios called at the hotel apartment of a much-married woman whose name still spells glamour to any serviceman of World War II. His mission was to sound her out about doing a TV show. She greeted him in a bathrobe and asked him to run the hot water for her before they talked business. She locked the outside door behind him. The following morning his conscience began to stir. "I'd better leave now," he said. "The office will think I died."

"You can't go," she cried. "I'm so lonely." She kept him there three days.

The town has always been full of lonely, frustrated women who have let their few years of basking in the sun as movie queens blind them to reality forever. You can start with Mary Pickford, who used to talk a blue streak about a wonderful girl protégé whom she said she was going to make over into a movie sensation. I had to try to disillusion her. "You're fooling yourself, Mary. What you should do is hire a press agent. All you really want is to keep your name alive."

Gloria Swanson is another who can't see straight today where her career as an actress is concerned. As a businesswoman in the dress industry she's not nearly as sharp as Joseph P. Kennedy was when he was a movie tycoon and she was his reigning queen. She'd made a hit in *Sunset Boulevard* and her reputation was on the rise again when I suggested she might do a movie version, written by Frances Marion, of Francis Parkinson Keyes' *Dinner at Antoine's*. Not a chance. "I couldn't possibly play the mother of an eighteen-year-old daughter," she snapped. "The part's too old for me." At the time, she was the mother of two daughters and a son, and she had two grandchildren.

34

Most of the unhappy ones have no husbands. One unfailing cause of that brand of misery is lack of female charity. They turn their backs on the facts of life and refuse to forgive their husbands a single act of infidelity—I believe every man married to a movie queen deserves one break in that department.

Barbara Stanwyck lives in a two-story mansion with her only company an elderly maid, the books she reads by the score, and the television set which hypnotizes her into watching old movies into all hours of the night. You don't see her around town much any more because people forget to ask her down from the ivory tower in which she's locked herself. When you do invite her out, there are roses from her the next day and thank-you notes so pathetically grateful they'd melt a stone.

Up to the day in 1951 that she divorced Robert Taylor, she was one of the happiest women alive. He was such a handsome slice of man, highly desirable, a full-size star. When he went to Rome for eleven months to make *Quo Vadis* with Deborah Kerr, women everywhere mobbed him. But Barbara loved to act. The Taylors didn't need the money, but she worked all the time, going straight from one picture into another, instead of taking time out to join her husband in Italy.

When he arrived home after nearly a year, Barbara disposed of him, while he found a much younger bride, Ursula Thiess. She has now had two children by him, although now they're having difficulty with an older child by a former husband.

At fifty-five, Barbara remains a talented actress and a mighty attractive woman, though she gets thinner all the time. She's kept her appetite for work, but suitable parts aren't easy to find—I don't rate her last role as a Lesbian madam of a New Orleans brothel in *A Walk on the Wild Side* as worthy of her. I have begged her to kiss Hollywood good-by and go to Europe. "There's nothing for you here. I guarantee you wouldn't be over there twenty-four hours without having at least two offers for pictures."

35

But Barbara stays on; with her maid, her books, and Helen Ferguson, her press agent and one of her closest friends.

Dinah Shore used to say, in one of those standard quotes that queens come up with when life is sunny, "My family means more to me than anything in the world—nothing will ever interfere with that." Then George Montgomery, her husband went off to work on his own, and seventeen years and 362 days of a good marriage went out the window.

Her place of purgatory now is an oversized mansion, built on a $75,000 lot, near that of Richard Nixon. There she sits in melancholy, alone much of the time, by the pool, which is equipped with a waterfall; or perhaps in the living room, which is proportioned somewhat like Grand Central Station. It's a great spot for brooding, but nevertheless she kept on singing on her shows "It's Great to Have a Man Around the House."

On the face of it, this used to be a couple that could never be divided. Certainly her reputation overshadowed George's, a situation which usually creates continual problems. It's hard on a husband when his house is invaded most nights by writers and directors who've come to discuss the new picture or new TV show with his wife. He has to sit and listen to them fuss over her with: "Now, darling, you're looking a little tired and you have to work tomorrow, so you'd better take a pill and go to bed early to catch up on your beauty sleep."

George, however, didn't resent Dinah's success. Though he never quite made film stardom and his own Western series died young on TV, he had his furniture factory, where he worked alongside his employees, and he went on making low budget pictures. He steered clear of the parasitic life so many husbands enjoy when the woman is combination breadwinner, wife, mother, and working head of the family.

When the husband carries the title of "agent" in Hollywood, it's a safe bet that he knows next to nothing about the business and is living off his wife. It's also odds that he has a mistress to while away those long afternoons when he isn't at the race track or propping up a bar. What can the wife do about it? If she wants to keep her home and family together in some semblance of order, she's powerless. Daddy must be allowed to continue as "agent," even if it ruins her.

When you're a wife as well as an actress, you have to think of your husband, too, not only about your career. Maybe Dinah didn't think hard enough. George, who in the past had given up several jobs to travel with her, went to the Philippines alone to make a picture and was gone three months. While he was away, she heard rumors that he was seeing a great deal of his leading woman. He hadn't been back in Hollywood long before she released the announcement that she was filing for divorce.

Only minutes after she'd finally decided on that step, she went on the air with no detectable strain showing as she sang and clowned in her TV show.

She is a forty-five-year-old woman with two children still in school. She is up to her ears in work most of the time. The fact that good men don't grow on trees is something most women don't realize until it's too late. Chances are that a new husband would be second-rate by comparison with George. Could be that thought has struck home with Dinah, too.

Inside the blonde head of tragedy's child, Marilyn Monroe, fame and misery were mixed up like tangled skeins of knitting wool. She was an unsophisticated, overly trusting creature whose career was always professionally and emotionally complicated beyond her power to control it. She was used by so many people.

She let herself be surrounded by such a clutch of nudgers, prodders, counselors, and advisers that the poor child developed an inferiority complex so ruinous that she was terrified to walk onto any movie set for stark fear she'd fluff a line or miss a cue. She never did have confidence in herself. Toward the end of her life, she couldn't sit and talk to you without her fingers twisting together like live bait in a jar.

37

That wasn't surprising in light of the words of wisdom her confidantes poured into her ears: "You cannot worry about unhappiness. There is no such thing as a happy artist. They develop understanding of things that other people don't understand."

Marilyn wasn't visibly suffering from anything the night she stopped off at my house for a last-minute talk on her way to Los Angeles Airport and New York for *The Seven Year Itch.* Her husband of that era, and one of the real men in her life, Joe DiMaggio, drove her over, but he wouldn't come in. "I'll knock on the door when it's time to go," said Joe, whom I'd known long before Marilyn.

She was wearing beige—beige fur collar on her beige coat, beige dress, beige hair. "You look absolutely divine," said I. "Are you beige all over?"

She had started to lift her dress before she murmured: "Oh, Hedda, that's *vulgar.*"

"Just thought I'd ask."

I was a booster of Marilyn's as far back as *All About Eve,* when she came on for a few minutes with George Sanders and glowed like the harvest moon. She had an extraordinary power of lighting up the whole screen. No one in my memory hypnotized the camera as she did. In her brain and body, the distinctions between woman and actress had edges sharp as razor blades. Off camera, she was a nervous, amazingly fair-skinned creature almost beside herself with concern about her roles, driven to seek relief in vodka, champagne, sleeping pills —anything to blunt the pain of her existence. When the camera rolled, everything was as different as night from day. Then she became an actress using her eyes, her hands, every muscle in her body to court and conquer the camera as though it were her lover, whom she simultaneously dominated and was dominated by, adored and feared.

She was the original Cinderella of our times, the slavey who'd washed dishes, swept floors, minded babies, been pushed around from one foster home to another without anybody caring for or loving her. But she was always as honest about her whole ugly past as an ambitious actress can be who smells good copy in her reminiscences. She was simultaneously lovely and pathetic most of the time, but she kept a sense of humor. I asked her once about a man alleged to be looming large in her life. "Is this a serious romance?" was the question.

"Say we're friendly," she said, "and put that 'friendly' in quotes."

The girl who was rated as the sex goddess supreme used to fight tooth and nail to hang onto the career which she was afraid might slip away from her at any moment. But there was an air of impregnable innocence about her in those calendar pictures. The innocence showed, too, in shots very much like them that her first husband used to carry around when he worked in an aircraft plant in World War II, to flash them in front of his workmates. One of the workmates was Robert Mitchum.

In the first great picture she made, *The Seven Year Itch*, the same charm of ignorance let her spout double-meaning lines as though she didn't know what they implied. She had that superb director Billy Wilder telling her what to do. "You had the innocence of a baby," I told her. "We knew the words were naughty, but we didn't think you did."

"I didn't know?" she said, bewildered. "But I have always known."

Soon after that picture, she lost the little-girl quality. She was surrounded by people all telling her how to act. They worked up her dissatisfaction with her studio, Twentieth Century-Fox. It's an old pitch that sycophants make to a star: "You don't need your studio. You're bigger than they are. You can have your own production company." She believed it. Basically simple women like Marilyn, who rise as fast as she did, are pushovers for this kind of mad propaganda.

A leading figure in her new circle was Milton Greene, the New York photographer who set up Marilyn as a one-woman corporation to do battle with her studio, meantime driving himself close to bankruptcy. Milton could take credit for getting her on Ed Murrow's "Person To Person" television program. After that painful evening I asked her: "How could you possibly go on TV looking like that?"

"Everybody said I looked good."

"Everybody lied then. You were a mess. You don't look well in skirts and heavy sweaters because you're too big in the bust. On that show you should have been the glamour girl you always are. But the glamorous one was Mrs. Milton Greene. This kind of thing will destroy you."

She spent part of the time during those rebellious days living in Connecticut with the Greenes, the rest in a three-room suite at the Waldorf Towers. She told me about the joys of adventuring around New York in dark glasses and turban with built-in black curls, going off on a cops-and-robbers round of cafes, theaters, the Metropolitan Museum. Meantime stupid rumors circulated that she was being kept in fantastic luxury by one millionaire or another, but nobody bothered to deny them.

"Didn't it occur to you," I wrote, "that great stars pursue their careers in conventional fashion, accepting the experienced judgment of good producers? . . . How did you rationalize the idea that a photographer who'd had no experience in making theatrical pictures could do better by you than the men who had made you famous?"

Then along came Arthur Miller, a writer held in awe by most of Hollywood, who ended a fifteen-year-old marriage to marry her. They were deeply in love and happy at first. When that ended, she came and sipped a martini in my home. He was, she said, "a charming and wonderful man—a great writer." And Joe DiMaggio? "A good friend." I believe Miller loved her, though it was Joe who turned up trumps in the end when she lay dead and deserted in Westwood Village Mortuary. One other man loved her, too—Miller's father, Isadore.

She said: "I have only married for love and happiness. Except perhaps my first one, but let's don't discuss that ever . . . I still love everybody a little that I ever loved." And about being the ex-Mrs. Miller? "When you put so much into a marriage and have it end, you feel something has died—and it has. But it didn't die abruptly. 'Died' isn't the right word for me," she said when we talked. But I think she was already dying inside her heart.

She went into *Let's Make Love*,—it was a terrible script, in her opinion—out of shape physically and mentally. As her leading man, she had Yves Montand, who was Lucky Pierre himself in getting the role, being choice number seven after Yul Brynner, Gregory Peck, Cary Grant, Charlton Heston, Rock Hudson, and Jimmy Stewart had all turned down the part. Montand had performed beautifully in his own one-man theater show, though three quarters of his American audiences obviously hadn't the least idea what he was talking about, since it was all in French. Opposite Marilyn, he thought he had only a small part after Arthur Miller had been asked to write additional dialogue for the heroine.

During shooting I detected that something strange was happening to Mrs. Arthur Miller, who hadn't announced yet that she was going to get a divorce. She was falling hard for this Frenchman with the carefully polished charm. Between the end of that picture and the start of her next, *The Misfits*, the stories spread that he would divorce his wife, Simone Signoret. M. Montand scored high in the publicity sweepstakes. The gossip spread all over town, with some help from the Twentieth Century-Fox promotion department and no hindrance from himself.

Before the prophetically titled *Misfits* was finished, she became so ill she was flown in from Reno and put into the Good Samaritan Hospital for a week's rest. She couldn't even reach Montand on the telephone, and she called him repeatedly, day after day.

The night before he left to rejoin his wife in Paris, I received a tip that he could be found in a certain bungalow in the grounds of Beverly Hills Hotel. "Just knock on the door; he'll let you in."

I did precisely that. He was astonished to see who had

rapped on his door, but I was invited in. The telephone started to ring almost immediately. He wouldn't accept the call. "I won't talk to her," he told the switchboard operator.

"Why not?" said I. "You'll probably never see her again. Go on. Speak to her." But he couldn't be persuaded. He suggested a drink, and I offered to mix them. I stirred up one hell of a martini to get him talking.

"You deliberately made love to this girl. You knew she wasn't sophisticated. Was that right?"

"Had Marilyn been sophisticated, none of this ever would have happened. I did everything I could for her when I realized that mine was a very small part. The only thing that could stand out in my performance were my love scenes. So, naturally, I did everything I could to make them good."

I'm sure that he knew what he was saying no more than half the time. She was "an enchanting child" and "a simple girl without any guile." He said: "Perhaps she had a schoolgirl crush. If she did, I'm sorry. But nothing will break up my marriage."

The last time I talked with Marilyn, there was no new man in sight. She owed Twentieth Century-Fox another picture, *Something's Got to Give,* under her old contract, but even if she'd finished it it would have paid her only $100,000, where she could have made at least $500,000 elsewhere. Her courtiers made her feel sore over that, though the only thing on her mind should have been the need to make a movie that was good for her after *Let's Make Love* and *The Misfits.* Three flops in a row, and anybody's out. Marie Dressler said it best years ago: "You're only as good as your last picture."

I believe Marilyn realized that the end of her acting career was waiting for her just around the corner. The last scenes she did in *Something's Got to Give* looked as though she was acting under water. She was sweet as ever, but vague, as if she were slightly off center. She did little more than the near-nude bathing shots, and she gave a still photographer who was on the set exclusive rights to pictures of the scene be-

42

cause "I want the world to see my body." Newspaper and magazine readers around the world were promptly granted that opportunity, needless to say.

Arthur Miller once called her "the greatest actress in the world." She was far from that, in my book. In spite of all her talk about playing Dostoevski heroines or some of Duse's roles, the sex-appealing blonde remained her stock in trade. And there was something else missing among her ambitions. She ached to have children, though she was physically incapable of it. Twice she lost babies through miscarriages when she was Mrs. Miller. She told friends that she longed for a baby on whom she could shower the attention she never had.

On June 1, 1962, she reached her thirty-sixth birthday, married three times, with still no baby and no husband. Two months later the end came, and all the sob sisters of the world fell to work explaining why. Of course, we shall never know. She took that secret with her. When you're alone and unhappy, the past, present, and future get mixed up in your brain. You say to yourself: "What's the use of it all? Nobody loves me. Perhaps I shall never find happiness again."

She seemed to be touched by forces that few human beings can bear, and her life turned into a nightmare of broken dreams, broken promises, and pain. In a way, we were all guilty. We loved her, yet left her lonely and afraid when she needed us most. Now she is gone forever, leaving us with bitter memories of what might have been. Dear Marilyn, may she rest in peace!

One of the men I loved most above all others was Gene Fowler. He once wrote me a letter from London. "What is success?" he asked. "I shall tell you out of the wisdom of my years. It is a toy balloon among children armed with sharp pins."

How can anyone say it better than that?

Three

Much as I regret it afterward, I all too often speak before I think. And too many years have gone by for much to be done about it now. For better or worse, I'm doomed to shoot from the hip, to be a chatterbox who'll fire off a quip if one comes to mind, without much thought about the consequences.

I love to laugh and to make other people laugh. That's what we're put in the world for. But I sometimes don't realize how thin some skins can be. I talked my merry way out of a tête-à-tête with Frank Sinatra, whom I've always liked, and I'll be sorry to my dying day for what was said on the spur of that moment.

The place was Romanoff's penthouse; the occasion, the crushingly dull farewell party that Sol Siegel, then head of MGM, and his wife gave Grace Kelly before she sailed off to be a princess.

To start with, the arrangement for welcoming guests was peculiar, to say the least. Instead of standing beside Mr. and Mrs. Siegel to say hello, Grace stood in solitary state in the middle of the floor. She was dressed up, rightly, for the fray—white gloves, a beautiful coat and dress. But she stood with her handbag hanging over her arm as though poised for take-off at the flash of a tiara.

Like all the rest of us, I went up alone to wish her well for her future in Monaco. She was regal already, smiling as benignly as Queen Mother Elizabeth opening a charity bazaar.

"If you'll excuse me," said I, after three minutes of nothing much, "I think I'll go and have a glass of champagne."

That party never did pick up. As the hours dragged by,

it grew stiffer and duller and colder, though the champagne flowed and the orchestra played its head off.

Come eleven o'clock I was dancing with Frank. *Confidential*, the scandal sheet which was the scourge of Hollywood in those days, had very recently printed the doleful reminiscences of one young woman whose expectations, she confided, had been aroused when Frank whisked her off to his Palm Springs hideaway. But hope had crumbled when he spent the night constantly getting up to eat Wheaties.

As the Siegels' guest, he was as bored as I was. "Let's blow this creepy party," he said, "and go down to my Palm Springs place."

"Why, Frank, I couldn't do that; I didn't bring my Wheaties." The wisecrack popped out without a second's consideration, and he nearly fell down on the floor. So ended the chances of getting the name of Hopper on the roll call of Sinatra dates, which has included Marilyn Maxwell, Anita Ekberg, Gloria Vanderbilt, Kim Novak, Lady Beatty (who became Mrs. Stanley Donen), and, according to witnesses, a master list of conquests among the female stars at MGM that he used to keep behind his dressing-room door.

He continues to send me gorgeous flowers for Christmas and Mother's Day, so I guess I'll be content with that. I got asked up to his handsome new house on top of a Beverly Hills mountain, equipped with lights that fade at the touch of a switch and a telescope through which he studies the stars (celestial variety) in their courses. But I haven't been invited to Palm Springs again.

Maybe it's for the best. I consider Frank the most superb entertainer of this age. When he's in good voice and a good mood, he's ahead of the field, and nobody can equal his charm. Like almost everybody, his nature has many sides to it—more than most people, because he has more talent than most. But on a host of subjects, we're far apart, not omitting politics. If I'd gone to his desert house and written about it, we might have seen a beautiful friendship dented.

When Charles Morrison, owner of our best night club, the

Mocambo, died, he left a mourning wife, Mary, with a mountain of debt. Like Sinatra, he'd spent it when he had it and also when he hadn't. Frank telephoned Mary and said he'd like to bring in an orchestra and sing for her, free for a couple of weeks. On opening night he caught fire, and his quips were as good as his singing.

He never worked harder than he did for two months arranging President Kennedy's inaugural ball. He wanted Ethel Merman and Sir Laurence Olivier for the show, but they were playing on Broadway in *Gypsy* and *Becket*, respectively. So Frank closed the two theaters for a night and refunded the price of the tickets to every disappointed theater-goer. After the inauguration Frank and most of his co-workers—including Janet Leigh, Tony Curtis, Roger Edens, and Jimmy Van Heusen—went to Joe Kennedy's Palm Beach home for a weekend's rest. I don't think the President has fully repaid Frank for that memorable evening.

Sinatra swears his private life is his own. Until the recent era of peace with the press dawned, he'd let fly with his fists to prove his point with some reporters. He once told me: "If a movie-goer spends $2.00 to see me in a motion picture, or $10 to watch me perform in a night club, then he has the right to see me at my best. I do not feel, however, that I have any responsibility to that movie-goer or that night-club-goer to tell him anything about my private life."

He likes to quote something said by Humphrey Bogart, one of his good friends: "The only thing you owe the public is a good performance." He must have remembered that when Bogey's widow, Betty Bacall, announced that she was going to marry Frank. A pal with him at the time—he was staying in Miami Beach—told me: "He was so angry he blew the roof off the hotel." That marked the end of that romance.

Frank has let his temper and temperament explode too often for his relations with many newspapermen and women to be anything but spotty. Believe it or not, that has him chewing his fingernails sometimes. "There are a handful of people who won't let go of me and won't try to be fair," he

46

said, defending himself one day. "And after a thing is over and I fly off the handle, I feel twice as bad as when I was angry. You get to think, 'Jeez, I'm sorry that had to happen!'"

He isn't the man he's usually painted to be. The brandy drinker who shrugs off advice? He was a guest of mine at a small dinner party for Noël Coward, along with the Bill Holdens, Clifton Webb, and one or two others. Over the liqueurs Noël, who'd spent the previous weekend with Sinatra at Palm Springs, said: "I'm very worried about you, Frank. You're the finest singer since Al Jolson. But unless you cut down on drinking, your career won't keep going up—it's going to start running downhill."

Frank listened as attentively as a new boy getting the business from his headmaster. "I think you're right, Noël," he said quietly. And for a long time his drinking tapered off.

Is he the headstrong egomaniac who thinks he owes nothing to anybody? "You know, there's one thing I wanted to say when I accepted the Oscar for *From Here to Eternity*," he said on another day. "I wanted to thank Monty Clift personally. I learned more about acting from Clift—well, it was equal to what I learned about musicals from Gene Kelly."

He sits up to take notice of his children, too, if they criticize him. There are three of them, Nancy, Jr., Frankie, Jr., and Tina. He drove up to see me once in a new fish-tail Cadillac that, he said, his son despised. "Frankie wondered what I wanted with all that tin on the back." Father Frank dragged me out to take a look. I knew he couldn't live with the car after his boy's jeers. He sold it one month later.

Can he be at heart the willful, adult version of Peck's Bad Boy that millions of women have adored since those days when he had them swooning by their radios? Bet your boots he can. As for example . . .

Earl Warren was still governor of California when Frank was working at Metro on *Take Me Out to the Ball Game*. The studio boss was Louis B. Mayer, a big Republican with ambitions to be bigger. Louis was thrilled to bits when a spokesman for Warren asked if Frank could go to Sacramento to attend a convention of governors of all the states which was meeting there. They were eager to have him sing for them as the sole representative of the motion-picture industry. Warren would have his own private plane fly Frank there and back if he'd agree to the trip.

Louis went to work on everybody who was close to Frank, pressuring them to persuade him that the honor of Metro—and the ambitions of Louis—demanded his presence at Sacramento. Frank, for once, seemed reasonable about it. Be glad to go, he said.

Louis was delighted. He gave orders that the picture was to be closed down at two o'clock on the auspicious afternoon. That would give Frank plenty of time to clean up and change out of his baseball suit to catch the governor's plane, which would be waiting for a three o'clock take-off. "Get a picnic basket made up," Frank told Jack Keller, his press agent, "with cold chicken and wine, silver and napkins and everything, so we can eat on the plane."

Keller and Dick Jones, Frank's accompanist, were ready early, waiting with the basket in his dressing room. Two-thirty came, but no Frank. Three o'clock; not a sign of him. A worried call to Dick Hanley, Mayer's secretary, established that work on the picture had stopped punctually at 2 P.M. A check of all the gates showed that Frank hadn't left; his car was parked outside the dressing room.

"He's probably up in some dame's dressing room having a little party," somebody suggested. So a squad of security guards, standing on no ceremony, went bursting in on the stars and starlets, searching for him. Not a trace. By four-thirty Louis was having apoplexy. By five o'clock all hope of delivering Frank to Sacramento had vanished. An hour later Louis was swallowing his rage and his pride, to call Governor Warren and explain that Frank had suddenly and inexplicably taken sick.

The following morning the mystery was solved. Sinatra, in make-up and uniform, had decided at two o'clock that Sacramento wasn't for him. So he hid in the back of a workman's truck and rode unseen through the studio gates, hopped off at a stop light, and flagged down a cab to take him home.

After *The Miracle of the Bells,* which he made for RKO on loan from Metro, he was ordered to San Francisco for a charity opening of that hunk of religious baloney. Frank, who harbors an almost fanatical resentment against being told what to do, went to Jesse Lasky, the producer, whom he admired, and asked: "You won't be paying the bills?"

"Not I. RKO."

"That's all I want to know. I'll go for you."

Frank hadn't taken off his hat and coat after checking into his four-bedroom suite at the Fairmont Hotel before he called room service. "Bring up eighty-eight manhattans right away." Jack Keller, manager George Evans, and composer Jimmy Van Heusen, who'd all gone along on the trip, were determined not to ask Frank why he'd ordered the cocktails, and he never explained. Four days later, when they checked out, the eighty-eight manhattans stood untouched on the waiter's wagon.

Meantime, he'd taken the three of them on a shopping spree in the most expensive men's shop in San Francisco, to buy them alpaca sweaters, $15 neckties, and socks by the box, while the cash register clicked up a score of $2800 for one member of the party alone within forty-five minutes. "Send the lot up to the Fairmont and have 'em put it on my bill," Frank said.

Fog covered the city the morning they were due to leave, and every air liner was grounded. Mad as a caged bear, Frank tried to argue Jimmy, who is a trained pilot, into chartering a private plane. "You think I'm nuts? Take a look outside," Jimmy said.

"Forget it then," Frank snarled. "I know what to do."

He had one of his favorite picnic baskets assembled by the Blue Fox restaurant, then hired a car and chauffeur to drive Jimmy and himself to Palm Springs, five hundred miles away. But the limousine got stuck in the mountain snows and Frank and party were marooned in a farmhouse for three days. Jack Keller and George Evans caught a noontime plane when the fog lifted and were home in Los Angeles by mid-afternoon.

The car-hire bill by itself ran to $795. Like everything else in the trip, it was charged to RKO.

When Frank originally moved out to California, he picked up his own bills. They ran high. He had a weakness for showering his friends and hangers-on with such trinkets as gold cigarette lighters lovingly inscribed. He imagined that every thousand dollars of salary was worth that much money in the bank, never realizing that in his tax bracket, and with his agents' cuts, a thousand dollars probably gave him no more than ninety to spend. The more he made, the more he owed the government, until the total tab ran to nearly $110,000. It took his switch from Columbia to Capitol Records to settle the tax score. That was part of the price Capitol paid out for him.

His first full-length picture, *Higher and Higher* for RKO, brought him out to live in the Sunset Towers apartments as a grass widower, leading a life as respectable as a church warden's. No girls, no drinking except an occasional beer. When his wife, Nancy, arrived and they bought the house at Toluca Lake that Mary Astor once owned, they kept up the same, small-town ways. Their wildest parties were devoted to gin rummy at half a cent a point. Frank was as happy with Nancy as he could be with anybody for long.

Fireworks usually start to sizzle in a marriage when the husband pulls himself ahead and the wife lags behind. But Nancy, the plasterer's daughter from Jersey City, kept pace with Frank's growth as an entertainer. She's maintained her patience and her dignity over the years, saying not a malicious word about any of the women who've cluttered up Frank's life.

The first feet of film in which he appeared were actually shot for Columbia Pictures in a little low-budget item entitled *Reveille for Beverly*. Harry Cohn, boss of Columbia, thought so poorly of him that he let him escape without optioning him. Frank couldn't let him forget that.

At the Toluca Lake house, Frank, Nancy, and their friends used to stage little Christmas Eve revues, running for an hour and more, complete with scenery, costumes, props, original score by Sammy Cahn and Julie Stein, sketches and performances by anybody with a mind to pitch in and work. The jokes were all "inside" humor, drawing a bead on the members of the group.

One sketch set its sights on Peter Lawford, a celebrated party-goer from the day he arrived in Hollywood and an actor whose performances in some pictures would scarcely show up under a microscope. On the stage built in the Sinatra living room, he sat at a table entertaining a girl while Frank, dressed as a waiter, served drinks to the pair. "Give me the check," said Peter as the skit ended. "I'll take care of it."

Frank's eyeballs revolved. "You mean you'll *pay?*" he gasped as he dropped his tray on Peter's head and staggered offstage.

When the bigwigs at Columbia heard about the shows, they asked Frank to put on a similar affair at Harry Cohn's house to celebrate his birthday. It turned out to be quite a party. The guest list included Rita Hayworth, José Iturbi, Al Jolson, and the Sinatra regulars. On the temporary stage, Phil Silvers acted the part of Cohn. Al Levy, Frank's manager who went on to found Talent Associates, took the role of agent and Frank played himself. "Mr. Cohn," said Al, introducing Frank, "I have a boy here I think has great talent."

"Can't use him," growled Phil Silvers.

"But at least listen to him. Give him a chance."

"No. Too Jewish."

Al (bewildered): "He's too *Jewish?*"

"No, you are. Get out of here." Everybody had a wonderful time . . . except Harry Cohn, who didn't crack a smile.

The woman who came within an ace of wrecking Frank Sinatra sat on my patio fresh from Smithfield, North Carolina. "What do you do down there?" I asked Ava Gardner, as beautiful then as she was frank about how dirt-poor she'd been until Hollywood whistled at her.

"Oh, I just went around picking bugs off tobacco plants," she said.

The earliest matrimonial picking she made was Mickey Rooney. She was twenty and he was a year older when they married. He had what she wanted, which included his limousine, the first she ever rode in. Though they were separated some frantic years later, they remained friends and he couldn't break old habits. They were sitting side by side and directly behind me at a premiere after their divorce. I heard her whispering: "Don't do that. Stop it. People will see."

Turning around, I spotted that he had his hand down the low-cut neck of her dress. "Aw, let him play," I said. "It'll keep him quiet." He gave a grin as broad as a barn door and left his hand where it was.

Frank's passion for Ava dragged him halfway around the world: to Mexico, Spain, Africa, England, France. It broke up his marriage to Nancy in 1951; it plunged his spirits and his bank balance so low that in December 1953 he had to borrow money to buy Ava a Christmas present.

Their jealousy of each other passed the raw edge of violence. At one point in their teeth-and-claw romance Frank was hired to sing at the Copacabana in New York, while the two of them stayed in Hampshire House. While he worked nights, Ava got bored and started running around town with her friends. She strayed one evening into Bop City, where Artie Shaw, ex-husband number two, was starred with a jazz band.

The following afternoon, when Frank discovered where she'd been, the fur began to fly in his hotel bedroom. When she screamed that she was sick of his jealousy and was going to leave him, he pulled out the .38 he carried and threatened to blow his brains out. She stalked toward the door. He fired twice—into the mattress of the bed. Ava didn't turn her head; she kept right on walking.

David Selznick, in the suite next door, heard the shots and

called the front desk. The clerk there telephoned the police. Mannie Sachs, the king of talent scouts for RCA, who had a permanent suite down the hall, had also been startled by the explosions, and came running. He and Selznick hurried into Frank's room, listened to what had happened. Then they grabbed the mattress with the two holes in it and toted it down the hall, to exchange it for one on Mannie's bed. When the police arrived to search Frank's suite without finding a trace of bullets, Frank was as cool as a cat. "You're dreaming," he told them. "You're crazy."

He had already applied to Harry Cohn for the featured role of Maggio in *From Here to Eternity* when he flew to Africa in 1952 to be with Ava while she made *Mogambo* with Clark Gable and Grace Kelly. Cohn had originally doused cold water on his ambition. "You're nuts. You're a song-and-dance man. Maggio's stage-actor kind of stuff."

Frank had been in Africa five days—days of sitting around with nothing to do but watch his wife work. He killed time by building an outside shower in the woods for her. He rounded up fifty native singers and dancers for a party for cast and crew. He worked harder than on any sound stage to keep from going crazy. Then his agent, Bert Allenberg of MCA, called him back to test for *Eternity*. Frank told me the whole story later:

"I left Africa one Friday night. I had a copy of the scene and I sat up all night on the plane. Didn't sleep the whole trip. Monday morning I made the test. I finished at 3 P.M. and that night flew back to Africa. My adrenalin was bubbling. I waited five days, ten, then got a letter they were testing five or six other guys, among them Eli Wallach.

"I'd seen him in *Rose Tattoo* on Broadway, and I know he's a fine actor. So I thought: 'I'm dead.' Then I got a wire from Allenberg: 'Looks bad.' My chin was kicking my knees. But Ava was wonderful. She said: 'They haven't cast the picture yet. All you get is a stinking telegram, and you let it get you down.'

"Clark would say: 'Skipper, relax. Drink a little booze.

53

Everything will be all right.' I left Africa and went to Boston for a night-club date. I got a call another Monday morning that they'd made the deal. I told Allenberg: 'If you have to pay Harry Cohn, sign the contract; I'll pay *him*.'"

For Maggio, Frank's fee was $8000 instead of the usual $150,000. He flew off to join Ava for a few days of fun and fury in Paris. "Then I got a cable from Harry Cohn: 'Clift already proficient in army drill. Seeing as how you have same routine, suggest you get back a few days early.' I wired back: 'Dear Harry—will comply with request. Drilling with French Army over weekend. Everything all right. Maggio.' I talked to his secretary later, and she said when she opened the wire she screamed. But Cohn didn't crack a smile. He had a sense of humor like an open grave."

Unpredictable as always, Frank went with his family to the Academy Awards show when he collected an Oscar for Maggio. "The minute my name was read, I turned around and looked at the kids. Little Nancy had tears in her eyes. For a second I didn't know whether to go up on stage and get it or stay there and comfort her. But I gave her a peck on the cheek and reached for young Frankie's hand.

"When I came back, it was late, so I got them home and sat with them for a while. Then I took the Oscar back to my place, where a few people dropped in. I got Nancy a little miniature thing for her charm bracelet, a small Oscar medallion. The kids gave me a St. Genesius medal before the Awards, engraved with, 'Dad, we will love you from here to eternity.' Little Nancy gave me a medal and said, 'This is from me and St. Anthony.' That's her dear friend. She seems to get a lot done with St. Anthony. I guess she has a direct wire to him."

There's a show-business legend that, abracadabra, Frank's career started going up like a skyrocket from that moment on. It's a legend, nothing more. Turning the corner was slow going for him. He still had to play in such flops as *Suddenly* and find he was turned down for *Mr. Roberts* because Leland Hayward thought he was too old. He still had night-club tours to make under old agreements. And he still had to work out the switch to Capitol which eventually made him a best seller on records.

It took him a long time, too, to recover from Ava. She hasn't yet recovered from him. Holed up in Spain, she has been outcast to most Spaniards, who don't tolerate her flouting of their social rules. Recently she went back to work again, talking a comeback, as so many like her do. The proof, as always, lies in the performance they can deliver before the cameras.

Frank came near the end of the road he'd traveled with her when he returned unexpectedly early one day to his Palm Springs house and overheard her talking with another woman star whom she'd invited down there while he was away. The subject they were discussing, I understand, was Frank's lovemaking, which they were downgrading. Those two would do just that. "Pack up your clothes and get out," Frank yelled. "I don't want to see either of you again."

I sat in his dressing room at Paramount in December 1956 when the Ava era finally ended for him. A Hollywood reporter had taken her out driving one night in the desert around Palm Springs, gotten her drunk, and recorded what she told him over a microphone hidden in his car. The magazine story that resulted had appeared that day. Frank sat with a copy of it in his hand, cringing silently in his chair. Ava was quoted as complaining: "Frank double-crossed me . . . made me the heavy . . . I paid many of the bills." Even the ashes were cold after that.

That was the year he waged a busy-beaver campaign for Adlai Stevenson, just as he had worked for Franklin D. Roosevelt, Harry Truman, and, four years later, would slave for John F. Kennedy. He was in Spain, filming *The Pride and the Passion*, when he was asked to assist the Democratic convention in Chicago by singing "The Star-Spangled Banner" on opening night. Eager to oblige, he flew for thirty-three hours through appalling transatlantic weather and reached the convention platform at 8 P.M., a bare thirty minutes before Sam

Rayburn, late Speaker of the House of Representatives, was scheduled to gavel the session to order.

No more than four hundred people had filtered into their places in the 25,000-seat auditorium when Mr. Rayburn, fortified by bourbon, started banging away with his gavel. Frank had no choice but sing to a virtually empty hall, while his fine old Sicilian temper flamed.

During the anthem somebody alerted Sam Rayburn to his error. He went over to Frank as soon as he'd finished singing and put his hand on Sinatra's sleeve to apologize. Frank brushed him aside. "Keep your arm off my suit," he snapped, and stormed away.

When Bill Davidson wrote the story, Frank had his attorney, Martin Gang, file suit for $2,300,000. He was armed with a telegram from Rayburn asserting that the incident was undiluted imagination. All Davidson had was the word of Mitch Miller, who'd been close enough on the platform to overhear what had gone on there. There didn't seem to be any other witnesses.

But on a visit to New York soon after, a Hollywood press agent who was close to Davidson bumped into a Madison Avenue advertising man whom he hadn't seen for years. The old friend happened to tell the press agent about a funny thing he'd seen on the platform at the Democratic convention, which he'd attended on agency business: He'd watched Sinatra giving Rayburn the brush-off. Needless to say, the suit was dropped.

Politics are serious business to Frank—they used to be to me until I got tired of the game and decided to give the young ones a chance. I was doing a bit in a picture at Las Vegas while he was there making *Oceans 11*, and I wanted to talk to him. But he was always too busy. After the 1960 conventions came and went, he was off on the island of Maui doing *Devil at 4 O'Clock* before he could keep a promise to come over to my house.

From Maui he sent me a letter "giving you all the answers to the questions you would have asked me if we actually did an interview." He's a John F. Kennedy man and I was a Robert Taft woman; what better subject for a letter than politics, Sinatra version?

"Every four years," he wrote, "the same question arises: Should show-business personalities become involved in politics? Should they use their popularity with the public to try to influence votes?

"My answer has always been 'yes.' If the head of a big corporation can try to use his influence with his employees, if a union head can try to use his influence with his members, if a newspaper editor can try to use his influence with his readers, if a columnist can try to use his influence, then an actor has a perfect right to try to use his influence.

"My own feeling is that those actors who do not agree with my point of view are those who are afraid to stand up and be counted. They want everybody to love them and want everybody to agree with them on everything.

"I am not sure whether they are right or whether I am right. I only know what is right for me . . ."

I almost tore up the letter as soon as I'd read it because of its last paragraph: "Maybe it will make a good Sunday piece for you. If you think so, then please don't start to edit it. These are my thoughts, and if you want to pass them on to your readers, let them stand as is." I haven't edited; I've quoted, but not all five pages. Life's too short for that, and you probably wouldn't read them, anyway.

Though he's proud to be a Democrat, he's uneasy about being called a "Clansman." The Clan consists of the men with which this mixed-up, lonely talent has surrounded himself—Dean Martin, Sammy Davis, Jr., Joey Bishop, Peter Pentagon Lawford.

"I hate the name of Clan," Frank once said.

"Did you ever look the word up in a dictionary?" I said. "It means a family group that sticks together, like the Kennedys you're so fond of. They're the most clannish family in America. I don't like Rat Pack, but there's nothing wrong with the name of Clan."

57

What is wrong with the Clan and the Leader, as his gang have christened Frank, is the pull they both have over young actors who would give their back teeth to be IN. Membership dues include generally behaving like Mongols from the court of Genghis Khan.

The Clan was riding high the night Eddie Fisher opened his night-club act at the Ambassador Hotel here, before the *Cleopatra* debacle got under way. I was in New York at the time. Frank and his henchmen took over and mashed Eddie's performance. "This was a disgusting display of ego," snorted Milton Berle, sitting in an audience that included comedians like Jerry Lewis, Danny Thomas, and Red Buttons, any one of whom, if he'd tried, could have joined in and made the Clan look silly. Elizabeth Taylor, on Eddie's side that night, raged: "He may have to take it from them, but I don't. One day they'll have to answer to me for this."

Steve McQueen was one young actor I managed to extricate from the Clan. I took him under my wing when he was driving racing cars around like an astronaut ready for orbit. "You could kill yourself when you were single, and it was only your concern. But you've got a family and responsibilities now. Think of them." Between his wife and myself, we got him away from overpowered automobiles.

I took to Steve as soon as I saw him in "Wanted Dead or Alive." I liked his arrogant walk, the don't-give-a-damn air about him. So did Frank. When he sent Sammy Davis, Jr., into temporary exile for indiscreet talk to a newspaper about other Clansmen, Frank had Sammy's part in *Never So Few* rewritten for Steve. When Frank is in a movie, he becomes casting director, too.

He took Steve on a junket to New York when the picture ended, and Steve took along a big bundle of Mexican fire-crackers, which he cherishes. He hadn't previously been any kind of drinker, but in Frank's crowd you drink. From the tenth floor of his hotel Steve had a ball tossing lighted fire-crackers into Central Park. When the police ran him to earth, it took all of Frank's influence to keep him out of jail.

As a peace offering, Steve had a live monkey delivered to my office in advance of his return. He wasted his time. I don't like monkeys, so I gave it away and summoned Steve for some Dutch-aunt lecturing when he got back. "I know all about your trip. You were loud, boorish, and probably drunk. You have to make up your mind whether you'll have a big career as Steve McQueen or be one of Frank Sinatra's set. Think it over."

Twenty-four hours later he gave me his answer. "I was out of line. I was flattered that Mr. Sinatra wanted me, but I'd rather stand on my own feet."

I sometimes wonder about the Leader. His face lit up like a neon sign when he broke the news to me that he was going to marry Juliet Prowse, the South African dancer to whom he was engaged for an hour or so. "I haven't seen that light in your eye for ten years," I told him.

But I suspect the men around Frank went to work against Juliet. It's easy enough to work the trick if you're determined and unscrupulous. A word dropped into the conversation here and there will plant the doubts. "Do you think she really goes for you, Frank?" "She'll probably figure on keeping her career." "You should have met that family of hers—strictly nothing." Frank was convinced eventually that Juliet wasn't for him.

With all his talents and power, I sometimes wonder who's the Leader and who's being led.

Four

When Louella Parsons heard that I'd started work on this book, she telephoned to ask what its title was going to be. "Come, Louella," I said, "you don't expect me to reveal that to you, do you?"

"I hoped you would. And I hope you'll be kind to me in your book because I was very nice to you in mine."

"You certainly were—you got the facts about me so mixed up that I haven't finished reading it."

"Well, anyway, what are you going to write about?"

"I'm just going to tell the truth."

"Oh, dear," she wailed, "that's what I was afraid of."

In the days when I earned my living as a motion-picture actress, I was one of Louella's regular news contacts. I had an insatiable curiosity about the town I'd known for years. I got around a lot, and lots of people talked to me. I salted down stories by the barrel load.

Louella would call up and say: "I understand you went to so-and-so's party last night. Tell me something about it." I was glad to oblige. Payment came in kind, not cash, when she inserted my name in her column, which helped a working actress.

She really was the First Lady of Hollywood then, for one good reason which nobody was allowed to forget. She was William Randolph Hearst's movie columnist, and he was lavishing millions of dollars and acres of publicity space on his motion-picture properties, bent on making himself the greatest of all impresarios and Marion Davies the greatest star.

With the Hearst newspaper empire behind her, Louella could wield power like Catherine of Russia. Hollywood read every word she wrote as though it was a revelation from San

Simeon, if not from Mount Sinai. Stars were terrified of her. If they crossed her, they were given the silent treatment: no mention of their names in her column.

When Hearst let himself be lured by Louis B. Mayer into putting his own production company, Cosmopolitan Pictures, under MGM's wing, Louella's power was apparently complete. She could get any story she wanted front-paged in the Los Angeles *Examiner* and all other Hearst papers, none of them accustomed to making much distinction between real news and flagrant publicity.

At San Simeon, Hearst's $40,000,000 Shangri-La in San Luis Obispo County, Louella mingled with the stream of visiting celebrities, stars, and producers that poured every weekend into the fabulous, twin-towered castle or the surrounding marble "bungalows" at the summons of W.R. or Marion. So did I. At the fifty-four-foot table in the Renaissance dining hall, you'd see Garbo, John Gilbert, Errol Flynn, Norma Shearer, Nick Schenck, Beatrice Lillie, Cissy Patterson, Frank Knox, Bernard Baruch. Name the biggest and they'd be there, including, on one occasion, Mr. and Mrs. Cal Coolidge and Bernard Shaw.

Nobody would deny that Louella has talent. She showed at her best with GBS, who was writing some articles for Hearst. All of us invited to San Simeon that weekend had been warned against asking Shaw for an interview. That didn't stop Louella. He yielded to her persuasions only on condition that he have the right to approve every word of her article after he'd talked to her.

When she went back with the typescript, he had her read it to him. After the first few words, he interrupted sharply: "But I didn't say that."

"Oh, Mr. Shaw," she said, batting her big brown eyes, "I'm so nervous just being in your presence. What was it you said before?" He repeated the sentence, which she carefully inserted, and then read another line or two before the irate Irishman pulled her up short again.

This performance went on for some minutes longer before

61

GBS took the manuscript from her hand. "Give it to me—I'll write it myself," he said firmly, proceeding to do just that. But Louella wasn't through yet. When he handed back the completed article to her, she asked: "Oh, Mr. Shaw, won't you please autograph it for me? It will be such a wonderful keepsake for my daughter, Harriet."

He couldn't refuse; he was writing for Hearst, too. So Miss Parsons scored in a triple-header. She collected the only interview Bernard Shaw gave in the United States. She subsequently sold the article to a Hearst magazine. And she has the autographed interview, which someday will sell for another tidy sum.

Some of us San Simeon regulars discovered that Louella isn't slow to take credit. When W.R. and Marion went abroad on one of the many voyages they made together, we decided to throw a party for them on their return. We intended it as a gesture of thanks for all the parties of theirs that we'd enjoyed. We put on a terrific evening at the Ambassador Hotel, with its rooms crammed with flowers and cockatoos, and split the bill between us: $175 apiece. Louella was one of the party, and I'll be damned if she didn't write an article for a national magazine taking credit for it.

She owed a lot to Marion Davies. It was an article praising Marion in *When Knighthood Was in Flower* that got Louella started with Hearst. It caught W.R.'s eye and prompted him to hire her away from her $110 a week as movie reporter on the New York *Telegraph* into working for him at more than twice the salary. Over the years Marion shielded Louella from boss trouble more than once. After W.R. died in 1951, she was among those who didn't exactly hurry to give Marion sympathy.

She did ring the doorbell, however, immediately after Marion had appeared on my television show. She arrived at her house bearing as a gift a photograph of herself in a heavy silver frame. She proceeded to place it in full view on a table in the front hall, taking star position ahead of an autographed portrait of General Douglas MacArthur.

Marion asked me to take a look when I arrived soon after Louella had left. I carried it back to the library, where Marion was sitting. "Do you want this?"

"No," she said quizzically. I took the frame home to substitute a photograph of Marion standing beside me on the TV show, returning the old frame and new picture to her the following day.

Louella didn't regard me as a serious rival when I got started as a columnist in 1938. Andy Harvey, in MGM's publicity department, had recommended me to Howard Denby of the *Esquire* syndicate: "When we want the low-down on our stars, we get it from Hedda Hopper." I was signed by Mr. Denby and sold to thirteen papers straightaway, the first to buy being the Los Angeles *Times*.

The betting in town after column number one appeared was that I wouldn't last a week. My mistake was being too kind to everybody. I didn't tell the whole truth—only the good. I set out to write about my fellows in terms of sweetness and light, not reality. I began:

Just twenty-three years ago my son was born. Since then I've acted in Broadway plays. Sold Liberty Bonds in Grand Central Station. Knitted socks for soldiers—which they wore as sweaters. Made very bad speeches on the steps of the New York Library. Helped build a snowman on Forty-second Street . . . when the streetcars were frozen solidly in their tracks. Earned money for one year as a prima donna in *The Quaker Girl* with only two tones in my voice, high and low—very low. Played in *Virtuous Wives*, Louis B. Mayer's first motion picture.

I've worked with practically every star in Hollywood. Sold real estate here—made it pay, too, but not lately. Was a contributor to one of the monthly magazines. Did special articles for the Washington *Herald*. With a friend, wrote a one-act play. Through pull had it produced at the Writers' Club and was it panned! Ran for a political job here; thank goodness the citizens had a better idea! Coached Jan Kiepura in diction. Learned about the beauty business from Elizabeth Arden in her Fifth Avenue salon. Made three trips abroad, one to England on business. Put on fashion shows. Have a radio program.

And today I begin laboring in a new field and am hoping it will bring me as much happiness as that major event which took place twenty-three years ago. I can only write about the Hollywood I know. About my neighbors and fellow workers. Amazing stories have been written—many true. Hollywood is mad, gay, heartbreakingly silly, but you can't satirize a satire. And that's Hollywood . . .

I was green as grass, and the town jeered at me. Luckily, I had a good friend at my side. Wonderful Ida Koverman carried the title of executive assistant to Louis B. Mayer, but she was the real power behind his throne. To all intent and purpose, she ran MGM. Two months after my launching, when I was sinking slowly in an ocean of kind words for everybody, she gave a hen party for me. On the guest list were Norma Shearer, Jeanette MacDonald, singer Rosa Ponselle, Claudette Colbert, Joan Crawford, Sophie Tucker, press people, public-relations people—every woman you could think of. There was only one holdout—Louella.

It was a night to remember. A forest fire was blazing in the hills, and the sky was lit with flame. I was burning, too. Ida had just set me straight about column writing. "They've laughed at you long enough. You've been too nice to people. Now start telling the truth."

That was the best advice she ever gave me. It marked a turning point. My telephone started ringing like a fire alarm every day soon after.

"Hedda," the callers would moan, "how can you print such things about me?"

"It's true, isn't it?"

"Yes, but you're my friend. I didn't think you'd tell."

"I'm earning my living with my column. I've got to tell the truth. You didn't call when I wrote sweet nothings about you, did you? If you can't face facts, then I'm sorry."

The column began to grow almost instantly, on the way up to its present readership of 35,000,000 people, which came

64

about after I switched from *Esquire* to the Des Moines *Register & Tribune*, then in 1942 to Chicago *Tribune*-New York *News* syndication. (If I stop to think of that audience figure, I get so scared I can't write a line until I've pushed the arithmetic out of my mind.)

Louella prepared for a fight. She had an intelligence service that included telegraph operators, telephone switchboard girls, beauty-parlor assistants, hotel bus boys, doctors' and dentists' receptionists. Her medical-intelligence chief was her husband, Dr. Harry Watson Martin. She called him Docky or Docky-Wocky. He was often known as Lolly's Pop. His special field earlier had been venereal disease and urology, his hobby was show business, and he retired as head of the Twentieth Century-Fox medical department.

Docky had the friendship of everybody, along with a certain nonchalance. He once took a dive into the Bimini Bath pool when it lacked a single drop of water, broke his neck, and lived to marry Louella in 1929. He displayed a similar unconcern about water one morning when Louella, dressed up to go ashore for Mass, made her cautious way down the gangplank of a yacht in Catalina Harbor straight into the sea. Docky was waiting in the dinghy, engrossed in the Sunday papers. "Ready to go, dear?" he asked, not raising his head until her splashing drew him to her rescue.

Leaving a party, Docky once fell flat on the floor and lay there, comfortable enough. When a friend came forward to hoist him up, Louella put out a restraining hand. "Oh, don't touch him, please. He has to operate at eight o'clock this morning."

Through Docky's good offices, Louella had a tie-in with testing laboratories, notably those making rabbit tests for pregnancy. This private line into the womb could give her news that a star was pregnant before the girl knew it herself.

But I had sleuths on my side, too. As an actress, I knew directors, producers, stars, and the men and women who worked on the other side of the cameras. One special ally was Mark Hellinger, a hard-boiled columnist for the New York

Daily News before he became a gentle, kind, and great producer for Warner Brothers and Universal.

He called me over to his house for an off-the-record conference and offered to help "because you're going to need it." He said: "I don't somehow care for what Miss Parsons stands for. Whenever I hear a story at the studio, I'll pass it on to you. I shan't be able to call you through the switchboard, so I'll give it to you from a private booth. There won't be time for questions, but you'll get the truth."

The scoops I had on the affairs of Warner Brothers nearly drove Jack Warner out of his cotton-picking mind. He could never make out how it happened. When he reads this, he'll know.

Louella watched her monopoly start to crack. If she was asked to a party, she'd want to know whether I was going to be invited. If I was, she'd demand that I be excluded "or else I certainly shan't come." Some timid hostesses fell for that. I laughed in their faces for their cowardice.

Anxious to break her hold, producers were steering my way more and more of the items that had previously been hers alone—the news of engagements, weddings, pregnancies, and divorces that made up a fat share of her daily diet. An engagement announced first to Louella had been good for six months of smiles for the happy couple. An exclusive on a pregnancy was even better—the mother-to-be could count on nine months' favorable notice, which could be extended if she gave Lolly a beat on the birth announcement, too.

The competition she was getting didn't make her any fonder of me. When Jean Parker was about to marry for the second time, she telephoned me: "I want you to have this exclusively."

"No," I warned her, "you must tell Louella."

"But I don't want her to have it."

"You can't afford to give it to me alone. Call her and tell her I have the news, too. For your career's sake, you must."

Ten minutes later she called back, weeping. "I did what you said and told her I'd given it to you. She said: 'Get it back from her, or I won't print it.'"

"Tell her she's got it exclusively, if it means so much to her," I said. "What's one story among friends—and you'll need friends."

If a studio passed along a story to me that Louella thought she should have, she raised the roof, if necessary going over everybody involved to the studio head himself: "Hopper was given that. I should have had it. Don't let it happen again."

Even a producer as peppery as Darryl Zanuck had reservations about doing anything that might antagonize her. Zanuck, at that time Twentieth Century-Fox production chief, thought nothing of squaring off and mixing it in a fist fight with a director who argued with him. But when Bill Wellman, after three days of shooting on *Public Enemy*, urged that Eddie Wood, who was the star, should be replaced in that gangster epic by a newcomer who had the second lead, Jimmy Cagney, the fiery Zanuck flinched.

"My God, we can't do it, Bill. Eddie's engaged to Harriet Parsons, Louella's daughter. Parsons will raise hell."

"You son of a bitch," answered Bill, who's a flinty character. "You mean you're going to let that decide it?"

"Damn it, no," said Zanuck, put on his metal. "You go and put Cagney in." And that's how two men with guts turned an ex-chorus boy into a star.

Harriet married not Eddie Wood but King Kennedy. There were more stars in attendance than there are in the Milky Way when the two of them became man and wife at Marsden Farms in the San Fernando Valley in September 1939. Some of the guests were old-timers like Rudy Vallee, Billy Haines, Aileen Pringle, Frances Marion, and myself. The photographers ignored us completely, to the point where Billy got spitting mad.

He went up to Hymie Fink, who had been the town's best still photographer since Valentino's day. "We'll each give you five bucks if you'll take a picture of us," Billy offered. But Hymie couldn't do it. He had his orders, he said. After Mr. and Mrs. Kennedy were divorced in 1944, King came to work for me as leg man, covering the studios for a while, but I insisted that he get Louella's consent before I hired him.

Not many men had the courage of Bill Wellman and Darryl Zanuck. I was in a roomful of faint hearts at a party the Gary Coopers gave when Gene Tierney made a beeline for me: "I've been trying to get you all afternoon to tell you I'm going to have another baby."

That was wonderful news. Louella and I both knew that Gene's first child, a beautiful little girl, had been born with a sleeping mind—it was one of the many blows that life dealt Gene, who finally cracked under the torment and needed psychiatric care. I hustled to the telephone, but it was tied up with a call to Henry Hathaway, who was a patient at the Mayo Clinic in Rochester, Minnesota. By the time I got through to the *Times* night desk, Gene was nowhere to be found to verify her news for the paper. But Louella had barged over to me and was hanging on like a limpet.

Next morning I heard what had happened. Gene's studio had given the story of the forthcoming baby exclusively to Louella the previous afternoon. When she heard Gene had told me, she had flounced over to the poor girl and delivered a tongue lashing so violent that Gene had collapsed into tears. Gary Cooper had been in another room and didn't hear it, but of the whole mob of Hollywood heroes who listened to Louella, not one lifted a voice or a finger to help Gene. Fear of their own precious skins kept them as dumb as mutes at a funeral.

Even Frank Sinatra had to come to terms with Louella in her heyday. He stood high in her disfavor for months. It seemed there was nothing he could do to stop the attacks she made on him. I thought I might be able to help, so I suggested through Perry Charles, his agent, that Frank should call Marion and arrange to meet Hearst. The meeting came about, and Frank made a good impression. The order was passed down from San Simeon, and Miss Parsons suddenly discovered that Sinatra was nowhere near as black as she'd imagined him.

Clark Gable and Carole Lombard flouted the "first to know" rule Louella had laid down when they set their wedding day to coincide with Louella's absence from town—she'd gone off on a trip to San Francisco. She was on the train coming home when she got the news that they were married. "It can't be true," she gasped. "They would have told me first."

But Clark had given the story to all newspapers simultaneously to avoid any bickering over who should have first whack. She took such a dim view of that, though, that the Gables felt they had to make up to her by means of a distinctly unusual present: They had her bathroom done over with mirrored walls and brand-new plumbing.

Orson Welles is one of the few who never gave a damn for her. When he was making *Citizen Kane*, a picture with a striking resemblance to the life of William Randolph Hearst, he persuaded Louella that the story was something entirely unconnected with her chief. I wasn't convinced so easily, and Orson finally agreed to let me see the first screening of the finished product in a private projection room of RKO. What I saw appalled me.

W.R. had been a friend to me for years. So had Orson, ever since I'd been a struggling actress and he'd gone out of his way to be kind to my son Bill, who was a struggling young actor. When Hearst learned that I'd been hired as a columnist, he said: "Why didn't you come to me? I didn't know you wanted to write a column. I'd have given you one."

"Have I ever asked you for anything?" "No," he said. "What makes you think I'd ask for anything as important as this is to me?"

"Everybody else asks for things. Why not you?"

"I don't ask," I said. Then he wrote me this, to which I didn't reply:

My dear Hedda:
I am glad you are going to do some work for the *Esquire* Syndicate. The *Esquire* people are very clever. They produce a fine publication and they know good stuff.

I always thought that the stuff you did for the Washington paper was extremely good.

It was accurate, interesting, and high-grade. It appealed to intelligent people, who like the movies—and there are lots of them. So many moving-picture commentators write down to the level of the movies, as they call it.

I always figure, however, that these commentators write down because they cannot write up.

Best wishes. I will look for your column.

Sincerely,

(s) W.R.

After the screening Orson asked how I liked it. "You won't get away with it," I said. But he arrogantly insisted that he would. It was his arrogance that decided which of two friendships had to come out ahead. I put in a call to Oscar Lawler, a great friend of mine and one of W.R.'s attorneys, to tell him about *Citizen Kane* and what Orson was up to.

As soon as word was passed along to W.R., he telephoned Louella. When she heard I'd seen the picture already and that, contrary to the assurances she'd given him, it had a great deal to do with the chief's affairs, the sky fell in on her. He commanded her to have it screened for Oscar Lawler and herself. After the showing she begged the attorney to go home with her to help describe to Hearst what they had seen, but he declined. She had to get on the telephone herself to San Simeon, just as later she made many calls, including one to Nelson Rockefeller, in a battle royal to keep *Citizen Kane* out of Radio City Music Hall, which is part of Rockefeller Center, and every other movie theater.

If W.R. had taken Oscar Lawler's advice to ignore *Kane*, it might never have received the attention it won when, breaking the boycott ten months later, it was shown around the world, won a Best Picture of the Year award, and, as late as 1958, was named as one of the greatest movies ever made. But on W.R.'s orders Orson Welles' name went on the Hearst Silent List of people about whom Louella could never say a kind word.

The black list constantly makes its presence felt. When Nunnally Johnson aided and abetted in a blistering article

70

about her that appeared in the *Saturday Evening Post*, she hit back at his wife.

"I ran into Dorris Bowdon last night," she wrote. "She used to be such a pretty girl before she married." Joan Crawford, Nelson Eddy, Jimmy Cagney, and Ava Gardner have all had the treatment.

Bette Davis and I were administered a slap on the wrist after I tracked her down to Laguna, where she holed up, refusing to talk to newspapers, following the birth of her May Day baby in 1947. The door of the cottage was open, so I walked in, and we talked for hours. The next week Louella wrote: "Since Bette Davis has had so many unwelcome visitors, she has had to have her gate padlocked."

As a present for the baby, Jack Warner sent Bette an add-a-pearl necklace with five pearls on it and space for the donor to add another each birthday. Recently I asked Bette if her daughter's necklace was still growing. She gave that raucous laugh of hers and replied: "It's just the size it was the day you came to visit me."

Personally, like Louella, I've found that silence is the greatest blow you can deliver to a Hollywood ego when it needs whacking down to size. Not to mention the name of a star drives him half out of his mind; they live and die by publicity. Not even producers are immune, as Sam Goldwyn demonstrated. He cabled me once from Hawaii, where my day's eight hundred words apparently were read so faithfully that even when wartime restrictions limited the paper there to four pages, I had to be squeezed in somehow. Sam complained: NAME NOT IN COLUMN FOR WEEK STOP THEY DO NOT THINK I'M IMPORTANT OVER HERE STOP PLEASE DO SOMETHING ABOUT IT.

Ginger Rogers and Ronald Colman were both excommunicated by Louella for years for their effrontery in refusing to appear on her former radio show, "Hollywood Hotel." As mistress of ceremonies, she collected $2500 a week and the stars appeared free. If any star balked, the producers hastened to Louella's aid by putting the pressure on until that star was convinced of the error of his ways. Total value of the free talent has been estimated by better mathematicians than I at $2,000,000. For a while, her sponsor, a soup company, was delighted to pay a weekly tab of about $12,000 for a show which, without her, would have cost well over $30,000.

But after the soup maker had been replaced by a soap maker and the show had been restyled as "Hollywood Premieres," the Screen Actors Guild plucked up its corporate courage to do what only Ginger and Colman had dared. The Guild ruled that Louella had to pay her guests, and thirteen weeks later the program was off the air.

She showed her power when Mary Pickford organized a radio spectacular, to be sponsored by a milk company, to benefit the Motion Picture Home, where poverty drives so many veterans of the movie business. Gable and dozens of other stars wanted to appear, but Louella got busy on her telephones. Mary had to back down and cancel the program with the stars in her living room waiting to go on.

For one of my radio series I wanted to hit up the competitive theme, which press agents had originally invented. They rubbed their hands when I got started because, by having us fight, they thought they could get double space and play off one columnist against the other.

Louella didn't seem to sense what they were up to. I said: "Let's take a tip from Jack Benny and Fred Allen and whip up a feud. We could have a mountain of fun. It would increase our audience ratings, and we might get a salary increase out of it. Supposing on the first show we staged a battle royal and both got carried out on stretchers . . ." But Louella wouldn't play.

Habit dies hard with her if she is invited to appear with me for a photograph, still shot, or movie. When Charles Brackett and Billy Wilder wanted us to appear together in *Sunset Boulevard* as reporters breaking the news of the murder, they extended the first bid to me. I began scheming a scene in which she and I would rush for a telephone simultaneously.

Then I would trip and say sweetly: "After you, Louella."

When she got her invitation and was told I had already been signed, she stormed: "Get her off. I won't be in it if she is." They would have none of that, so Miss Parsons did not appear in *Sunset Boulevard*. And she didn't mention the picture in her column for months.

She didn't know what to do when *Time* ran a cover story and a cover portrait along with ten columns of some highly flattering prose about yours sincerely. (Hopper "is a self-appointed judge and censor of all that goes on in Hollywood," said *Time*, "and she carries out her assignment with a hey nonny-nonny and the old one-two.") In frustration, Louella took to her bed.

The studios were in a panic. They couldn't afford to have Louella out of action. She's too useful to them. They know how to handle her, where I'm a tougher nut to crack. If she lays hold of a scandal, she does not print it unless the studio involved is willing. When scandal comes in range of my telescope, I'll print it so long as it's news and true. Press agents can't stand it; the business they're in should be called suppress agentry. They've suppressed far more than they've ever passed out as news. In the olden days, when Louella reigned alone, there was a mighty loud to suppress, too.

As she slid into a decline through sheer aggravation over *Time*, her spirits were rapidly restored by a suggestion put up by Adela Rogers St. John, the magazine writer: "Give Louella the most wonderful dinner party Hollywood has seen, then maybe she'll forget about the cover story."

Now Louella has accepted every conceivable and inconceivable degree, doctorate, scroll, and plaque held out by college or corporation. Testimonial dinners to her are routine, though Eddie Cantor may have said a little more than he meant at a Masquers Club event celebrating her thirtieth anniversary as a columnist when he conceded: "I am here for the same reason everybody else is—we were afraid not to come."

The idea of putting on a super-size testimonial caught on

with every producer who heard about it. The Ambassador Hotel's Cocoanut Grove was hired and treated to a face lift for the big event. It was originally planned to collect $25 from each of the hundreds of guests who sat among the papier-mâché monkeys and imitation palm trees, but when Hearst heard about it, he footed the whole bill.

Daily Variety did the evening up proud: "The guest list was the Who's Who of motion pictures, and even the oldest old-timer could not recall when so many reigning stars of the past, present, and future, in toto, as well as agents, press agents, producers, directors, authors, distributors, studio chiefs, maîtres d'hôtel, the mayor, and governor all got together in one room. Flanked by industry leaders, Miss Parsons sat on a garland-strewn dais and listened to oratory in which no adjectives were spared."

As a climax, Louella collected a gold plaque with an engraved inscription to her "courage, accuracy, fairness and curiosity." *Time's* account noted: "Such well-established stars as Clark Gable and Cary Grant allowed themselves the liberty of not attending."

All I know about it, I read in the papers. I wasn't invited. Neither was Adela Rogers St. John.

My modest contribution to the welfare of Louella and her family took the form of some column paragraphs that appeared soon after the Cocoanut Grove whingding: "*I Remember Mama*, and you will, too, when you have seen the film. With all the elements of good theater and good cinema, humor, humanity and hominess, it will be hard to forget . . . to Harriet Parsons, who found the story and produced the picture, must go a lot of credit . . ."

That was the final chapter in a story that had started four years earlier. Harriet is an only child; her father was John Parsons, who died following the breakup of Louella's first marriage, before Docky came on the scene. RKO had signed Harriet as a producer, and she set to work delving into the studio's files, looking for likely properties. She dug out *The Enchanted Cottage*, had it prepared for the screen, arranged a deal with Sam Goldwyn to borrow Teresa Wright as the heroine. Then suddenly it was snatched away from her and given to another writer-producer.

Undeterred, she went back to the files and excavated a story called *Mama's Bank Account,* which was retitled *I Remember Mama,* and lined up Katina Paxinou to play in it. That, too, was grabbed from her by RKO. At that point, I stepped in with a column item relating Harriet's misfortunes and asking: "What goes on? Harriet's clever, and I think this is shabby treatment, even for Hollywood."

The day after the item appeared *The Enchanted Cottage* was returned to her—it was a big success when she produced it—and she got *I Remember Mama* back, too. Louella had been restored in health and spirit in time to attend the preview, though in a seat removed from mine. "I expect Harriet's picture will be very good," she confided to a friend, "but I know one person here who won't give it a good review."

Harriet was in New York, where she read my notice in the *News.* She telephoned her mother. "Have you read Hedda's column?"

"No, I never read that column," Louella sniffed.

"She's done what nobody else would do for me. I want you to call her and thank her for me." Louella did, and we arranged a peace parley over a luncheon table at Romanoff's for one o'clock the following day. When she walked in, a bit late as usual, every chin in the place dropped. Hasty telephone calls brought in a mob of patrons who stood six deep at the bar to witness our version of the signing of the Versailles Peace Treaty. Nobody moved until we left arm in arm two hours later.

Harriet, whom I'll always like, wired: YOU AND MA WOULD MANAGE TO TOP ME STOP YOUR HISTORIC LUNCH HAS NOW CROWDED I REMEMBER MAMA OFF THE FRONT PAGE STOP YOU GALS MIGHT HAVE WAITED FOR BABY. After that, she won a ten-year contract at RKO. But peace between Louella and me wasn't wonderful enough to last very long.

The flames of our relationship blazed merrily one Christmas when a studio head unwittingly poured fuel oil on. Louella and I are on the same list for good-will offerings from studios, which fill my living room from floor to ceiling every season.

One Christmas just before Ernie Pyle went off on his last visit to the South Pacific, he came to call on me with some friends. After a few drinks in the den, I said: "Ernie, do you want to see what fear can bring a female in this town?"

We went into my living room. He looked in wonder at the loot and said softly: "I don't believe it. I just don't believe it."

Not every female star gets carried away with generosity. Doris Day once sent me boxes of gift-wrapped chocolate-covered pretzels, and Rosalind Russell a fist-sized hunk of coral such as you'd find in a fish bowl. Louella's loot exceeds mine. Once, I'm told, she collected an automobile.

One unlucky studio chief had bought expensive handbags for each of us, but they got switched in delivery. When I telephoned to thank him and included a glowing description of the bag, I could hear his face fall. "But that's Louella's," he moaned. "Will you be a doll and send it on to her and explain?"

"Like the devil I will," I countered crisply. Louella is certain to this day that I got a better present than she did. Another store's mistake brought me two handsome cut-crystal decanters for another Yuletide, one engraved HH, the other LOP. "Would you return hers to me?" said their donor.

"Not for the world. It makes such a gay conversation piece when I can ask a guest: 'Would you like some Jack Daniels out of Louella's bottle?'"

I regard her ungrudgingly as a good reporter, though she doesn't always get her facts straight where I'm concerned. (Nor do I sometimes.) She invariably pretends that I am published only in the Los Angeles *Times*, so her followers won't know about the syndicate, which gives Hopper a considerable edge in readership.

She has sometimes been tripped by her own prose. When

Warners years ago chose Alan Mowbray to play George Washington in *Alexander Hamilton,* she took aim and fired: "It seems strange to me that an Englishman would be cast as the father of our country." During the days when Mussolini invaded Albania and lives were snuffed out by the thousands, she decided: "The deadly dullness of the past week was lifted today when Darryl Zanuck announced he had bought all rights to *The Blue Bird* for Shirley Temple."

In a reminiscent mood she noted: "I don't know how many of my readers remember John Barrymore and Dolores Costello in *Trilby,* the George Du Maunier story, but my mind goes back to John just loving the part of Svengali, wearing a black beard and hypnotizing the artist's model who could only sing when he cast his baleful eye on her." As Irving Hoffman recalled: "There wasn't a thing wrong in the story except that the name of the picture was *Svengali,* not *Trilby,* the leading lady was Marian Marsh, not Dolores Costello . . . du Maurier wrote it, not Du Maunier."

Louella left me with egg on my face with her exclusive story that Ingrid Bergman was going to have a baby by Roberto Rossellini while she was still the wife of Dr. Peter Lindstrom. This, a few months after I'd interviewed Bergman at the scene of the crime and left Rome convinced by her that Italian newspapers had lied in their linotypes when they called her pregnant!

I will always believe that Joe Steele (the press agent employed both by her and her studio boss, Howard Hughes) subsequently told the truth to Louella. When her scoop appeared and the newspapers were hunting for Joe, they couldn't find him. Seems she had persuaded him he was in bad shape, made sure he didn't suffer thirst or hunger, then kept him safe and sound for three days away from her competitors.

After her story had been spread to the world, it seemed like a good idea to do something to help Ingrid, who wanted a quick divorce so that her baby could be spared at least a part of the stigma. I thought that perhaps she could be smuggled by plane out of Italy to some other country, where only

77

friends would know exactly when or if the child was born.

Plans were going beautifully when the plan was broached to Ingrid. She refused to have anything to do with it. She would have her child proudly, she said, and if anyone didn't like the idea he could lump it.

In 1951, Docky Martin died of cancer in Cedars of Lebanon Hospital. It was a crushing blow for Louella. Not long ago, she found herself there, too, for an operation. The feebleness in her voice alarmed me. "I'm so tired of this place," she said, "and I'm so sick."

I had a word with Harry Brand, publicity director of Twentieth Century-Fox and a good friend to Louella and Docky: "If you want her to live, you'd better get her out of that hospital. Either she's in the same room that Docky had or one exactly like it. She'll never recover until she's moved."

Nobody apparently had thought of that. She was out of there and into the Beverly Hills Hotel the next day. Her column power is still potent, but the times and temper of Hollywood have changed. Though she doesn't change, you can't help but feel sorry for her. She still belabors her enemies and coos over her intimates: Mervyn LeRoy, Jimmy McHugh, Cobina Wright, all the Catholic "A" group that includes Loretta Young, Irene Dunne, Dolores Hope. She still pretends not to read Hopper, but when I broke the news of Kay Gable's pregnancy, on the strength of a tip from a crew member on *The Misfits*, Louella must have read the item and put in a call instantly to Kay, begging to be the child's godmother. At the baptism her hands were so shaky we were scared stiff she'd let young John Clark Cable fall on the floor by the font.

Louella claims that the people she writes about are all her dear, dear friends, a total she once estimated at 312. My taste runs closer to that of Dema Harshbarger, my manager, whom I have known since she first put me on radio. "I have three friends in the world," says Dema, "and I don't want any more. The average Hollywood friendship today wouldn't buy you a ham sandwich."

Five

One of the legends that haunts the typewriters of most of Hollywood's five hundred resident reporters and columnists insists that our town is just like Podunk, a typical American community with a heart as big as Cinerama. (Are you there, Louella?) This is true, of course—give or take a few billion dollars a year. Provided Podunk can muster three dozen and more Rolls-Royces outside a movie house for a new picture opening. And pay a good cook $500 a week to steal her away from the best friend. And produce half a dozen houses with built-in pipe organs and one with wood-burning fireplaces in both the master and children's bathrooms—it used to belong to Maggie Sullavan and Leland Hayward but Fred MacMurray owns it now.

If the majority of people in Podunk worship money like a god, then there isn't much to choose between us. Take a man like Dean Martin. If Podunkians judge their fellows by how many dollars they earn, then Dean would be right at home. There was the day he got to arguing with his press agent about Albert Einstein.

"I made $20,000 last week," Dean said. "What do you think he made?"

"You're right," said the press agent, a thoughtful soul. "That Einstein's a dummy. I bet he never earned more than $12,000 a year in his whole life. He's got to be an idiot." Dean had the grace to grin. In Hollywood, where the love of money can change people's nature every bit as fast as in Podunk, he has a reputation for cool blood behind his beaming Italian charm.

He isn't alone in his class. It's an obvious weakness among singers. Perry Como, for instance, sets few records for making appearances for charity. Bing Crosby, who enjoys almost noth-

79

ing about his profession except the income it brings him, can't be dragged to a benefit. It took his fiery little Irish mother, Kate, to push him out of his house to one Academy Awards show when he was at the top of his career. "You'll go," she threatened, "or you'll never hear the last of it from me." Kate was a woman to be reckoned with and still is. That was the night Bing got his Oscar for *Going My Way*.

Jerry Lewis on one occasion begged one big star to join him in New York on an all-night telethon to raise funds in a muscular-dystrophy drive. "You know what you can do with those crippled kids," was the response he received from this father of a big family, who has a reputation for charming birds off trees.

Some of our inhabitants cherish the quaint idea that the number of charity performances he gives is an accurate yardstick for measuring an entertainer's heart. More accurate, anyway, than the size of his bank account. It's easy to sing a song or two, harder to stand up and be funny for half an hour. Yet the comics measure up well; Jack Benny, Red Skelton, Jerry Lewis, George Burns—all knock themselves out in the sweet cause of charity.

Our number-one citizen on that score is Bob Hope, and we're proud as peacocks of him. There isn't a place in the world he wouldn't fly to for charity and work without drawing a nickel. He's ham enough to love the publicity it brings him, but he does a monumental amount of good. Bob has literally made the millions that everybody believes Bing has stashed away in the vaults.

Money is talked about in our town more than elsewhere, perhaps, because there's more of it around. Bob, who could safely be called thrifty, has splurged on a private three-hole golf course valued at more than $100,000. Elvis Presley owns fifteen automobiles, including an all-pink Cadillac with a television and hi-fi set. Beverly Hills High School has an oil well on its campus which brings in $18,000 a year.

Beverly Hills is an oasis of thirty thousand inhabitants and thirty thousand trees set in the steppes of Los Angeles. Many of its people earn their living in the entertainment industry or as doctors, lawyers, agents, soothsayers and headshrinkers, living on the backs of the others. Most of the trees that line the sidewalks are palms, though magnolias, eucalyptus, and acacias thrive in the gardens, and the evening scent of pittosporum drifts over the streets as sweet as the song of nightingales.

It's a separate community with its own schools, police, firemen, and local government. As a contented resident, I'm happy to say that it enjoys the lowest tax rate for miles around. I am not so happy to report that in our town, where there's at least one Olympic size pool to the block, and sometimes five, Esther Williams found nobody she asked would give her the regular use of one for classes in teaching blind children to swim. She finally found a pool in Santa Monica, thirty minutes' drive away, two days a week.

Acting as a kind of buffer between Beverly Hills and Los Angeles proper is Hollywood, with a population of some quarter of a million, which is the workplace of most of the stars who live in Beverly Hills. The rest of our population seems to be Texans, who are flocking in and who can usually leave the movie colony standing with dust on their faces when it comes to worshiping the golden calf.

Up until the early days of this century, Beverly Hills saw more coyotes than dollar bills. It was a Spanish-owned wilderness of remote canyons and tumbleweed. Then in 1906 it was bought for $670,000 by its American founders, who sold off lots at $1000 apiece on the installment plan, $800 if you paid cash; those lots sell now for $50,000. The big spending didn't start until soon after World War I ended, but long before that Mary Pickford and Douglas Fairbanks had bought a whole hilltop on Summit Drive together with the hunting lodge that stood there. They spent hundreds of thousands on the place that we called "The White House"—Pickfair.

Doug itched to put a wall all the way around Beverly Hills, but he compromised by simply encircling their estate. He and Mary literally made their home a palace. They were America's royalty and were treated as such in their own country and overseas. Kings and queens entertained them; they rode in Mussolini's private train. At Pickfair they entertained visiting bluebloods.

The Duke and Duchess of Alba stayed there, but they left a week early because the duke discovered, to his chagrin, that the armfuls of cuddly Hollywood blondes he'd been expecting were not permitted through Pickfair's portals.

Pickfair had some rich neighbors. Carl Laemmle, the half-pint immigrant from Bavaria who founded Universal-International, built an estate. So did Will Rogers, Gloria Swanson, Charles Chaplin. Chaplin is notoriously tight-fisted. After he'd furnished most of his home on Summit Drive, including his own bedroom, four or five other bedrooms remained empty. He had the head decorator of our biggest furniture store come to see the rooms and suggest their decor. Charlie had all the recommended furniture delivered and kept it for six months, ignoring the bills. Finally, the store repossessed everything it had "lent" him. He applied the same treatment to another store, with the same final result.

During this period, a titled Englishman with wife and entourage wired the Douglas Fairbankses that they'd be arriving at Pickfair with ten in party; could they be accommodated? Pickfair hadn't room for everybody, so Mary telephoned Charlie, who said he'd take in six of the visitors.

But he'd forgotten that the furniture in his guest bedrooms had been carted off, leaving only an old chest of drawers and mattresses and bedsprings on the floor of each otherwise empty room. When the guests saw the accommodations he'd provided for them, they were astounded; imagined he must be some kind of crazy health faddist, and departed after one night for a hotel.

Harold Lloyd bought his acreage direct from Mr. Benedict himself—that's the old-timer who put his name on Benedict Canyon. Then Harold bought more adjoining land from Thomas Ince until he had twenty acres of lawns and woodlands. After he married Mildred Davis, his leading woman in

Grandma's Boy, in 1923, he built a forty-room, Spanish-style mansion on the place, with ten bedrooms, two elevators, a theater seating one hundred guests, and a four-room dolls' house complete with electric light, plumbing, and grand piano. Around the house he had kennels for his great Danes, a swimming pool with fountain, two reflecting pools, and a Greek temple.

Mildred loved it all, then took a second look at the front door and burst into tears. What was the matter? "No keyhole!" she sobbed.

The Lloyds still live there. When he opened the grounds for a local charity a few years ago, today's generation of stars gasped at this glimpse of how thick the luxury could grow before income taxes gobbled up your pay checks. "How can he possibly afford to keep up this place?" Frank Sinatra asked me.

"Because he's worth millions," I said, "and he holds on to them." That afternoon, though, $69,000 was raised for the Nursery for Visually Handicapped Children. At the suggestion of Walter Annenberg's mother, when things got dull, I sold endowments for thirteen scholarships to the school at $1000 apiece.

Harold, who is in his late sixties, believes that you can take it with you. There is one servant, a helper and nurse for their grandchild, on the place which used to employ twenty gardeners. Mildred Lloyd does most of the cooking.

Stores and services soon crowded into and around Beverly Hills, to tap the golden stream that poured into the motion-picture industry. You could buy any kind of merchandise or service at a price. Saks Fifth Avenue, J. W. Robinson's, W. & J. Sloane eventually opened up on Wilshire Boulevard. One lady got in ahead of them with a different kind of establishment on Sunset Strip, just beyond the town line; her girls, dressed to the teeth, were once taken on a conducted tour of the MGM lot. A Metro executive was appalled when, in a moment of confidence, she showed him a wad of rubber checks she'd been given by various male customers. They would have been a prize package for any autograph hound. He offered to collect the debts and split the proceeds with her.

"Oh no, I couldn't allow that," she said, shocked to the marrow. "It wouldn't be ethical."

She had a competitor in the same line of business who one evening telephoned a visiting English knight in the middle of a dinner party to say she'd seen his name in the papers and could she provide him with a steady companion for his lonely hours.

In Beverly Hills you can call on furriers who'll be glad to sell a mink coat at $20,000, a chinchilla wrap for $15,000, or an ermine-covered toilet seat. You can have your hair dressed by George Masters, who'll bill you up to you-name-it for a home appointment, or a make-up by Gene Hibbs, who invented an ingenious, invisible bit of nylon mesh with a rubber band suspended from tiny hooks pulled up through your hair which, for special occasions, takes more years off your looks than plastic surgery.

If you're a celebrity anywhere, your cost of living takes a leap, but in our town it jumps sky high. Any star looking to buy a house tries to keep his identity secret until closing day or else the price will be doubled. A star of the opposite sex will be charged $5000 by her obstetrician for delivering a baby.

When Norma Shearer was first pregnant, she was aghast to hear what the bill would be. "Very well," the doctor compromised, "I'll gamble with you. I'll charge $5000 for a boy, $1000 for a girl. Okay?" Norma lost the bet when Irving Thalberg, Jr., was born.

Some of our citizens fall into the habits of European royalty and carry no money whatever in their pockets. Shirley MacLaine was working on *The Children's Hour* when Sam Goldwyn invited her to dine tête-à-tête with him and see a private showing of his old-time movie, *Stella Dallas*. It provided an evening out as unsophisticated as a flour sack.

She told me: "While we were looking at the picture, I started to scratch. I was wearing a wool dress I hadn't had on for months and apparently it had gotten moths or something. I was afraid he'd think I wasn't enjoying *Stella*. When we got out, he said, 'How about a soda?' "

In his Thunderbird they drove to Will Wright's on Sunset Boulevard. At the next table some youngsters were having a ball burning holes in soda straws to make improvised flutes, then blowing tunes on them. Sam asked for a lesson and soon sat in to play his own straw flute.

"The girl came with our orders," Shirley reported, "and we ate them. Then he went through all his pockets before he finally said, 'You got any money on you?' But I'd left my bag at the studio."

He called over the waitress, who wore her name on a lapel pin: "Nancy, have you ever been out with a male friend and been so embarrassed because he didn't have any money with him?" Nancy smiled sympathetically. "How about if I sign an I.O.U. and have my wife, Frances, come down tomorrow to pay you?"

That was agreed. Sam leaned over confidentially toward Shirley. "Since we're getting 'em free, let's have a couple more." They had three each before they went outside and flagged down his chauffeur, who'd followed them in another car.

"You go up and tell Mrs. Goldwyn what happened here tonight," Sam instructed. "Say Nancy had to trust us for six sodas at thirty-five cents apiece. You come back with the money and see if you can't scrounge seventy-five cents for a tip—but don't tell Frances about the tip."

Evenings were known to be gaudier in the old days. The Basil Rathbones gave a Louis XIV masquerade, and I was set to go as a shepherdess complete with live lamb, who had his hoofs gilded and fleece shampooed. I didn't get there, but that's a later story. Mrs. George Temple, Shirley's mother, went to her first and only big Hollywood party and left a new ermine coat on a bed on top of a pile of others. When the time came to leave, she discovered that one distinguished guest had been taken violently ill in the bedroom with disastrous results to the furs, her ermine suffering most of all.

For one revel at his Mulholland Drive home, Errol Flynn imported a transvestite fairy dressed so skillfully as a girl that nobody guessed the secret. Errol had his swimming pool lit from below and brought on a team of high divers to brighten the evening. When his guests went on chattering, taking not a blind bit of notice of the performance, he dived headlong into the water in protest and refused to speak to anybody except the divers for the duration of the party.

"You're so generous in many ways and so stingy in others," I told him, years later. "You spent thousands on those parties, yet you wouldn't buy a girl a box of candy or send her flowers when you could have saved yourself at least five lawsuits with a single rose each time."

He worshiped John Barrymore and deliberately started the rumor that he was John's illegitimate offspring. They came to a parting of the ways, however, when he invited "Father" up to Mulholland Drive. John, who was incontinent toward the end, forgot himself as he sat on a beautiful settee in the lavishly furnished living room that was Errol's pride. That was the last time John was invited.

Water, as well as drugs and alcohol, attracted Errol. He was sun-bathing mother-naked one day on a sailboat in the Mediterranean when a sight-seeing craft loaded with American schoolteachers came by. He chose that moment to stand up and stretch. One gasping teacher fell overboard, covered in blushes, and he promptly plunged in to retrieve her.

Errol used to live directly across the street from me during his marriage to Lili Damita. All I had to do to pick up an item or two for the column was sit by my bedroom window and listen to them shrieking at each other. I got the low-down on their separation by just lying in bed and listening. It was a screaming, juicy bout.

I was all set to put it on the wire the next morning, when Errol came over in dressing gown and slippers at 7 A.M., got me out of bed, and begged me not to print it, saying they hadn't even talked about a property settlement. Like a fool,

86

I promised to keep silent until he gave me the cue. But he couldn't keep his own secret and told Louella, who scooped me with my own story. I could have throttled him—but that's Hollywood.

The last time I saw Errol was in Paris, when he was making *The Roots of Heaven*. He wanted his teen-age popsie to stay in the room while I interviewed him. She wouldn't go, so I did, interview or no interview. But I kept a soft spot for him in my heart in spite of the several kinds of ruin he brought on himself.

After ten o'clock on a weekday night, Podunk would probably look like Broadway compared with Beverly Hills, which is strictly a roll-up-the-sidewalk community. After that witching hour, police in prowl cars stop anyone they see out walking to ask if they're residents and, if they're not and have no good reason for being around, escort them to the nearest bus stop.

By ten-thirty virtually every household has gone to bed. Working actors and actresses have to be up by six or six-thirty. Then it's a cold shower to get the eyes open, a shampoo and a finger wave in the case of actresses. Most women have a shampoo every morning; blondes from necessity because they use gold dust in their hair, brunettes to make their hair shiny. Half a dozen eggs makes the basis of many a brunet shampoo.

Under the dryer, the Beverly Hills workingwoman takes the juice of a lemon and a cup of hot water. Then a look over the script for the day's shooting while she downs orange juice and black coffee. After leaving instructions for the cook and servants—and nurse, if there are young children—she drives to the studio, where curls are combed out and make-up applied. If she's wearing an evening gown, she's whitened to the waist; it's cold and sticky.

She's squeezed into her costume, and a stand-by car takes her to the sound stage. Director, crew, and rest of the cast say their good mornings. Because their moods will be affected by hers, she has to set the emotional climate for the day—no headaches, heartaches, or bellyaches for her.

If she knows her lines, some other cast members may not. So the company rehearses until everybody's letter perfect. Lights are set, sound adjusted, cameras roll. Then somebody fluffs a cue or a move, and that's contagious. "Dear God, don't let it happen to me," she mutters. The same scene may be done over forty times before the director is satisfied. Some of them are sadists, who'll keep their players sweating just to prove who's boss.

At noon, lunch is called. Her dress is usually so tight that a cup of hot soup, green salad with cottage cheese, and more black coffee is as much as she can stand. It's hard to relax after that bit of bunny food.

Maybe there's a long-distance call waiting from some relative who never did a lick of work, complaining that the allowance will have to be upped because baby Peggy needs braces or the car has to have new tires or Auntie May has set her heart on a Florida vacation.

Then she hurries back to work. If she happens to have a crying scene to do, it will be easy. When she comes out of it, she catches the eye of an extra whose thoughts are as plain as if shouted aloud: "Were you ever rotten in that! I could show them how to handle it." When our girl's nose, eyes, and mascara are all running simultaneously, the head of the studio walks on with a banker from New York.

So it goes until six o'clock, when she goes to the projection room to see the previous day's rushes, then back to the dressing room to remove make-up. If she's a blonde, the gold dust is brushed out, hot oil applied, and her head's wrapped up in a bandanna like a Christmas pudding.

Home at last, where the servants are eating high on the hog, but she has a tray with hot broth, one lamb chop, spinach or string beans, and perhaps a dab of apple sauce. There's time to play with the children for half an hour, look over tomorrow's script, sign dozens of checks a secretary has laid out in a folder for her. Then a body massage, and what's left of her crawls to bed.

Is it any wonder that there hasn't been a real, big-star hostess in our town since Doug Fairbanks deserted Mary Pickford? Hundreds have tried, but nobody's succeeded, not even Mary. As Mrs. Buddy Rogers, she lost the glory.

Mrs. Kirk Douglas and her friend, the present Mrs. Gregory Peck, have their dreams along those lines. Veronique pretended to be a writer so she could get a private interview with Gregory when he visited Paris with his first wife, Greta, and openly told a companion, Brenda Helser of *Diplomat* magazine: "I'm going to be the next Mrs. Peck." Her plan worked like a charm.

The current Mrs. Edward G. Robinson would like to be a hostess with the mostest, but she has not attained the status of Gladys, his former wife, who entertained in great style and set him going on his way to being a great art collector. It was Gladys who had the knowledge and chose most of the paintings. Collecting pictures is a neat trick for cutting down on income tax, highly recommended by financial consultants if you can afford it. You donate the paintings to a museum as an act of charity, but have the pleasure of them hanging on your walls for a lifetime.

The William Goetzes mix social ambitions with art collecting and what may be lightheartedly called "cultural leadership." The walls of their home—it takes seven servants to run it—are adorned like a museum with works by Monet, Matisse, Roualt, Dufy, Lautrec, and a reputed Van Gogh, which Bill bought for $50,000 in 1948 from a New York gallery. When the painter's nephew had doubts about its authenticity, the Metropolitan Museum assembled a jury of three experts. After they'd pored over the canvas, they declared that they, too, were unwilling to accept it as an original. A European art critic, Dr. Jacob Bart de la Faille, who had vouched for the picture's genuineness in the first place, insisted that he'd made no mistake and the buyer hadn't been taken. Then five European experts took a look and said it was a Van Gogh, sure enough. Where that leaves Bill Goetz, I don't know, because he hasn't told me. We aren't in each other's confidence and never have been.

He married Edith, Louis B. Mayer's older daughter—Irene, the other, became David Selznick's wife. When Edie's engagement was announced, Louis put Ida Koverman in charge of wedding arrangements, with orders to invite all the old-line Los Angeles socialites. As Herbert Hoover's former aide, Ida knew them; Louis did not. Edie was always drawn by pictures of one sort or another. She paid almost daily visits to Ida's office, whose walls were hung with autographed pictures from the biggest people in America, to bombard her with fresh instructions.

She stopped in front of the then President's photograph ("To my dear Ida . . . Herbert Hoover") and asked: "Have you invited him?"

"You don't know him," Ida said.

"You do and father does. Send him an invitation. I'd like to see what he sends me."

"But he's the President of the United States."

"Invite him, anyway."

Hoover didn't attend the wedding, but Edie got a present from him. She got presents from everybody. There must have been twenty showers given for her. If you were on the MGM payroll, as I was as an actress then, there was somebody to tell you what to take or send for all occasions.

Came the night of the wedding and sit-down supper in the Biltmore ballroom. I was seated at a side table when Ben Meyer, a local banker, came over and asked me to join his group at a more elevated spot. "We don't know any of these people," he said. "Will you point out the stars for us?"

Partly as a result of making my first visit to the place as DeWolf Hopper's wife when he was an idol in the theater, partly as a result of having Harry Lombard, the Boston banker, and his wife as friends, I knew my way around Los Angeles society. But I had to tell Ben Meyer: "I'll have to get Mr. Mayer's permission first."

"You'll have to what?" he exploded.

"He employs me, remember? Social or anything else, I'll have to ask him."

Louis couldn't understand how I could have a banker asking after me.

"These are my friends, Louis: lawyers, doctors, professional people. They've no idea who your stars are because they never see your pictures." Permission granted, grudgingly. With the Meyers, I sat at the gayest, most gossipy table in the room. At the end of the evening they knew the names of all the stars and most of their historics.

Louis and his son in law were thick as thieves for years. Mayer bought race horses, Goetz bought race horses. At one Academy Award banquet Louis put his arm around Bill: "If you just go on the way you're going, you'll be a greater man than I ever was."

William wanted to head his own film company just like his brother-in-law, David. With Louis behind him anything was possible. It looked like a wide-open opportunity when Darryl Zanuck left Twentieth Century-Fox to join the Army in World War II. Louis began maneuvers with his partner at Metro, Nick Schenck, of Loew's Inc., whose brother Joe was board chairman at Fox. Goetz would replace Zanuck while Darryl was in Washington, D.C. in uniform.

I got wind of it and flashed a "hurry home" message to Darryl, who was on duty in Washington. He raced back three days before the intended change-over. Shortly thereafter it was announced that Mr. Goetz had resigned from Twentieth Century-Fox, to become production chief at Universal-International.

Ten years later, in 1953, he quit that job, too. A controlling interest in the studio had been bought by Milton Rackmil, who found in the course of negotiating a new contract for his head of production that Goetz set his price at $5000 a week while fellow executives got less than $2000. Later he had a spell at Columbia, and now Bill Goetz sits on a bank's board, has real-estate interests. The movies lost their attraction when he underestimated Louis, a fierce Republican, and backed Adlai Stevenson in 1948 despite his father-in-law's pleas. Louis did not speak to him after that. When he died in 1957, his will left $500,000 to his daughter Irene and similar bequests to her sons by Selznick. He cut out Edie and Bill Goetz and their children entirely.

Los Angeles society is much like the frog that wanted to inflate himself bigger than a bull. New York, San Francisco, Chicago, Detroit all have social leaders with recognizable names that stand for something in America and, in some cases, around the world. Los Angeles is different, for all its size. Outside our city limits, its "society" with few exceptions doesn't mean much, primarily because our standard isn't "Who are you?" but "How much have you got?"

In the early days Los Angeles socialites lent their gardens and exteriors of their houses to movie making on a business basis, donating proceeds to charity. But they didn't invite picture people in to dine with them. The dividing line still exists, though it's narrower than it used to be. For one thing, international leaders and celebrities don't give a damn about Los Angeles society when they visit here. They want to meet and be entertained by the stars, because they give the best parties and are more fun to be with.

Now Sam Goldwyn mingles with Mrs. Norman Chandler and the music crowd since they're both deeply involved in fund raising for the music center housing the Los Angeles Philharmonic and the San Francisco Opera Company. Danny Kaye and Jack Benny conduct concerts for the symphony. One that Danny did brought in $185,000. But movie people can no more get into the Los Angeles Country Club for either love or money than they could when Cecil De Mille battered in vain on its doors.

Harpo Marx, whom I adore, once told me he couldn't understand why he couldn't join a local country club. "That's easy," was my reply. "You belong to a different club, where they don't take in Christians. So in a way they're sort of even."

"I never thought of that," said he. The following day, Eddie Mannix, a feisty Irishman, joined Harpo's country club.

Generally speaking, Los Angeles society in the beginning would have nothing to do with the movie crowd; now the movie industry has little to do with Los Angeles society. In some cases the bar went up because they worked in movies, sometimes because they were Jews. Our town and every suburban Podunk across the nation have something in common with that prejudice.

Hollywood treats the subject simultaneously as a joke, a jinx, and a business risk. Sinatra and the Clan allow themselves the privilege of kidding each other as "wops" and "kikes" but protest publicly against racial discrimination. One comedy star doesn't wince when men on his payroll refer to him as "Super-Jew."

When Louis B. Mayer first saw Danny Thomas, who is a professional Lebanese, on a night-club stage, he liked everything about him except his looks. "I would put you under contract immediately," he told Danny, "except you look too Jewish. I want you to have some surgery to straighten out your nose."

He imagined it was doubt about the possible result that made Danny decline with thanks. "Well, then, I understand you have a brother. Here's what we'll do for you. We'll have his nose done *first* as a sample." He was amazed when that offer was turned down, too.

Because of his "lady complex," I was approached by Louis, who begged me to get his daughters into our most private private school, whose principal was a friend of mine. There was no point in mincing words. "Mr. Mayer," I said, "they don't accept them."

"But they'll take my daughters," he snapped. "Can't you tell the head mistress how important I am?"

"It won't do any good. You can't win that one. They will not take Jews." He had no choice but to accept the truth, no matter how disagreeable.

When Samuel Goldwyn was preparing *Guys and Dolls*, I heard he was talking about having Frank Sinatra play Nathan Detroit, the gambling man, brilliantly played by Sam Levene on Broadway. I bearded Samuel in his den. "Sinatra's no more fitted for that part than I am. He's a great entertainer, but not in that role. Nobody but nobody can play it like Sam Levene. Why don't you get him?"

"You can't have a Jew playing a Jew," Sam said calmly. "It wouldn't work on the screen."

I couldn't believe my ears. "What was that you said?" He repeated his words. "I could slay you for that remark," I exploded.

"But you won't."

"But someday I might," I warned.

So in Hollywood only Christians are allowed to portray Jews. Gertrude Berg was thrown out of *A Majority of One* to make room for Rosalind Russell—Gertrude read about the switch in the New York *Times* after she'd been promised the part by Dore Schary. Otto Preminger's casting transformed *Exodus* into a Protestant epic. *Anne Frank* emerged as milk-and-watery Millie Perkins. *A Catered Affair* served Kellys instead of Cohens.

Sam stayed on speaking terms with me until *Porgy and Bess* came along, and he hired as director Rouben Mamoulian, who had performed the same task for DuBose Heyward's *Porgy* as a straight play, before it was converted into a musical. During the following eight months Mamoulian had fresh arrangements orchestrated, persuaded a distinguished list of Negro players to forget their fears that the movie would be an "Uncle Tom" show.

Sidney Poitier, Dorothy Dandridge, Pearl Bailey, and others had turned down Goldwyn's approaches. Only Sammy Davis, Jr., had agreed to perform. Mamoulian explained individually to each holdout how he would direct, with full recognition of the fact that humanity has come a long way since Porgy first saw the light of Catfish Row. Satisfied that there'd be no reflection on their race, they signed contracts with Sam—who decided to fire Mamoulian and hire in his place Otto Preminger, whose style is distinctly Prussian. He engaged Preminger before he told Mamoulian he was through.

Outraged, I let fly at Sam in a column. I admired this talented, foxy man from the days when he was Sam Goldfish, an immigrant from Poland. I knew him as Jesse Lasky's partner when Geraldine Farrar came out from New York to make *Joan of Arc* in 1915. In fact, I made a couple of silent pictures for him. I helped get an honorary Oscar for Harold Russell, the miraculous, handless ex-GI in Sam's *Best Years of Our Lives*. Harold also collected one as best supporting actor, thus squeezing out Clifton Webb, who was the favorite that year in that category.

Samuel was Mr. Charm himself then; we were friends, especially if he'd had a tiff with Louella. But a few lines in print ended our life-term friendship. He hasn't spoken to me since. It's gall to him that *Porgy and Bess* was one of his few failures, a dull, photographed opera with no heart, soul, or finesse, where Mamoulian could have made it a thing of beauty, like the original *Porgy*, which had me weeping tears of compassion as I first saw it in a New York theater.

Beverly Hills is my home. I've lived in the same house there for twenty-two years. When I walk my gray French poodle, Beau Beau, a gift from Ann Sheridan, I pass the house of Ned Washington, who wrote such scintillating songs as "My Foolish Heart," "I'll Walk Alone," "When You Wish Upon a Star." Across from him resides Pete Smith, retired now, whose movie short subjects had audiences in gales of laughter for more than a generation.

Then there's the home of Ann and Jack Warner, with its private golf course and tennis court. In the drawing room hangs her portrait by Salvador Dali, the finest he's painted. . . . There's the house of Mr. and Mrs. Bruno Pagliai. We knew her first as Merle Oberon, then as Lady Alexander Korda. After their divorce she married Lucien Ballard, one of our finest cinematographers. She longed for children but could have none, even after several operations. So after her marriage to Bruno, she adopted a boy and a girl.

Next to the Pagliais live Ketti and Kurt Frings. Ketti adapted for the stage *Look Homeward, Angel*, which boosted Tony Perkins to stardom. Kurt is the agent who got Elizabeth Taylor the first million-dollar picture salary in our history.

Turning into Roxbury Drive, I pass the home of Lucille Ball, who knew joy and sorrow there with Desi Arnaz and now is happy as a lark with her new husband, Gary Morton. Tallulah Bankhead and I were among the dinner guests in that house once, when Tallu was appearing the following day on "I Love Lucy." Desi seated me on his right, a place which Tallu insisted should be hers. But Hopper can be stubborn as an Amish mule, and the brickbats started to fly. We couldn't get her out of the house until 1:30 A.M. At the "Lucy" filming Lucille was nervous as a cat over the events of the previous night. She forgot her lines for the first time in her life. Tallulah, who'd been appalling during rehearsals, sailed through her performance like Eleanora Duse.

Lucy's neighbors are Mary and Jack Benny, who've never changed marriage partners or their way of life. Jack doesn't stop working; Mary, like Gracie Allen, refuses to set foot on a TV sound stage again.

Up the street, you find Jeanne Crain and Paul Brinkman and their six children, all happy as hooligans. Better look sharp as you pass or you'll trip over roller skates, a tricycle, or a baseball bat on the sidewalk.

Next door is a house of sorrow Rosemary Clooney and her five children live there with no husband or father to guide them. José Ferrer moved out. Also on this street are the Ira Gershwins; the Thomas Mitchells; Aggie Moorehead in the house where Sigmund Romberg used to make music and feed us every Sunday night. In this block, too, stands the Spanish house where Liz Taylor lived with her parents when she was making *National Velvet*, too young to be interested in men or even boys.

Then I pass what was once the home of Sir Charles and

Lady Mendl, a monstrous Spanish affair that Elsie Mendl made over into a thing of beauty. Never was an off-color joke allowed to be told when she was present. Ludwig Bemelmans, who had a Rabelaisian sense of humor, repaid her hospitality by adorning the powder-room walls with some outrageous pictures. She took one horrified look and ordered the walls repainted immediately. Elsie, ninety-five pounds of energy, fun, and good taste, received Sir Charles in her bedroom only after she had granted him permission via his valet.

Charles and I used to walk by the mile together, apparently the only residents of Beverly who applied their legs to such purpose. Though he'd known seventeen European monarchs in his day—including the Duke of Windsor, whom Charles didn't much care for—he steadfastly turned down my pleas for him to write the Mendl memoirs.

Charles earned his knighthood as press attaché to the British Embassy in Paris when Ramsay MacDonald was Prime Minister. MacDonald, unsophisticated as a newborn baby, fell into the clutches of a wise and beautiful woman. He was indiscreet enough to write her letters that a schoolboy would have blushed over. The problem was how to recover them without scandal or the outlay of a mint of money.

Someone thought of Charles Mendl, who had a way with the ladies and adored them one and all. He was delighted to accept the assignment. The lady was so pleased with him that she produced the letters for them to read together, roaring with laughter. She presented them to him as a souvenir of many happy hours, and she collected a few thousand pounds for her trouble. The Empire was saved; Charles was knighted.

No wonder psychiatrists flourish in our town. There are nearly two hundred of them. Bedford Drive and Roxbury Drive, where their consulting rooms are concentrated, are known as Libido Lane and Couch Canyon. Louis Mayer once had his whole family analyzed by the same woman. I went to her once to see how she'd react to my being a patient.

"You'd have me on the couch in nothing flat," she said. "Out you go." I went.

Six

The one and only exclusive interview I had with Marlon Brando lasted half an hour. As the minutes ticked by he sat posed like Rodin's "Thinker" contemplating a bust of Stanislavski. He paid no more heed to me than if I'd been a ladybug squatting on the back of his canvas chair. With a snap of the fingers, I brought him out of his trance. "Have you been listening, Mr. Brando?"

"Sure."

"Do you care to answer my questions?"

"I don't believe so."

"Then may I tell you that I didn't want this interview? Your producer, Stanley Kramer, insisted that I do it. You needn't submit yourself to further agony. Thanks for nothing, and good day."

I walked off the set of *The Men*, and I haven't set foot on any Brando set from that day on. Every studio he has worked for has tried to coax me back. But I can't be insulted twice, not if I know what's going to happen.

I regard him as a supreme egotist, for want of a better term, whose good performances, like those in *On the Waterfront* and *A Streetcar Named Desire*, I recognize. I understand that he refers to me as "The One with the Hat." He has been known variously as "the male Garbo" and "Dostoevski's Tom Sawyer." He's doing extremely well without my support in piling up millions. He's a dedicated ringleader in a current melodrama which can be called "Viva Brando; or, The Actor's Revenge."

When he originally landed here in 1950, he carried his entire wardrobe in a canvas satchel: two pairs of blue jeans, four T shirts, two pairs of socks, and the works of the philosopher Spinoza, who teaches that everything is decreed by God and is therefore necessarily good. Marlon immediately labeled Hollywood a "cultural boneyard."

He said then: "My objective is to submit myself to what I think and feel until I'm in a position to think and feel as I please." It took ten years to do it, but he made it in spades in *Mutiny on the Bounty*. He also said: "The only reason I'm here is because I don't yet have the moral strength to turn down the money."

When Stanley Kramer telephoned him in Paris about doing *The Men*, Marlon had two questions: "Do you want me for more than one film? How much will you pay?" From a $50,000 fee for *The Men*, he went, via *Streetcar*, to $150,000 in *Viva Zapata*. More recently, he held out for every cent of net profits, leaving the studio to collect nothing more than a percentage of the gross as distributor. His asking price now is a million dollars a performance.

The town should have known what to expect on the strength of reports from Broadway and his nerve-racking portrayal in the theater of Stanley Kowalski, the cave-man lover of *Streetcar*. Irene Selznick, who produced the play, gave an opening-night party at "21" which Marlon reluctantly attended. Jerome Zerbe, the society photographer and columnist, was there, and Irene asked it he'd invite Marlon over to be photographed with her, not for publicity but for her personal album.

Crossing the room, Zerbe passed on the request to Marlon, who turned him down flat. "Why should I be photographed with her?"

"Well, she's your producer, after all."

"Means nothing to me," said the newest sensation of Broadway, aged twenty-three. Zerbe broke the news to Irene and exchanged no more words with Marlon until Gertrude Lawrence and Beatrice Lillie, arriving late, picked their way through the crowd to Zerbe and made a fuss over him.

Now Marlon could see that Jerome was socially "in"; he

made a beeline for him. "I'll pose for that picture now," he offered.

Zerbe, a proud man, was halfway toward the door on his way out. "You won't pose for me," he said flatly. "I wouldn't photograph you if you were the last man on this earth."

I once put a question to Marlon asking his opinion of acting as a profession. "If you're successful," he replied, "it's about as soft a job as anybody could ever wish for. But if you're unsuccessful, it's worse than having a skin disease."

Social ailments of various kinds hold a strange attraction for him. When reporters used to ask him about some chapters of his younger days, he would tell them he couldn't give an adequate answer because at the time he wasn't feeling too well. The favorite theme cropped up again when he was making *Mutiny on the Bounty* in Tahiti. By then, the joke was on him, but he was drawing $5000 a day overtime and spouting another favorite thought in slightly altered words: "After you've got enough money, money doesn't matter."

He arrived in Hollywood with a hole in the knee of his only pair of pants, and a large-sized chip on his shoulder. Though there were stories of such generosity as tipping a New York shoeshine boy with a five-dollar bill "because I felt sorry for him," he appeared to resent spending money, even a dime. If he could get an agent or reporter to buy him a dinner, a drink, or even a cup of coffee, he was in a good mood for hours. He refused to load himself down with a house, swimming pool, convertible, fancy wardrobe, or any such items which the "cultural boneyard" usually regards as the accompaniments to a soaring career.

Producers, if they can, cultivate extravagance on the part of the stars. They see to it that their puppets stagger under piles of possessions and towering stacks of bills. Studios will lend money so it seems easy to buy the house with the swimming pool at $200,000. The debt becomes a sword to dangle over the star's head if he shows signs of resentment about making a particular picture. Arguments about "artistic integrity" are as effective as paper darts against a studio that holds the mortgage.

To his credit, in more ways than one, Marlon was in no danger on that score. "Just because the big shots were nice to me," he told a reporter, "I saw no reason to overlook what they did to others and to ignore the fact that they morally behave with the hostility of ants at picnics."

He is turning the picnic tables with a vengeance on the "ants." Their one-sided admiration of Brando (they used to call him "the best actor in the world" on weekdays and a "genius" on Sundays) got chipped when Twentieth Century-Fox cast him in a stinker called *The Egyptian*. He objected, but they imagined they had soothed him and went ahead building sets, making costumes, signing other players. When the first day of shooting arrived, Brando did not. Instead, his New York psychoanalyst sent a telegram: BRANDO VERY SICK.

Breaking a contract is a refined art, which skillful performers conduct with the finesse of brain surgeons. A classic case is provided by Jerry Lewis after he broke with Dean Martin when they were under contract to make three more pictures for Hal Wallis.

Wallis had the legal right to have them complete the contract, no matter what carnage would have resulted. Martin and Lewis' agents, the Music Corporation of America, talked to him but they got nowhere. Attorneys tried to argue with him, but Wallis is, among other things, a stubborn man. It took a press agent to recall the time-tested formula.

"You call Mr. Wallis," the agent told Jerry, "and invite him to lunch at the Hillcrest Country Club. Sit him down and say: 'Have you ever had a picture that began, Scene one, take eighty-five?' Tell him that you're ready to devote six months of your life to his next Martin and Lewis picture; that you understand his problem, so you've reserved a suite at Mount Sinai Hospital for him as your guest. Because you know he's going to get a coronary from the aggravation that's coming to him."

The press agent continued: "Also tell Wallis: 'You know my own medical history. I only pray to God we don't get in the middle of this thing before I have to take to my bed again.'"

Jerry took Hal Wallis to lunch at Hillcrest and said his piece. Wallis heard him out, then conceded: "I get your point. I'll start with you alone in a new picture next month." No further movie with Dean Martin was discussed.

Marlon didn't get off so lightly when he tangled with Fox. The studio pushed Edmond Purdom into *The Egyptian*, which was a great mistake, and sued Brando for two million dollars. He settled by agreeing to play Napoleon in a turgid flop called *Desirée*.

The studio bosses are proof positive that you can fool yourself most of the time over stars who, when the fancy strikes them, delight in doing in the people who put up the money. The producers ignore any flop these highly prized players make and hypnotize themselves by repeating over and over: "We can't go wrong this time; it's our turn to be lucky." They blind themselves to the fact that these stars jeer at the money men, make fools of them, regard them deep down as their sworn enemies with the I.Q. of idiots.

Marlon got into stride when he made *One-Eyed Jacks*, a simple Western that was going to cost no more than $1,800,-000 and a few months to complete. First casualty was the director, Stanley Kubrick, who retreated in the early stages of production and abandoned the field to Brando. On his first day as director, Marlon threw away the script and announced: "We're going to improvise." For the next half year, he and his crew ran up production bills of $42,000 a day.

He had them spending hours on the shores of the Pacific waiting for the water to "look more dramatic." He'd start the cameras, then sit with his head between his knees for twenty minutes or more until he got in the mood. As a good democrat, he let his actors vote for the last reel they liked best, and that was the ending he used, though he didn't care for it himself.

When the front office at Paramount got uneasy and costs passed the $6,000,000 mark, Marlon turned surly: "I'm shooting a movie, not a schedule." There were days, I'm sure, when Y. Frank Freeman, head of Paramount, would have liked to clobber him, while Marlon went on playing his favorite mumbling, lurching, behind-scratching character—himself. Paramount has long since given up hope of getting its money back, much less of making a profit.

But when *Mutiny* came around, Metro recited the old mumbo jumbo: "We can't go wrong on this." Sol Siegel, who ran the studio, would settle for nobody but Marlon as top star. That little decision, along with several other lulus along the way, cost well over $20,000,000 before the picture was wound up. Marlon enjoyed $1,250,000 for his contributions, along with ten per cent of the gross and an incredible contract giving him the final word on scenes taken on Tahiti.

Screen rights to the original novel by Charles Nordhoff and James Norman Hall were bought by the late Frank Lloyd, a fine, free-lance director, for only $12,000. In order to make the picture and gather the cast he'd set his heart on, he was compelled to sell those rights back to Irving Thalberg at Metro for precisely what they had cost.

Metro's first flash of creative genius called for Wallace Beery to play Captain Bligh in the breath-catching tale of eighteenth-century mutiny on the high seas aboard the British merchantman *Bounty*. They envisaged the sadistic captain as a comical old coot pursued by his wife and twelve children. Talked out of that, Thalberg signed Charles Laughton, who for weeks had to be rowed slowly around Catalina Island, flat on his back on the floorboards, to teach his protesting digestion that seasickness was not permissible during working hours.

Louis B. Mayer didn't think much of the script: "Where's the romance?" he demanded. Gable didn't like the idea of playing Fletcher Christian, leader of the mutineers and his finest role up to that date. Eddie Mannix talked him around: "You're the only guy in the picture who gets anything to do with a dame." I'll never know why they didn't reissue the old *Mutiny* after Clark's death—it would have made $5,000,-000 and saved Metro a truckload of ulcers.

Frank Lloyd's picture was ten months in the making, from his first background shooting on Tahiti to its presentation in November 1935. The bills amounted to $1,700,000, the most expensive MGM production of those days. Front-office opposition grew stronger month by month. To satisfy Nick Schenck, a rough cut was sent to New York with the strict understanding that it would be run only for him to see. He had it screened before an audience of four hundred people and afterward delivered himself of this undying judgment: "Tell Thalberg it's the worst picture MGM ever made."

The second version of *Mutiny* got under way when an MGM expedition arrived on Tahiti at the height of the rainy season. It had to run before the weather and go back later for another try. The first of the thirty scripts to be completed by five writers, including Eric Ambler and Charles Lederer, was meantime coming hot off the typewriters.

Life on French Tahiti, where society is very proper and the caste system very strong, livened up considerably when Marlon debarked. He unearthed a series of hide-outs to which he would retire when the mood came upon him. On bad days hours would roll by while messengers tracked him down so that filming could resume.

His taste in girls has always been off-beat, from the Hindu impersonator, Anna Kashfi, whom he married and divorced; through the fisherman's daughter, Josanne Mariana-Berenger, to a barefoot waitress whom he found on Tahiti.

The first major casualty among the company was Oscar-winning Hugh Griffith, who was eased off the island by the French authorities after some spectacular high jinks. Another Briton, Sir Carol Reed, hired to direct, was replaced when it developed that he saw Captain Bligh as the hero, not

Fletcher Christian. At the speed at which he was shooting, it would have taken years to finish the picture.

Sir Carol had also made the basic error of believing that when he told Marlon to do something in front of the camera, Marlon would obey. Reed was succeeded by Lewis Milestone, director and diplomat, who grew accustomed to handling difficult situations with kid gloves.

There were plenty to handle. The movie makers hit the South Seas like a typhoon. Liquor poured over the island like the Johnstown flood. A French naval lieutenant ran off with the second native lead halfway through filming, so that in one version two girls mysteriously alternated in playing the romantic scenes without a word of explanation being offered.

Marlon at one point was bowled over in a double feature by a popular local infection and a virus, forcing him to take to his bed for three weeks.

Aaron Rosenberg, the producer, couldn't make a move without being balked and countermanded by cable and telephone from Metro's front office, where Siegel found his reputation at stake. On Tahiti there was panic at the lack of a script. A succession of writers, concluding with Lederer, worked against the clock to get out scenes, often only one day in advance of shooting, sometimes rewriting lines at lunch time for the afternoon shift.

"In one two-week period we shot only two small scenes," Richard Harris told me during filming—he came close to stealing the picture as one of the mutineers. "That wasn't surprising since Brando was constantly demanding that scenes be rewritten. You never knew where the hell you were." Marlon added his own seasoning to the stew by toying with the idea at one point of abandoning the part of Christian and taking on a different role in the picture.

Trevor Howard, playing Captain Bligh, left for home swearing: "Never again will I take part in an epic," and to prove his point he turned down *Cleopatra*. He thought it was "the greatest travesty in the world to allow Brando to snap and snarl at me."

In their steamy tents the sweating writers invented a game to preserve their sanity. They made up imaginary labels to hang on the cast. Trevor Howard: "a deafening answer to no question." Aaron Rosenberg: "the persistent marshmallow." For Brando, they had a tag so obscene that he brooded for days, trying in vain to think of some way to strike back at them.

At work, on a typical morning, he'd stand on the *Bounty* deck, draw his cutlass, and yell at the ship's company: "I now take command of this . . ." At that second, his memory would falter. The crew and other cast members filled in for him. "Train?" somebody suggested. Marlon nodded his thanks and take eighteen began. This time he got it right . . . "command of this ship."

Charles Lederer insisted: "Brando is responsible for a great deal of whatever brilliance the picture has. But neither he nor anybody else I know can improvise and be better in five minutes on the set than a writer with three weeks at a type-writer."

Marlon's enthusiasm touched rock bottom when it came to playing scenes supposedly on Pitcairn Island, where the *Bounty* mutineers landed. Rosenberg ordered him to perform. Richard Harris related the rest of the story: "Brando fouled it up good. He came to work for a few days, but I thought he was acting as though he wanted to scuttle it. So I finally told him: 'When you're willing to perform like a pro, I'll be in my dressing room.' The picture was suspended for three days, while they tried to get him to resume, but not a word about it got into print—it was all suppressed."

The cast didn't know what they were doing most of the time because the next scene usually contradicted whatever they were trying to play. Harris had another clash with Brando. He told me: "Brando said: 'This is the final script. I want nothing changed, not a line, not a comma.' On the strength of that, I memorized eight pages. We rehearsed it in the morning, went to lunch, and prepared to shoot in the afternoon."

The company returned after the break, and the cameras rolled. Then "Cut!" Harris related: "They told me I was wrong. When I asked why, I found out they'd changed the script during lunch. I demanded that the producer be brought to the set."

Aaron Rosenberg didn't know that changes had been made. "Actors," said Brando to Harris, "are paid to do their jobs without opinion."

Harris exploded. "You like to pull the strings as though others are puppets. This scene was changed because you demanded it." At that point, Lewis Milestone walked off the set. So did Harris, who's an outspoken Irishman. "When Mr. Brando is ready to perform, I'm available," he said once more.

"It was a long way to my dressing room. You'd have thought I was radioactive the way everybody backed away from me. I lay down on my couch and closed my eyes. Presently the director stuck his head in the door to say *sotto voce*: 'Everybody in the company wants to applaud. You were great.' But still no one came in until Rosenberg shook my hand, said he was sorry this had happened, and added: 'Thank you.'"

Eighteen months after the start, when MGM had poured more than $20,000,000 into this bounty on the *Mutiny*, Marlon was still acting up. The final scenes, months behind schedule, were being shot in Hollywood, costing still another two million. With the financial future of Metro itself at stake, with millions tied up in a picture which still had no ending, Marlon played Fletcher Christian in such a manner that, although the cameras turned, the film was unusable. He overplayed; he underplayed; he mumbled; he minced. It was a unique moment in our town's history. Nobody before him had dared take hold of a mammoth studio, swing it by the tail, and make the bosses like it. The actors' revenge was complete.

It takes avaricious agents with calculating machines for

hearts to encourage stars like Brando to behave as they do. Now that no studio any longer has its own roster of stars tied by contracts, the agents and actors run Hollywood, as they always threatened to. The studio has to go cap in hand to the agent to sign up the big star for a single picture. No more than a half dozen actors and actresses alive today can attract an audience big enough to give a picture a hope of success at the box office.

The first giant among ten per centers hated producers and made no secret of it. Myron Selznick held it a point of honor to wring every dollar he could get out of the studios to settle the score for the wrong that had been done his father, Lewis J. The louder the bosses yelled "Murder!" the harder Myron squeezed.

Lewis J. was nicknamed "C.O.D." for "cash on delivery" by starlets he lured to that notorious item of studio furniture, the casting couch. He lured plenty when he owned a $60,-000,000 film corporation in the silent twenties. But as a financier he overreached himself. His sons, Myron and David, blamed rival movie makers for plotting the ruin that overtook old "C.O.D."

Myron's first client was Lewis Milestone, who must have smiled philosophically to himself when he saw what Brando was doing to MGM. Acting for Milestone, Myron left his mark on the Howard Hughes studio when, in 1927, he squeezed out of them exactly twice the salary the then young director had anticipated receiving. Alva Johnston recalled the time when Myron went home rejoicing: "Remember what those bastards did to my father? They paid more than a million dollars for it today."

Bill Wellman was Selznick's second client. After him, everybody who was anybody—Carole Lombard, William Powell, Pat O'Brien, to name just a sample—rushed to get Myron to do battle for them.

But neither he nor the mob of imitators who followed him in business managed to hold the entire industry up to ransom as it is being done today. One reason was that under the star system of that era, contracts came up only once a year for negotiation, not before every picture. Another reason: producers and directors, to a great extent, could make or break a star.

As a tribe, actors and actresses seldom know what's good for them. They usually judge any script solely by the number of lines of dialogue they get. Greer Garson announced to one and all that she wouldn't be playing in *Goodbye, Mr. Chips*, one of the finest pictures that came her way, because "I'm only in a few scenes."

The day before she left town for England to make the picture, she poured out her woe to me. "I've sat here for months doing nothing," she said, "and now I'm going back to my native land in a picture that gives me a very small part. When I left England, I was a star there; my friends will think I'm coming home a failure."

I wrote the story, but before she stepped on the train the next day, she begged me to kill it: "What if the picture's a hit? I'd look like a fool." So I kept a friend by sitting on the interview. *Mr. Chips* made her an international name.

Vanity takes all kinds of shapes. In one of his earliest pictures Gary Cooper played a location scene so well that it was shot in a single take. That night Coop went diffidently to the director's tent. "If you don't mind, I'd like to do that scene over again in the morning," he said. "I seem to remember at one point I picked my nose I was so nervous."

The director knew better. "Listen," he said. "You were so damn nervous you were great. You keep acting that way and you can pick your nose into a fortune." That bit of advice registered with Coop. After he'd belly-flopped trying to dive into the deep end of acting with pictures like *Saratoga Trunk*, he saw his old director again. "Guess I'll have to go back to my nose," he said.

It took an eye doctor from South Bend, Indiana, to set up in the agency business and put the hammer lock on Hollywood; by comparison Myron only twisted arms. Dr. Jules Caesar Stein is the founder and board chairman of MCA, a flesh-peddling octopus with approximately one thousand clients ranging from actors to zither players, before it got rid of them all in a hurry under pressure from Washington's trust busters. He and his wife, Doris, are also devout collectors of antiques; European furniture dealers used to rub their hands when they saw them coming, but they were soon crying in their porcelain teacups, because Jules had set up his own antique shops.

Dr. and Mrs. Stein have climbed so high since his college days—he worked his way through by playing the violin in little jazz bands—that they are now helping to refurnish the White House. Mrs. John F. Kennedy was pleased to announce last year that the Steins, as a gift to the nation, "will contribute pieces from their collection of eighteenth-century antiques as well as new acquisitions."

Soon after the Steins moved to California—they now live in a beautiful Beverly Hills hilltop mansion—the good doctor told me at a party: "I'm going to be king of Hollywood one day."

"You and who else?" I laughed. But I underestimated him. He succeeded, thanks to the shortsightedness of the producers when big stars are in short supply and desperate demand.

Besides Brando, MCA spoke for Marilyn Monroe, Ingrid Bergman, Burt Lancaster, Montgomery Clift, Dean Martin, Jack Benny. That's just a sample. Agents used to hustle for salary and billing. Jules Stein's poker-faced assistants demanded lots more than that. They often weren't satisfied until they got a fat slice of the picture's profits for their clients.

The first deal like that was made for Jimmy Stewart, whom I originally recommended to MGM after he and I played on Broadway together with Judith Anderson in *Divided by Three*. The slice that MCA carved for him out of Universal-International's *Winchester '73* brought him more than $600,-000. Now he's a millionaire on the investments he made on the advice of a keen-brained business friend from Texas and he's become a sober-sided industrialist as well as a fine actor.

With Kirk Douglas as a client Jules Stein did even better at Universal. After running up costs of $12,000,000 on *Spartacus* in which Douglas starred and also produced with Universal's money, the huge, 400-acre studio fell into a situation where it had to sell out, lock, stock, and acreage. MCA bought the place for $11,250,000 and set to work churning out television series. Now it's called Revue Productions and it's the best-run studio in Hollywood. If MCA plans work out now it has beaten the anti-trust suit—it is concentrating on production and stripping itself of the agency business— millions more dollars will be invested in an effort to make Hollywood the movie capital of the world once more.

Once an actor has seen his agent put the pressure on and turn a geyser of cash into Old Faithful itself, the sky's the limit where his greed for money is concerned. Everything else is forgotten, including, of course, gratitude. William Holden, an MCA prize winner, did mighty well with *The Key*, though Trevor Howard stole the notices; and much, much better before that from *Bridge on the River Kwai*, which brought him millions. The producer of *The Key* was Carl Foreman.

When Foreman had another picture in the works, *The Guns of Navarone*, he wanted Holden for his hero. "My price," Holden declared, "is now $750,000, plus ten per cent of the gross."

"But not with me, not after *The Key*," Foreman said.

"With you or anybody else, that's my price," Holden replied.

Foreman had a few forceful words to say on the subject of gratitude, then hired Gregory Peck, David Niven, and Anthony Quinn together for less than Holden demanded. To keep his bulging bank account safe from the hands of tax collectors, Holden moved his family to Switzerland, that temporary haven of fugitive American fortunes—temporary because I understand that President Kennedy has some fancy plans for correcting that state of inequity.

William doesn't spend much time in his Swiss home, though his wife, formerly Brenda Marshall, does, together with their two sons. Her daughter by a previous marriage preferred staying behind in Hollywood as an interior decorator. When Brenda Marshall married, she was a happy, fun-loving woman. The last time I saw her, at a party Norman Krasna gave for me at Lausanne, Switzerland, her old contentment had gone bye-bye.

When Tony Curtis was fourteen, he wrote me a six-page letter from his family's one-and-a-half-room flat in the Bronx, where his father worked as a tailor. The boy was then Bernie Schwartz, and he wanted to know how to become a movie actor. He'd beaten a path to Hollywood, but he wasn't rated as much more than a curly haired pretty boy by most people when MCA started to steer him. No matter how hard he was asked to work to promote his career, he gave the same answer: "I'd love to." He was eager and fun to be with, and I invited him to all my parties. There he got to know, among others, suave, immaculate Clifton Webb, whom he looked up to as the epitome of social form.

"You're getting up there," Clifton cautioned him as the months rolled by, "so you must dress better. That suit isn't good enough for you, and your tie is awful."

As soon as Tony could afford it, he bought himself a custom-tailored suit, which he christened at another party of mine where Webb was a guest. "Look, Hedda," Tony said with pride, "isn't it wonderful? All hand-sewn."

"Lovely," I agreed, "and that's a good-looking pair of shoes, too."

"A producer I know couldn't wear them, so he gave them to me. They pinch a little, but aren't they beautiful? They cost him $75."

Clifton wandered over to add a word of praise for the suit. "But you can't wear that tie with it."

"What kind should I wear, Mr. Webb?"

"Come over to my house tomorrow and I'll give you some."

Tony found a wife who was used to being kept on a tight financial rein when he married Janet Leigh in 1951. Her father, Fred Morrison, who ten years later took an overdose of pills that ended his life, held the purse strings after her career got going. I remember coming across her at Rex, the mad hatter, where she was aching to buy a sweater for $75, but her dad said no. When he died, she was on the French Riviera with Mrs. Dean Martin, guests of Joe Kennedy.

Tony and Janet bought an eighteen-room house in 1958. ("Did you ever believe I'd end up a country gentleman?" he asked me.) They had enough money left to furnish the dining room, but not enough to buy much else. He was around at my house when I mentioned that I had a handsome, carved oak chair down in the basement, which I couldn't use. "If you want it, take it. Go down and see."

He came back conveying the heavy chair in his arms. "It's wonderful," he said. "I'll put it in my car." He'd started the motor to drive straight home before I caught him. "Come back here. We've got a party going. Janet can see it when you get home." It still sits in their front hall, bleached and upholstered in white brocade.

MCA maneuvered Tony's affairs so astutely that he now owns his own picture company, makes millions, drives a Rolls-Royce. "I hope that in a few years I'll have enough security so I can drive around in an old battered station wagon if I want to," he says. He lost Janet Leigh after he made a picture in South America with Yul Brynner, which featured a girl named Christine Kaufman, to whose apartment in the Château Marmont, in the company of her mother, Tony would go to have coffee on his way home.

He sent me another letter after I'd criticized him in the column last year over the postponement of *Lady L*. "I wonder," I'd asked, "if actors realize they're killing the goose that laid the golden eggs and are ruining their careers."

"You might well have asked whether the studios realize what they are doing to actors," Tony wrote back. "Because of the delays and stalling on this project, I have not made a film for eight months. True, I was paid a salary for part of that time but money alone can never make up for the fact that I might have two films during that period, that I could have been working in my chosen profession, could have been improving in the only way an actor can improve—by working.

"As a star, I have the right to pick my own parts, to decide whether or not a script is right for me. That is clearly understood by everyone who seeks to employ me.

"If the final script does not meet my requirements, the burden must remain with the company and not with me. The studio did submit a script I liked, which is why I signed to do the picture in the first place. Before we could get into production, they began making changes and the script they were finally ready to shoot bore little resemblance to the one I had approved." He was right, the picture has never been made.

When press agents nudge an actor hard enough, he imagines he can write, produce, direct, and act simultaneously, as busy as a one-armed paper hanger. That was a delusion Clark Gable avoided.

"Why don't you want to direct, like everybody else?" I asked him not long before he died.

"It's hard enough to act without going into all those monkeyshines," he said. "I just want to act and get the money. Let them take the grief."

Clark loved money all his working life. I don't remember that he ever gave a party. He nursed a grievance against Metro from the time Mayer loaned him to David Selznick to make *Gone With the Wind*. Clark thought he should have received an extra bonus for that, not simply continue on his salary of $7000 a week, fifty-two weeks a year.

When he cast off from Metro in 1954 and entrusted his business affairs to MCA, he boasted that he had "never really made any big money" until then. Like the rest of the monarchs of the movies, he wanted what they call "the most"— highest salary, biggest percentage.

"Why do you fight so hard for those enormous salaries?" I asked him, as I've asked them all. "Why can't you put back some investment in the industry when it's done so much for you?"

"I want the most because you're only important if you get it."

Money helped kill Clark Gable. That and his refusal to acknowledge that he was growing old. He couldn't resist earning the most he'd ever get, when the offer came along for *The Misfits*; $750,000 plus $58,000 for every week the picture ran overtime.

On location in the Nevada desert, where the heat jumps to 130 degrees, he roped and wrestled with wild horses to prove to everybody who watched, including me, that he still had his old virility. "This picture will prove he is America's answer to Sir Laurence Olivier," said the ever-present Mrs. Paula Strasberg. He was encouraged by John Huston, a director with no qualms about making actors sweat. And he was outraged by the behavior of Marilyn Monroe.

He was habitually early on the set, ready to work at 9 A.M. Some days she wouldn't show up until lunch time, sometimes not at all. Though he seethed inside, Kay Gable told me, he curbed his feelings by iron self-control. Clark was not a pretty sight when he blew his top, as he did when *The Misfits* was completed, but Huston wanted one more retake.

The retake was never shot. Huston was still working the final cut of the picture when Clark died, nearly a million dollars richer, leaving a beautiful widow in Kay Gable and a handsome son he never saw.

Seven

Hollywood was always heartbreak town, though most of the world fancied it to be Shangri-La, King Solomon's mines, and Fort Knox rolled into one big ball of 24-karat gold. We used to see the hopefuls stream in from every state of the Union, tens of thousands of them, expecting that a cute smile or a head of curls was all it took to pick up a million dollars. Many were old enough to know better, but not the children.

They came like a flock of hungry locusts driven by the gale winds of their pushing, prompting, ruthless mothers. One look into the eyes of those women told you what was on their minds: "If I can get this kid of mine on the screen, we might just hit it big." I used to wonder if there wasn't a special, subhuman species of womankind that bred children for the sole purpose of dragging them to Hollywood.

Most of the women showed no mercy. They took little creatures scarcely old enough to stand or speak and, like buck sergeants, drilled them to shuffle through a dance step or mumble a song. They robbed them of every phase of childhood to keep the waves in the hair, the pleats in the dress, the pink polish on the nails. I've had hundreds of them passing through my office asking for help.

Stage mothers are nothing new. I remember as far back as the Tartar we lovingly called "Ma" Janis, who took care of all the cash her daughter Elsie earned. When "Ma" died, Elsie got so lost in the tangle of her financial standing that she wondered whether she had $100,000 or a million in the bank. She found she had little left except a note signed by "Ma" certifying that she owed Irving Berlin $10,000. Elsie had never made out a check in her whole life, never had more than $5.00 in her pocketbook.

What motion pictures did was to encourage the breed and give them better opportunities to ruin their children while they were beneath the age of consent. Peg Talmadge, mother of Norma and Constance, was a sweetheart. Anita Loos wrote her book *Gentlemen Prefer Blondes* from choice bits that fell from the lips of Peg, but even she ruled with a whim of iron. We all laughed at Peg when she said these things but didn't have the wit to write them down. Anita did.

Jackie Coogan's boyhood earnings were so scandalously dissipated by his family that the law was changed to protect child actors—but Jackie was left penniless.

When I worked for Metro, stage mothers lingered outside the gates at the Culver City studios, waiting to catch some dignitary's eye or for a chance, which seldom came, to slip past the guards into the maze of narrow streets that wound between the big barns plastered with stucco which were called sound stages.

Some children made it, though not by waiting like beggars at the gates of paradise. Louis B. Mayer needed appealing youngsters for the all-American family pictures which this Russian-born Jew from New Brunswick delighted in making because they earned fortunes for him. There were two children in particular, a boy and a girl, who captured the imaginations of all.

The boy had once had his hair dyed black by his mother so he could get a job in two-reel silent comedies. She wanted to change his name to Mickey Looney, but the "L" became an "R" when he was signed on at Culver City.

The girl's mother had seen her child walk out onto a vaudeville stage when she was two years old to join her two older sisters in a song-and-dance act. Mrs. Ethel Gumm took her three children slogging through West Coast theaters for years. Frances, the youngest, developed the hungriest drive of them all, battling to show her big sisters that she could sing louder and longer than either of them.

It was a cheap act, and it made very little money for anybody. One Christmas saw the traveling Gumms chewing on tortillas at a corner drugstore near the theater they were playing. Frances Gumm had been rechristened Judy Garland when Lew Brown spotted the trio playing The Lodge at Lake Tahoe and decided she might have something.

In the typical Tinker-to-Evers-to-Chance switching that usually makes it possible for half a dozen people to claim they "discovered" a star, Brown put Judy and her mother in touch with an agent named Rosen, who knew Jack Robbins, a music publisher with offices in Culver City.

With Rosen, Judy was in Robbins' office when he telephoned down to Ida Koverman, who made a point of hunting for fresh talent to keep the wheels turning at MGM. Judy was twelve; round as a rain barrel; stringy hair; dressed in an old blouse, blue slacks, dirty white shoes. Ida heard her sing with a zing in her heart, and she flipped. She called Mayer, who grudgingly came up to see what was causing all the excitement. Ida had got hold of the words to the Jewish lament "Eli, Eli" and coached Judy in the pronunciation. That's what she sang for Mayer, but he wasn't impressed. He tossed the ball right back at Ida. "If you want her, sign her up."

But Ida was too knowing about the foxy ways of Mayer to fall for that. She needed a second opinion, or else if Judy failed, Mayer would never let Ida forget it. She had Judy sing again, this time for Jack Cummings, a producer who just happened to be Mayer's nephew.

Jack was called one of the "Sons of the Pioneers," a walking testimonial to the fact that it never hurt to be somebody's relative at Metro. "A producer produces relations" was a stock gag. Later on, however, in pictures like Seven Brides for Seven Brothers, Jack proved that he could fly when they gave him wings.

Long before that, he made a picture with a young girl named Liz Taylor and a collie dog: Lassie Come Home. The picture was sweet, sentimental, and I went all out in praise of it. A loyal friend in Metro's New York office wired me after reading the review: YOU SURE STUCK YOUR NECK OUT THIS TIME HOPPER STOP IT'S NOTHING BUT A POTBOILER. But the picture made a fortune, got Lassie a lifetime contract, helped get Liz *National Velvet*.

Cummings could see the potential appeal of Judy, a roly-poly girl with eyes like saucers and a voice as clear as a gold trumpet. "This kid's got it," he told Ida. "Let's sign her up." While he went off to set the legal wheels in motion, Ida took Judy to the commissary for some ice cream.

She tried to introduce her there to Rufus Le Maire, head of casting, but she got the brush-off. Mr. Mayer hadn't given the little new girl the nod, so she wouldn't receive any favors. He was starry-eyed over another schoolgirl MGM had signed. Deanna Durbin was the real talent, in his book. The two children made a musical short together, *Every Sunday Afternoon*, but Deanna was the one given the big build-up. After that, Judy had nothing to do but hang around the lot—and get some education at the school Ida had established with academically qualified teachers to meet the requirements of California law.

Mayer had decided to let Judy go and keep Deanna, but the plan turned sour. Universal, looking for a youngster to play in *Three Smart Girls*, wanted Deanna. By a fluke, Metro had let her contract lapse. Mayer was away on one of his many trips to Europe. He knew nothing of this until he returned and found his prize pigeon had been allowed to fly the coop. He went berserk.

For days he ranted and raged at everybody in sight until some anonymous prankster won revenge. In Mayer's exclusive, private bathroom one morning, Louis found that on every sheet of toilet paper the face of Deanna had been printed overnight.

Deanna got stardom and the royal treatment from Universal with *One Hundred Men and a Girl*, which followed *Three Smart Girls*. There was a fancy premiere, and she planted her footprints in wet cement in the forecourt of Grauman's Chinese Theatre, a pastime which was one of the glorious bits of nonsense in those days. Deanna is now quite plump and leading a happy married life with husband and children in Paris. Once a year newspapermen descend upon her home, but she won't receive them or allow photographs to be taken. She's had her fill of Hollywood and you couldn't lure her back for a million dollars. The only singing she does is with her children.

Judy was living in a little rented house with her mother. Her father, Frank Gumm, was not in Hollywood. Judy's mother telephoned Ida the morning after Deanna's big show: "I can't do a thing with Judy. She's been crying all night. What shall I do?"

"Bring her right over," said Ida. With no children of her own, she was a mother hen to everyone who needed her. Judy was as close to her as a daughter. She fell into Ida's lap and buried her head on her shoulder, sobbing: "I've been in show business ten years, and Deanna's starred in a picture and I'm nothing."

Frustrated ambition has to be treated gently. "You'll get your feet in cement, too," Ida soothed her. "You'll be starred, you'll see. Don't forget, I've told you so."

Mayer schemed to turn the tables on Universal. Nobody was going to laugh at him for keeping the wrong girl. "I'll take this fat one, Garland, and make her a bigger star than Durbin," he boasted to his associates. How to start was the puzzle. He began by insisting that she be coached in acting and dancing, though she's never had a formal singing lesson in her life. She still doesn't know what key she sings in. She'll say, "Play some chords and I'll pick one." He had orders sent down to the commissary: "No matter what she orders, give her nothing but chicken soup and cottage cheese."

Her one dear friend in approximately her own age group was Mickey Rooney. They were nuts about each other. They went to school together, along with Metro's Jackie Cooper, Freddie Bartholomew, and other child stars whom Mickey rapidly eclipsed. Mickey, who remains today one of the greatest underrated talents in entertainment, was brash, cocksure, and growing up fast. He was doing calisthenics in the schoolyard one day under an instructor's eye when Frank Whitbeck, the studio advertising director, passed by.

"Hi, Uncle Frank," yelled Mickey. "Ain't this the damndest thing for a grown man to be doing?"

The crush Judy had on Mickey would have burned up a girl twice her age. An explosive mixture of emotion and ambition churns inside her. "I have to have a crush on somebody," she once cried to Ida, "but they don't last." Mickey had a shield of toughness, which she lacked, and a heart as big as Ireland, but he mostly regarded her as a kid, too young for him.

She'd played minor roles, two of them with Mickey as star, when *The Wizard of Oz* came along. Producer Mervyn LeRoy, typically, was all set to have Shirley Temple as Dorothy, but Twentieth Century-Fox wouldn't release her. So he reluctantly settled for Judy—and she had it made.

The top executive offices at Culver City are located in the Thalberg Building, otherwise known as the "Iron Lung" by reason of its much-envied air-conditioning system. Before it was built, Metro tried to buy a little piece of corner property, on which stands a long-established undertaker's parlor. He refused to sell, so today his establishment stands like a sore thumb next to the handsome structure named for Irving Thalberg. The undertaker occasionally peers into the "Iron Lung" and says: "Well, I'll get you all, sooner or later." He's had most of the old-timers already.

From the executive offices you could look across the street at four big twenty-four-sheet billboards standing side by side. On them were displayed posters that shouted the claims of the studio's newest hits, listing names of the stars, featured players, producer, director and, if they were lucky, the writers.

Since actors are vain, Mayer and his aides, like soft-spoken Benny Thau and burly Eddie Mannix, could sweet-talk them into accepting bigger billing in lieu of more money in many a contract. With *Oz*, Judy's billing grew like a mushroom. It jumped above the picture's title, making her technically a star. The size of the lettering that was used to spell out her name expanded year by year. Now she's reached the peak, where one name, *Judy*—like *Garbo* and *Gable*—does all the selling needed to pull in an audience.

Then Metro smelled gold in billing Mickey and Judy together for *Babes on Broadway*, and some of her cruelest years opened up for her. Compared with Mickey's greased-lightning ability to do everything and anything and get it right instantly, Judy was a slow study. Dance rehearsals were a torture. She was driven frantic, dancing, singing, improvising, putting a picture together. The director, Busby Berkeley, was a taskmaster who extracted the last ounce of her energy.

"I used to feel," she told me later, "as if he had a big black bull whip, and he was lashing me with it. Sometimes I used to think I couldn't live through the day. Other times I'd have my driver take me round and round the block because I hated to go through the gates."

I saw him work her over in one picture, where she stood on a truck and sang. He watched from the floor, with a wild gleam in his eye, while in take after take he drove her toward the perfection he demanded. She was close to hysteria; I was ready to scream myself. But the order was repeated time and time again: "Cut. Let's try it again, Judy."

"Come on, Judy! Move! Get the lead out." By now, she was determined to keep her name in the billing, but I doubt if she would have pretended to anyone that she enjoyed being an actress. She was jealous of Mickey, forever running to Ida to complain: "He got the break, I didn't." For all the friendship of the two young people, she wanted to best him in everything they did together.

The two of them sat together in the darkened theater. On one side of them was Irene Dunne; on the other, Sonja Henie; behind them, Cary Grant. When the house lights came on, Judy was crying through the applause. "I know what you're thinking," Mickey said. "We're two kids from vaudeville, and we didn't mean a damn thing for so long, and now it's happened to both of us."

Years later, after Judy had fallen into a bottomless pit and climbed out again, the Friars Club gave a banquet at the Biltmore Bowl and proclaimed her "Miss Show Business." She had just had the British eating out of her hand at the London Paladium, played the Palace in New York for nineteen sensational weeks; toured the United States and finished her triumph at the Philharmonic Auditorium in Los Angeles. Mickey's career was running downhill. Somebody remembered to send him an invitation to the Biltmore Bowl, but it was to sit way over in a corner.

"Everybody was slapping each other on the back," he reported without bitterness, "and I said to myself: 'Poor Judy, how many of these people really care about you?'"

I said. "You two were like ham and eggs. You helped her more than anybody."

"Yeah, but the people who gave the party forgot that. That was the only thing that hurt. Because I felt so close. I haven't seen her much lately. It's all a kind of whirl."

Adolescence can give a rough ride to any girl—and her mother, if she's around to share her daughter's fears and confidences and dry her tears. Judy's thinned-out body was not given time to readjust. The public idolized her. The exhibitors couldn't get enough Garland-Rooney musicals. She had to go on churning them out one after another. They'd been sent to New York for the Capitol Theatre opening of *Babes on Broadway*. They went back again and broke every house record.

"We'd been doing six, seven shows a day and having about forty minutes between shows," Mickey recalled. "This one afternoon we'd just gone off stage to come back and take a bow together, and she collapsed in the wings. I didn't know what to do. I filled up with tears. I felt as though something serious had happened. I came out on stage and just felt lost without her. She wasn't dieting at this time. She was just going too fast." And with the wrong companions.

That was Louis B. Mayer's doing. His suspicious brain came up with the idea that Ida had too much influence over Judy. She might be tempted to think of what was good for the girl before she thought of the studio, so he flatly told Ida: "You've got too much work to do to look after the Garland." By order, the old intimacy was ended.

The studio brushed off somebody else in Judy's life, too—her first husband, David Rose, the serious-minded, preoccupied composer to whom she was married at nineteen. She made two mistakes in that. She married him without consulting Mr. Mayer beforehand, which was a fracture of MGM protocol. Even worse was the fact that she married at all.

A star's life was supposedly controlled twenty-four hours a day by the studio. She was told what to do, both at work and after working hours; where to go; what to say; whom to mix with. Mayer didn't want any star to marry because that introduced a foreign influence in the control system. A husband could often influence a star against the studio for her own good and sometimes for his own power.

They turned on Judy like rattlesnakes. On Academy Awards night, she had sat for years at the number-one table along with the rest of the MGM stars. As Mrs. David Rose she was deliberately humiliated and seated at a much less desirable spot on the side and out of the spotlight. That year she called to ask if I'd like to sit with her.

"Love to," I said, then proceeded to give the tsar hell by telephone: "Louis, you are treating her outrageously. Even if you personally don't like her, think of what she has done for your company. You should be ashamed of yourself." But he was immune to shame or compassion. I wasted my breath.

They actually believed that she belonged to them, body and soul. They'd created her; why couldn't she show more gratitude? The marriage hadn't a chance. The studio told her so. David Rose was the wrong man for her, said the sycophants who clung to her like leeches. "He's trading on your popularity. You're a star; he's a struggling composer." If they passed the two of them in the Culver City streets, they'd greet her but ignore him.

After Judy left him, as she inevitably did, her private life changed in many ways. Her father had died and her mother remarried to become Ethel Gilmore. Both sisters were married, too. Metro assigned a publicity writer, Betty Asher, to stay with Judy, and they lived high, wide, and not particularly handsome.

She turned from her mother and her old friends. When they warned her about the new set she was going with, the rainbow girl screamed: "I'm old enough to know what I want. When I want your advice I'll ask for it."

The dismal cycle of benzedrine and sleeping pills began again. The studio kept up the illusion of Judy's perfect health. She plunged on, beating her thin chest and saying: "I feel fine." Of course, she knew she wasn't, but she was too riddled with ambition to let someone else take over a picture scheduled for her.

She listened to anybody who flattered her ego. Joe Mankiewicz, the director who suffered the tortures of the damned on *Cleopatra*, was a great ego booster. "You could be the greatest dramatic star in the world," he told her. "Anything Bernhardt did, you can do better. I'll write material for you, make you another Bernhardt." That was something he never did.

Metro smiled on marriage number two—to Vincent Minnelli, who had directed her in *Meet Me in St. Louis* and *The Clock*. They felt this gentle man would bring her under control. Judy was married in her mother's home. Louis Mayer gave the bride away; Betty Asher was matron of honor; Ira Gershwin the best man. Ida Koverman was not invited, nor was I. Judy was then twenty-three.

Minelli, ten years her senior, had never married before. Though he controlled hundreds on a sound stage, he wasn't successful in seizing the reins as husband. He was too gentle. She continued to mingle with her old crowd; sought and found her sensations; quarreled with her mother.

By this time, we knew many of Judy's problems and were delighted to hear that she was pregnant. Maybe motherhood would bring her back to her senses. Before Liza was born, I wanted to give her a different kind of baby shower, with only men invited. Judy was in a depressed mood. She bowed out with a note: "I'd have been a dull guest of honor, but it was a wonderful idea. Thanks for thinking of me. Forgive me, and after March I'll be rarin' to go. I'll be my old self again."

Unfortunately motherhood rarely produces miracles. Though the birth left Judy weakened, she scurried back to work again. Metro issued glowing reports about her health, but her previously ravenous appetite had strangely deserted her, and she stayed pathetically thin. She got through her pictures only on nervous energy and doctors' help. She was so near the borderline that when I visited her in her dressing room on the set of *The Pirate*, in which she was co-starring with Gene Kelly, she was shaking like an aspen leaf. She went into a frenzy of hysteria. Everybody who had once loved her had turned against her, she said. She had no friends.

Even her mother, Judy said, tapped her telephone calls. "She is doing everything in her power to destroy me."

I said: "You know that isn't true. Nobody in the world loves you as your mother does—and has all your life through all your troubles."

But she cried out against her mother; against Ida Koverman; against all those who had helped her out of so much potential trouble. She was carried out of the dressing room, put in a limousine, still wearing make-up and costume, and put to bed. But she rallied and finished the picture.

The gulf between her and Minnelli widened. He tried to force her to eat, but she couldn't. In fits of temperament, the couple parted many times. But he was always on hand to help.

The road got rougher. Something desperate was happening to her. The sad chronicle of studio suspensions began. Then Metro bought *Annie Get Your Gun* for her and assigned as director the "man with the bull whip," Buzz Berkeley. She went into a weeping rage when she was told she'd have to work for him again and refused point-blank to do it. So the studio gave her Charles Walters in his place. But then nothing could have improved the situation for her.

She recorded the songs which are collectors' items—I often sit and play them in my den at night. Then day after day, with a million dollars of Metro's money already invested, she didn't show up for work. Her bosses took her off the picture. Betty Hutton was brought in to replace her, which was one of their biggest mistakes. They should have waited until Judy got well.

When Judy walked into my den after hearing the news from Mayer himself, she looked middle-aged. She stared into space, blamed herself for her troubles. "I understand the studio's problems at last. I'd been there so long I'd forgotten you have to conform to their plans. Mr. Mayer promised to take care of me. He said he'd give me so much to live on while I'm out of work."

She was in the throes of another separation from Minnelli. "I'm broke. How can anyone save money in this business? When Vincent and I were together, I spent $70,000 decorating our house. Since our separation I'm paying $1000 a month rent on another. It's tiny; no nursery for my baby. But I have to keep working."

I begged her to go to the Menninger Clinic. Treatments there had done much good for Robert Walker, her co-star in *The Clock*. "There's nothing the matter with my head," she replied. "It's my body that's tired."

A few days later she entered the Peter Brigham Hospital in Boston, with Louis Mayer personally paying the bills, and stayed there for several months. Back in Hollywood, fighting to lose weight again, she finished *Summer Stock* with Gene Kelly. Then, during rehearsals for *Royal Wedding* with Fred Astaire, the headlines screamed that Judy Garland, suspended for refusing to work, had cut her throat in the house she'd spent $70,000 decorating. Stories told of her racing into the bathroom, breaking a glass, slashing her throat. In fact, the scratch could have been as easily made with a pin. The cut wasn't serious. It was more a case of nerves than anything else.

Her mother had long since given up the hopeless task of

staying close. She was working as a theater manager in Dallas. When she heard the news, she got in her little jalopy and drove thirty-six hours nonstop to go to her daughter. "Judy," she said enigmatically, "will never kill herself." She stayed on in California, working in a job in an aircraft plant that Ida Koverman helped obtain for her. She died of a heart attack in the parking lot there. Previously, she used to plead with her friends: "Please don't introduce me as Judy's mother."

Judy has walked the rocky road back to the top of the mountain with Sid Luft by her side for most of the miles. Sid is her husband, "manager," and a gambling man who can kill $10,000 in an afternoon. He loves horses and fast motor cars. It was Sid, with whom she has led an on-again off-again life as Mrs. Luft, who arranged her first tour that opened at the London Palladium, where she was an absolute sensation. She has two more children by him: Lorna and Joe.

"I don't think there's any actress in the world that can produce like she can when she's going," said one member of the group that accompanied her to London. "When she's going, she's the greatest thing on wheels. When you're with a dame that's fantastic like that, and you don't know if she's going to get on or off or anything, you're bound to crack under the strain."

Many people wondered how Judy Garland got her amazing contract from Jack Warner to make the musical version of *A Star Is Born*. There was a clause in it she didn't have to work before 11 A.M. If she was ill they wouldn't expect her to work. It was a fantastic deal. Here's the story.

When it came time for Jack's beautiful daughter Barbara to have her coming-out party, he promised to get her anything she wanted. What she wanted was to have Judy Garland sing at the party. Her father told her that was impossible. "But, Daddy, you promised to give me anything I wanted, and I thought you could do anything." Then she burst into tears and hung up the telephone.

Father went to work. He called Judy. Her answer was:

"Why would I do that? No." He called her again: "What would I have to give you to change your mind?"

Then it was that Sid Luft came on the phone and said: "We want *A Star Is Born*," naming an astronomical price for Judy and special clauses in the contract. Warner had to buy the story from David O. Selznick at a cost, I believe, of a quarter of a million.

But Judy survived the flop that *A Star Is Born* proved to be, as she has survived all the incredible excesses of her life. In every performance—at concerts, on television, in her new pictures—she has the power to stir an audience to the depths of their hearts, like an old-fashioned revival meeting. "We have all come through the fire together," she seems to say, "and none of us is getting any younger, but we're here together, and I'll love you if you love me."

This feeling she gives out to and gets back from an audience may be the one crush of her life that will last. She used to be her own worst critic. Before she went into a number for the screen, her co-workers had to keep telling her: "You're wonderful, wonderful!" But she never thought she was good. "I was awful" was her own self-judgment whenever she'd finished. But now, as she literally tears her way through her songs, her audiences go crazy listening to her. They crowd around to touch her, and she believes in what she can achieve.

Ethel Barrymore, one of her greatest boosters, told me: "I think she has a tremendous frustration. She's always felt she wasn't wanted. She has a complex common among women—she wants to be beautiful. I told her: 'God is funny that way. He divides these things. When you open your mouth to sing, you can be as beautiful as anyone I've ever known.' But you've got to keep telling her."

Judy suffers from nightmares concerning her mother. She has lost something of herself somewhere along the road. But so long as she has millions of people loving her and fighting for her, she'll keep the ghosts in the background.

Her performance in Carnegie Hall was one of the most amazing things I ever witnessed. Her fans screamed and applauded after every number. She gave encore after encore, promised: "I'll stay all night if you want me." She threw her head back and used the mike like a trumpet.

She repeated the same frenzied performance in the Hollywood Bowl, this time in the rain, and nobody moved. You sat enthralled because she'd cast her magic spell as she did first when she sang "Over the Rainbow." This was our little Judy, who came home and persuaded the natives that skies really were blue and that dreams really do come true.

Eight

One bright morning last spring, a fat young woman with a baby carriage ambled along Hollywood Boulevard. First to catch my eye were the pink Capri pants and her wabbling *derrière* that was threatening to burst right out of them. Next item I spotted was the cigarette dangling out of her mouth, sprinkling ashes on the baby. I put on speed to catch up with her, though I didn't know her from Little Orphan Annie.

"I wonder if you know how you look from the rear. You should be ashamed of yourself, and you a mother, too."

That stopped her dead in her tracks. "And who might you be?"

"Doesn't matter, but you're disgusting." With that, I walked on, feeling I'd done my bit for the cause. I wasn't exactly running any risk. Though she outweighed me by thirty pounds, I knew she couldn't leave the baby to come after me.

The cause is glamour, for which I've been fighting a losing battle for years. Our town was built on it, but there's scarcely a trace left now. Morning, noon, and night the girls parade in babushkas; dirty, sloppy sweaters; and skin-tight pants. They may be an incitement to rape, but certainly not to marriage. Unless the era of the tough tomboy ends soon, the institution of matrimony is doomed to disappear forever.

The geniuses who conduct the motion-picture business killed glamour when they decided that what the public wanted was not dream stuff, from which movies used to be made, but realism. They took the girls out of satin, chiffon, velvet, and mink, put them first into gingham and then blue jeans. So what happened? They converted the heroine into the girl next door, and I've always advocated that if they

131

want to see the girl next door, go next door. Now they've thrown the poor kid out to earn her living on the streets.

The milliners, especially the males, have helped stitch glamour's shroud. Deep inside whatever they call their souls, they hate women. They made the most ridiculous concoctions for women to wear on their heads. Hats like table doilies, little pot holders, coal scuttles, dishpans, crash helmets, bedpans. Husbands were ignored when they complained: "Where in God's name did you get that thing? Whoever made it must hate your sex."

Not until other women laughed at them did the glamour pusses discard their psychotic chapeaux and go bareheaded. By then the designers had ruined their own racket; they'd killed the sale of hats. I can walk six blocks today in any city and see nothing more than hair or a scarf covering anybody else's hair but mine.

Studio wardrobe departments that employed cutters, seamstresses, and embroidery hands by the dozens are empty, staffed by skeleton crews. The stock rooms were crammed with bolts of magnificent brocades, satins, laces; now most of the shelves are bare. One odd sight you'll see, though—rows and rows of realistic breasts cunningly contoured from flesh-colored plastic, complete with pink nipples, hanging in pairs, labeled with the name of the underprivileged star they were created for. Some deceivers are made of rubber and inflate to size.

Everything else in Wardrobe was real—furs, fabrics, and feathers. The cost of sheer labor that went into making the clothes drove the accountants cross-eyed. One costume Garbo wore in *Mata Hari* took eight Guadalajaran needlewomen nine weeks to complete. In my wardrobe I have the most beautiful coat I have seen anywhere, which Travis Banton of Paramount designed. The embroidery alone cost $4000.

The studio designers were brilliant men and would have succeeded as artists, painters, decorators. One or two were addicted to the bottle, but they all blazed with talent. Travis at Paramount, Adrian at Metro, Omar Kiam at Goldwyn,

Orry-Kelly, now free-lancing and making more money than ever. He designed the clothes for Marilyn Monroe in *Some Like It Hot*, but she recut them to suit herself, and he refused to do her next picture.

There are only two women associated with the movies now who make sure they look like stars, and they both live in New York. Joan Crawford won't venture out of her Fifth Avenue apartment to buy an egg unless she is dressed to the teeth. Marlene Dietrich does more—she's made herself a living legend of spectacular glamour around the world.

For her opening night the first year at the Sahara in Las Vegas I had a front-row seat. She came on in a white dress that was poured over her. She wore layers of sheer soufflé, infinitely finer than chiffon, but only one layer to protect her chest from the evening air. The audience let out a gasp that threatened to blow away the tablecloths. The next night she wore the same gown, but she'd had two little circles of seed pearls sewed strategically on the bodice and forever after swore she had never appeared any more naked than that. But I'd seen both of them.

Every year she outdoes herself. One season she succeeded with a full-length coat of rippling swan's-down that for sheer beauty surpassed anything in fabulous fashion. Jean Louis designed it, but it was made by my furrier, Mrs. Fuhrman. In her shop one day, where the coat was kept in cold storage, she asked me to try it on. I felt like a maharaja's mother.

"We had a terrible time getting the swan's-down," said Mrs. Fuhrman, as I preened my borrowed feathers. "You know, you have to pull the feathers off the living swans—"

"You what?" I gulped. "I don't want to see it again."

Marlene was invented as a fashion plate just as Pygmalion created Galatea. The first time Travis Banton saw her, I thought he'd pass right out at her feet. Soon after she landed here, as Josef von Sternberg's protégée, she turned up at an afternoon tea party wearing a black satin evening gown complete with train, trimmed with ostrich feathers. Her hips were decidedly lumpy. Except for her beautiful face and perfect legs, which we'd seen in *The Blue Angel,* she could have passed for a German housewife.

Travis, a Yale man, took her in hand, taught her everything he knew about art, clothes, and good taste. She slimmed down, was made over into the most strikingly dressed clothes horse on the screen. She had some keen competition to contend with at Paramount. Carole Lombard, Claudette Colbert, Kay Francis, Evelyn Brent, and, later, Mae West fought for Travis' most stunning designs.

For one picture Mae insisted upon having only French clothes. She had posed for a nude statue and sent it to Paris to have the clothes fitted on it. They were beautiful clothes that arrived back, but when they were tried on Mae, they didn't meet by ten inches. Everything had to be remade at the studio.

There aren't any Marquis of Queensberry rules when an actress wants to win, but Marlene walked off with the honors. She was Travis' favorite. Nothing was too good for her. As top star at Paramount, she allowed herself the luxury of a raging temper unless she got her own way, but she took care not to rage at Travis.

At Christmas time she showered him with presents by way of thanks. He invited my son Bill and me to help trim his tree one Christmas. I saw him unwrap twenty-two separate packages from Marlene, covering the whole gamut of giving, from sapphire-and-diamond cuff links with studs to match, to Chinese jade figures and a kitchenload of copper pots and pans.

She is a complex woman. A different side showed when she wanted a hat, made almost entirely of black bird-of-paradise feathers, which she was going to wear at the race track. Trouble was that federal agents had just swooped down on the Wardrobe Department and confiscated its entire stock of egret and paradise feathers—$3500 worth. The law said that importing, buying, or possessing them was forbidden, though these particular items had been carried on the inventory for years.

So Marlene's precious hat had to be made of substitute plumage by a staff of expert milliners—one of them even came out from New York for the occasion. Marlene took one look at the result, tried the fine feathers disdainfully on for size, then in silence ripped them to shreds. The milliners worked for days before they came up with a hat she'd wear.

The same perfectionism blazed again when Ouida and Basil Rathbone announced a costume ball they were giving at the old Victor Hugo Restaurant in Beverly Hills. This was going to be the diamond-studded social event of the season. Our hosts counted the invitations they'd sent out, then thoughtfully had the restaurant install extra plumbing and built two complete extra powder rooms, ladies' and gents'.

Marlene, as ever, was intent on outdoing everybody. She decided to come as Leda and the Swan. Paramount's sewing ladies labored for weeks on the costume. The studios in those days took care that wherever a star appeared, she lived up to the glittering image of a star that they—and the public—carried in their minds. If she showed up at a private gathering looking less than immaculate, she'd be hauled on the carpet next morning by a head executive and advised to mend her manners.

On the evening of the Rathbones' party Marlene made up at home and went to the studio at 8 P.M. to be poured into her Leda gown. She regarded herself in the mirrors, then cried: "It won't do. I can't possibly wear a swan whose eyes match mine." So the sewing girls fell to, and the embroidered blue eyes were picked out and green ones substituted. Marlene sent out for champagne and sandwiches for them all to have an impromptu celebration in Wardrobe. She arrived at the Rathbones' shivaree five hours late and was the sensation of the evening.

I'd intended to go in a borrowed brocade that had a coronation look, with a jeweled crown to match, toting a baby lamb with gilded hoofs on a leash. But the lamb submitted to his pedicure for nothing. I was working on a picture with Louise Fazenda until midnight. When I got home, I was too tired to look at the lamb or do anything but flop into bed.

Under the swan's-down and sequins, Marlene remains at heart what she was in the beginning: a *Hausfrau* with a mothering instinct a mile wide. She has mothered every man in her life. They've loved her for that, and much more. Mike Todd enjoyed a special place under her warm, protective wing. A great friendship started when he went to see her in Las Vegas to ask her to appear as a "cameo" star along with Frank Sinatra, Red Skelton, and George Raft in the San Francisco honky-tonk sequence in *Around the World in Eighty Days*.

She agreed and instantly took on the full-time job of mothering Mike. She saw to it that he ate regularly, and the proper food. She helped him with advice. She bought him his first matched set of expensive luggage when she saw the ratty collection of cheap suitcases in which he'd been living. "You are a very great man, Mike," she told him; "you must look and act like one." He bought her nothing in return. Every dollar he could scrape up had to go into completing his picture. He hadn't then met Elizabeth Taylor.

I watched Marlene play the honky-tonk scene, which wasn't suited to her—she could have written a much better script herself. Then Mike drove me over to Metro, the only place where Todd-AO equipment had been installed, to see José Greco, David Niven, Cantinflas, and Cesar Romero in the flamenco and bullfight sequences. I sat stunned. "If the rest is as good as this," I told Mike, "you've got one of the greatest spectacles ever made." Joe Schenck, who'd sat with us, agreed. "If you need money to finish it," he promised, "all you have to do is come to me."

Mike gave Marlene and me his word that we could see the first rough cut of the complete picture. He kept his promises with most people, certainly with us. We had a six o'clock date to attend the screening with him before the three of us ate a quick dinner at Chasen's and he flew to New York. He was late, as usual, but at six-thirty he was there to call: "Roll 'em."

When the screening ended, Marlene and I sat in total silence. Mike couldn't stand it. "Why don't you say something? What's the matter? I've never known you two broads at a loss for words."

"Shall I tell him?" I asked Marlene.

"Go ahead."

I gave it to him on the chin. "Who cut this picture? A butcher? Where are those wonderful scenes I saw in the gypsy tavern and the bull ring? Why have they been cut to bits?"

"She's right," murmured Marlene. "It doesn't make sense."

"The cutter said they ran too long," Mike explained.

"Well, fire him. Cut the negative put back together and start all over again. Pay him off and find yourself an artist, not the man who did this."

"I don't know if I can do it. I gave him a year's contract. It'd cost a fortune."

"If you don't, it will cost you a great picture."

"Who could I get?" he begged.

"You've got one friend in this town who wants to see you succeed, not fail," I said, "and that's Sam Goldwyn. He has saved his own pictures in the cutting room many a time. Go to Sam and let him find you the finest cutter in the business. It's the only way you can save it. You haven't got a picture unless you do."

Mike sat there churning with anger. This was his first picture. We made a sad threesome in the restaurant, with Mike complaining about how hard he'd worked already and us not listening to him. "You're going on a plane and you'll get no food there," Marlene interrupted. "I'll order dinner for you. Hedda and I will eat later."

He accepted that idea, then grumbled that he didn't feel like going to New York anyway and he'd cancel his reservation. "You must go. You've got money questions to settle there," said Marlene, the mother again.

After he'd left, she telephoned the airport: "Mr. Michael Todd will be a few minutes late for his flight, number ten, TWA, for New York. Would you please hold the plane for

137

him? It's very important." Then she asked me: "Are you hungry?" We hadn't eaten a mouthful with him.

He went to New York. On his return he saw Sam Goldwyn, who came through with the right cutter. The first real preview, loaded down with Hollywood and New York big shots, was a sensation. But by then Mike had met and been dazzled by Liz, who arrived late at that screening nursing a highball, and sipped her way through the performance. Marlene saw very little of him after that, and Liz got all the glory.

On the afternoon of March 22, 1958, I was in Havana, Cuba, bowing before Madame Fulgencio Batista, wife of the reigning dictator, who was guest of honor at a fashion show being staged to celebrate the opening of a new Conrad Hilton hotel. In my outstretched hand I held a hat for presentation to her. A newspaperman in the crowd couldn't wait until I'd finished. He hurried forward and whispered in my ear: "Mike Todd's dead—his plane crashed."

I quickly dipped my head to Madame. "Will you excuse me? I've had some very sad news."

When I flew back to New York next day, Marlene telephoned me at the Waldorf Towers, broken up by the news of Mike. We talked for ninety minutes. She wept for him, and so did I.

Over cocktails in Havana I'd met an ex-subject of my moviemaking days. Ernest Hemingway had cursed like a troop of cavalry in 1942 when my cameraman trailed him around Sun Valley and ruined a day's quail hunting for him. I wanted to bag him and the Gary Coopers on film for my series of two-reelers called *Hedda Hopper's Hollywood*. In Cuba I got very chummy with Ernest and his lovely wife, Mary. "We should have met twenty-five years ago," he said gallantly.

"Yes, I think we might have made some sweet music then."

"It's not too late now," the old flirt replied.

"It is for me," I said.

He sighed. "I was boasting a bit. I guess for me, too."

The following winter in New York I saw Mary at a Broadway opening. "Where's your ever-loving?" I asked.

"Out with Marlene Dietrich. He preferred dining with her to coming to see this play."

"Can't blame him. But how come I never get that much attention from your husband?"

"Because you don't do as much for him as Marlene," said Mary.

Where Marlene was a challenge and an inspiration to Travis Banton, Garbo was a challenge, exclamation point, to Gilbert Adrian at Metro. Marlene loves seductive glamour in clothes, and she finished up knowing as much as her master. The Swede hated dressing up, enjoyed wearing only her drab woolen skirt, turtle-neck sweater, flat-heeled shoes, and men's socks on her big feet.

Travis delighted in high fashion. Adrian came up with more fantastic designs, though when femininity was in order, his clothes dripped with it for Greer Garson, Norma Shearer, Jeanette MacDonald. He sized up Garbo like a bone surgeon, with his keen, kind, hazel eyes. She moved like a man, and she had a man's square shoulders. Her arms were muscular; her bosom—let's just say meager. Yet on the screen there was a commanding presence and luminous beauty.

She had an acting secret that only a few of us who watched her closely caught on to. In every clinch, a split second before the leading man put his arms around her, she would reach out and embrace him. It was one of the subconscious things that marked the difference between a European and an American woman—and Americans were always awed by Garbo. Her pictures are still earning lots more praise and money overseas than at home.

Her face hinted at sadness. She suffered her first bitter taste of that not long after she was brought over from Stockholm by Metro, to land in the middle of a New York heat wave, when she spent most of her days sitting in a hotel bathtub full of cold water. It wasn't Garbo that the studio wanted but Maurice Stiller, the Swedish director who had discovered her and refused to travel without her. But Stiller was subsequently fired by Irving Thalberg, and it was Garbo who was given the build-up. Stiller returned to Stockholm, a defeated, ailing giant of a man, and she was heartbroken.

She stored up bitterness against MGM. In her early days Pete Smith, head of publicity, had her pose for cheesecake shots wearing track shorts, to be photographed with another Scandinavian, Paavo Nurmi, the record-breaking runner, on the athletic fields of the University of Southern California. When she had made her name a household word and insisted on working in complete privacy on the set behind tall screens, Louis B. Mayer brought six important New York stockholders to see her. She sent them packing. "When Lillian Gish was queen of the lot, all I was allowed to do was show my knees. Now let these visitors bend their rusty knees to me, but they shall not watch," she said.

Once Arthur Brisbane, Hearst's top editor, came on the set to watch. When she saw him she walked out of the scene. "If he wants to see me, he can see me in the theater." She went to her dressing room and wouldn't come back until he'd gone.

Adrian accentuated Garbo's assets and concealed her liabilities. For her he devised the high-necked, long-sleeved evening gown that swept the world of fashion in the thirties. For *As You Desire Me*, in which I played her sister, he invented the pillbox hat with strings tied under her chin, which became part of every smart woman's wardrobe. He had her dripping in lace and melting costume lines for *Anna Karenina*, sent the dress industry off on an oriental kick with her exotic outfits for *The Painted Veil*. Her costumes in *Grand Hotel* could be worn today and still be high fashion.

He achieved much the same kind of fashion influence for Crawford. Her padded halfback's shoulders in *Chained* and a dozen other movies convinced half the women of America that this was exactly how they wanted to appear. His *Letty Lynton* dress, with wide sleeves and sweetheart neck, was a garment-center classic. "If Crawford has an apron," we used to say, "it has to be by Adrian."

His new clothes for any top star were guarded like the gold of Fort Knox. Until the premiere costumes were kept under lock and key so manufacturers' spies couldn't run off with his designs and pirate them. A new Garbo or Crawford or Norma Shearer picture carried the fashion wallop of a Paris opening today.

No more. The tradition that the designers fostered has vanished. Women used to follow Hollywood fashion as avidly as they copied Veronica Lake's peekaboo hairdo or dreamed that some miracle might endow them with legs like Betty Grable or Esther Williams' classy chassis. Now they haven't got much to build their diet of dreams on except Ben Casey's surgical smock—television doesn't go in strong for women, much less gals in glamorous gowns.

When I look at Jackie Kennedy these days I think: "If those fellows were around today, what they couldn't have done for her!" She'd be queen of fashion the world over. Oleg Cassini can't hold a candle to any of them, and he never had it so good, not even when he was married to Gene Tierney.

Who's left in motion-picture fashions? Nobody much outside the industry has heard of Irene Sharaff, or Helen Rose. Edith Head started as Travis Banton's sketch girl, and her designs continue to follow his lead. Jean Louis is the one designer that picture stars ask for today, just as stage stars beg for Mainbocher.

Sometimes Jean overdresses Doris Day, but the clothes he makes for her, at producer Ross Hunter's insistence, have transformed Doris from a plain Jane into a fashion plate. One difference between Jean Louis and Adrian: Doris Day and Lana Turner got all the clothes to keep, as a wonderful bonus from Ross Hunter. At Metro, the dresses belonged to the studio, and Adrian had to ignore the pleas from a New York socialite who, after every Garbo picture, used to send him a blank check, willing to pay anything for just one of the costumes Garbo wore.

Metro's meanness and lack of judgment was one reason he quit and opened his own salon. A New York wholesale house wanted him to design a total of thirty-five dresses a year and offered to pay $150,000 for the job, split between him and Metro. "What's that to us?" his bosses said. "That's peanuts. No, you can't take it, and that's final."

Reason number two was the reaction Adrian got from director George Cukor to the twenty-four beautiful costumes designed for Garbo in *Two-Faced Woman*. I saw them hanging in the Wardrobe Department and drooled over them. But Cukor made up his mind that for this picture she was going to look as she does in reality. No glamour; two fake diamond clips in her frizzed-up hair. No clothes to make an audience's eyes pop, but wool sweaters and sack frocks.

"After making her a fashion legend, you want to do *this* to her?" cried Adrian. "Won't you at least come and see the clothes I've made?"

Cukor refused even that. *Two-Faced Woman* was the last picture Garbo made. She respected Adrian, to the point where she'd sometimes eat her vegetarian lunch in his office. The picture was one of her few failures. He handed in his notice. Metro was burned to a cinder when it had to hire six people to replace him. He'd been in the habit of designing clothes not only for the stars but for the whole company in movies he worked on.

When Garbo retired from the screen, she gave only one autograph as a souvenir. It went neither to Adrian nor Louis Mayer. To her colored maid, the only living soul allowed in her dressing room, whom the studio paid for, she presented a framed photograph of herself on which she had written: "To Ursula, from your friend, Greta Garbo." I've heard of only one similar gesture of hers. Dr. Henry Bieler, of California, put her on a diet to which she's clung over the years. When he wrote a book, he asked her for an endorsement, which she promptly sent him.

Nowadays she's lost the passion for self-effacement that had her masquerading as "Harriet Brown," hidden in a floppy hat and dark glasses. Neighbors in the New York apartment where she lives are devoted to her. Their children exchange greetings with her on the street. Among those neighbors are Mary Martin and Richard Halliday. Their daughter Heller lived with them until she eloped last year.

One day Mary's front-door bell rang. Garbo was standing outside. "Forgive my intrusion," she said shyly, "but I have often watched from my window and seen you and your family. Sometimes going shopping. Sometimes getting into your car. You look so happy, and I feel so alone."

Over the tea that Mary insisted on serving for them both, Garbo found one more friend, to add to the precious few she's made in her lifetime. Two others, who are devotion itself, are the designer Valentina and her husband, George Schlee.

There was a Christmas Eve before Adrian resigned when I was the stooge in a plot to turn him green around the edges. Omar Kiam, who designed for Sam Goldwyn, was the one to arrange it. Adrian had just announced his engagement to Janet Gaynor. He was giving a party, and Omar was to be my escort. On December 22, Omar informed me that I had to have a new gown. But I hadn't time to get anything, I told him. "Then I'll make one. You won't even need fittings; I've got your dress form at the studio. You've got to be dressed to the teeth."

At six o'clock on Christmas Eve, ninety minutes before he was due to collect me to go to Adrian's, Omar arrived on my doorstep with the dress over his arm. I have never seen anything lovelier: American Beauty red velvet, tightly fitted, with a full, flounced skirt and train. "If this doesn't knock their eyes out, nothing will," he grinned.

"It sure will," I said. "I'll be ready sharp on time." But I was still waiting at eight-thirty. Wondering what went wrong, I telephoned Omar's house. His butler answered: "I'm terribly sorry, and I should have let you know. Mr. Kiam won't be able to come for you. He has retired for the night."

It dawned on me then what had happened. After delivering the gown he went home to celebrate, not wisely but too well, and had to be put to bed. I swept into Adrian's living room an hour late. My red gown dimmed everything else in the room. Ina Clair, who was there, said: "You did it on purpose."

I still have that red velvet—as the upholstery on two French chairs once owned by Elinor Glyn. Every morning when I open my eyes I see a memento of Omar Kiam. He did the clothes for both the pictures I made for Sam Goldwyn. In one of them, *Vogues of 1938*, which Walter Wanger produced, I played Joan Bennett's mother. She and I had a certain exchange of words some years later.

Two lines in my column brought me the gift of a skunk from her. Here's the story. Mothers usually had a tough time in pictures, especially with close-ups. They came almost always at the end of the day when you were tired and your make-up was messy. So it was on this picture.

It was not only the end of the day but the last scene in the picture and I was feeling desperately weary. I went to Walter Wanger and said: "I don't think I can do that close-up. If you'll let me come tomorrow morning, it won't cost you anything."

He said: "You'll have to do it—I'd have to bring the whole crew in; it would cost a day's salary for everyone."

So I finished the scene and went to my dressing room and for the first time in my life fainted. How long I lay there I don't know. When I woke I called for help. There wasn't a soul around; everybody had gone home. I finally found a telephone and got the gateman to order me a cab, which took me home. Then I sent for a doctor.

Years later, when Joan was playing mother to Elizabeth Taylor in *Father of the Bride*, I went on the set to interview Liz. There was Joan doing her close-up. I looked at my watch: it was 6:30 P.M. I remembered the misery I'd once endured, and in my column the following day, I wrote: "At last Miss Bennett knows how it feels to get her close-up at the end of the day and not at the beginning."

For that she sent me a deodorized, live skunk. I christened it Joan and gave it to the James Masons, who had been looking for one as a companion for their nine cats.

In its rosier days, Hollywood Boulevard saw glamour by the carload on Oscar nights. Movie fans drove in, goggle-eyed, from every state in the Union to see the stars; a hundred searchlights would crisscross the sky. Bleachers set up on the sidewalk overflowed. Flashbulbs flared by the thousands as the queens slid out of their limousines, owned or rented, in minks and sables, which the studio would lend to dress up the show if your wardrobe didn't run to such luxury. They'd glide across the sidewalk like some special, splendid race of the beautiful and the blessed; gowns swishing, hairdos immaculate; teeth, eyes, and diamonds gleaming together.

Just watching them walk in was as good as a ticket to a world's fair. They all had gowns made for those evenings, each trying to outdo the other. They'd pester the studio designers to find out what the other girls were getting. "You've got to top them for me," they'd all plead, and the boys would smile the promise to do their best with sketch pads and shears.

During World War II the women of Hollywood let the producers talk them into surrendering every shred of glamour even on Oscar nights. "If you go out, you mustn't be well dressed," the front-office men argued, "or else the public will be offended. What you've got to do is to look *austere*."

I knew this was malarkey. So did they. From the mail that poured in, it was as plain as a pikestaff that servicemen were starving for glamour. They wanted pin-up pictures of glamorous girls. I sent out ten thousand of them, until the studios rebelled and pretended they couldn't afford any more. But they didn't get away with that.

I waged a little guerrilla war of my own, too, to doll up the Academy Awards when the studio chieftains still wanted the presentation to look no dressier than a missionary's sewing bee. Telephone calls by the dozen worked the trick. "What are you going to do," I demanded, "let those clothes rot in your closets? You're not going to wear anything but your most beautiful gown."

"But nobody's going to be dressed," the girl at the other end would wail.

"Then set the style. Last year you looked like spooks: sack-cloth and ashes."

At least, we managed to re-establish the tradition that year that women should dress for the night they hand out the gold-plated little men who first saw life in 1927, when Cedric Gibbon roughed in the design for them on a tablecloth at the Ambassador Hotel.

But the Academy Awards I've cared about most over the years had nothing to do with glamour. They had to do with life, exclusively, in full measure. The first were the two Oscars that went to the crippled veteran, Harold Russell, who proved in *The Best Years of Our Lives* that a man can lose his hands but not his courage.

The second was willed to Howard University by Hattie McDaniel, who won hers for the best supporting role in 1939 for *Gone With the Wind* and died penniless in 1952 in the Motion Picture Relief Home.

The third was won by James Baskette for *Song of the South*, after a campaign in which Jean Hersholt, then president of the Academy, and Freeman Gosden gave their immediate support. Some members disdained my idea that a special Oscar should go to a man for playing Uncle Remus, a slave, and they fought at a meeting on the eve of presentation until 4 A.M. Jean finally sent them home with this warning: "If he doesn't receive an Oscar, I shall stand up tomorrow night and tell the world the whole disgraceful story."

After he received it from the hands of Ingrid Bergman, James Baskette carried his statuette everywhere he went, in a black velvet bag that his wife made. At night he stood it on his bedroom mantelpiece with a tiny spotlight shining on it.

He was slated to play "De Lawd" in a Broadway revival of *Green Pastures* when he was taken critically ill. As he lay dying, his eyes returned time and again to Oscar. "No colored man ever got one before," he said, "and I'm grateful, Lord."

Nine

Our town worships success, the bitch goddess whose smile hides a taste for blood. She has a habit, before she destroys her worshipers, of turning them into spitting images of herself. She has an army of beauties in attendance at her shrine.

Not many survive the encounter with success. Wreathed in smiles, she kills them in cars, like Jimmy Dean; or with torment, like Marilyn Monroe; or with illness, like Jean Harlow. She turns them into drunkards, liars, or cheats who are as dishonest in business as in love. This is the story of four women and what success did to them.

One of them who escaped in a single piece is Lucille Ball. She grabbed the prizes of talent, fame, and money, and Lucy is only slightly battered as a consequence. She even survived after she gave Desi Arnaz, with whom she was madly in love, the shock of his life by divorcing him.

Lucille had the sense to quit as TV's "Lucy" when she sat on top of the world. That show had an audience rating so high that America took time out for half an hour every Tuesday evening to look at that little black box. I remember that the 1952 inauguration party that Colonel Robert McCormick of the Chicago *Tribune* gave in Washington came to a temporary halt while everybody had to watch in silence. Lucy's baby was being born on the program that night and Bertie wanted to see.

But the time came when Lucy told Desi: "I won't do any more. The writers have run out of ideas, and I'm dead tired." They sold out the series to CBS for reruns and on the proceeds bought the two RKO studios for $6,150,000. These studios had a certain sentimental appeal on top of their commercial value. Lucy and Desi first met at RKO in 1940 when

147

they were filming *Too Many Girls*, a prophetic title. The former Earl Carroll chorus girl and the ex-bongo drummer from Cuba proceeded to spread themselves over a whole pile of enterprises that included a Palm Springs hotel, a golf course, and a $12,000,000 production contract for Westinghouse.

Desi took to putting a few drinks under his belt as a diet, and the fireworks started. They split up two or three times, but Lucy always forgave him and took him back. To save the marriage, as she hoped, she set up a trip to Europe for them both. "We'll take the children along, too," she said.

I begged her not to. "If you'd just try it alone, the two of you," I said. "Little Desi and Lucie are too young to enjoy a trip like that."

But Lucy can be stubborn. "I won't go without them," she said. So she took a maid along to look after them. For the voyage, which she hoped would be a second honeymoon, she bought clothes by the trunkload; big picture hats that she never put on her head; a magnificent full-length sable coat. "But it's May now, and you'll be running into summer over there," I said.

"I've bought it and I'm going to take it," she said. "Besides, Desi hasn't seen it."

They sailed aboard the *Liberté*. "We are having a wonderful crossing—so far—weather perfect," she wrote me. "Food divine—too divine. Eating ourselves out of shape. Everyone loves our kids—that makes us happy. They have even forgiven us our forty pieces of baggage and two trunks."

Just how wonderful the trip was I heard when she got back, scarcely speaking to Desi. He had been weary, resenting the presence of their children, though he's a loving father. He and Lucy collided head on in one quarrel after another. "What did he think about the sable coat?" I asked.

"Never saw it," she said. "I used it on the ship as a blanket for the kids."

The following Christmas, when the Westinghouse contract had three more months to run, she asked me to appear on a TV show on which she was making her bow as director; it included a dozen or more players she had been training in her school. Desi was just back from a solo trip to Europe, shooting a picture there.

On the set, Vivian Vance and Bill Frawley, veterans of happier "I Love Lucy" days, wanted to take cover along with me to shelter from the storms between Lucy and Desi. It was dreadful. "You can't insult him before the entire company," I warned her in her dressing room. "You're partly responsible for this show, too, you know."

It seemed we were doomed to have a flop on our hands. As director, Lucy was lost without a compass, too mad to see straight, and the show was going to pieces. In dress rehearsal Desi said mildly: "Lucy, dear, will you let me see if I can pull this thing together for you?"

"Okay, try it!" she snapped.

Desi was winning no medals as husband, but he shines as a director and producer. In ten minutes he had that Christmas program ticking like a clock. The New Year hadn't yet come around the corner before Lucy wanted to sue him for divorce, which was something Desi had been convinced she would never do.

"You can't," I told her. "You and Desi both signed the Westinghouse contract as partners. If you walk out, they could cancel and sue you."

She had to listen to the same tune from me every week. She was itching to dump Desi and so desperate to leave Hollywood that she'd have played *Uncle Tom's Cabin* if it would take her to Broadway. Instead she took on the next best thing—a musical called *Wildcat*, on which she staked money and her reputation.

Lucy hasn't many illusions about herself. "I'm not beautiful, not sexy, and I don't have a good figure," she says. She knows she can't sing and she admits that too many years have flowed under the bridge for her to dance like Cyd Charisse. But for *Wildcat* she had to sing, dance, and hold the show together. She tried to inject some sparkle by ad-libbing wisecracks à la Lucy. The author, instead of being grateful, was fit to be tied.

After a lot of her cash had vanished and she'd collapsed two or three times on stage, she returned to Hollywood. She licked her wounds and, with Desi down on his ranch breeding horses, earned fresh medals as a businesswoman by helping to put Desilu back on its feet.

In November 1961, I went to the wedding of Lucy and Gary Morton, a young man she met on a blind date while she was playing in *Wildcat* and he was telling jokes at the Copacabana. He makes her happy, and she told me that he'd be able to spend the summer at home while she started a new television series. No, Gary would not co-star.

Joan Crawford has been a priestess at the shrine of success since she was a hoofer named Lucille Le Sueur. She's been put to the sacrificial flames more than once, but has always risen like Lazarus and lived to burn another day.

She's cool, courageous, and thinks like a man. She labors twenty-four hours a day to keep her name in the pupil of the public eye. She'll time her arrival at a theater seconds before the curtain goes up and make such an entrance that the audience sees only her through act one, scene one. The actors on stage may hate it, but she's having a ball. If she has a surviving fan club in any city she's visiting, she'll carefully supply its president in advance with a complete schedule for the day, detailed to the minute, and collect such crowds that by evening there'll be a mob hundreds strong escorting her.

She was called box-office poison and couldn't get a job for years after her Metro contract ended. Out of money, she continued to play the star and hold her head high, and she had the town's sympathy. *Mildred Pierce* put her back in pictures and won her an Oscar, as much for bravery under fire as for her acting. The same gutsy quality showed when her husband, Al Steele, died and she took on a job as traveling ambassador for his company, Pepsi-Cola. Just before that, he'd arranged for her to visit the Strategic Air Command base at Omaha, Nebraska. Typically, she went through with the visit alone. Going on from there to Hollywood, she told me about it over dinner at the home of Billy Haines, once a picture star, now a top decorator with Joan among his customers.

Nothing would suit but I had to see SAC, too. She fixed it with General Thomas Power, the commander in chief. The Air Force flew me out from Los Angeles. Joan, who'd meantime returned to New York, came on from there on a commercial flight that got in an hour ahead of me. I found her waiting at the airport, with the mayor of the city in tow. She hadn't yet checked into the hotel suite we were sharing, so we went straight to SAC, where General Power took us through the most amazing setup you could dream of. Joan and I rode to town together in the chauffeured limousine Mr. Mayor had put at her disposal.

She had enough luggage and hatboxes with her to fill a department store. She carried a jewel case two feet long. "I always travel with it," she told us. "By the way [this to the mayor] would you be kind enough to provide someone to guard my jewels? I'll need two men—one for day and one for night."

"Certainly, Miss Crawford," he said, hypnotized. "Whatever you need, just ask for it."

Our suite consisted of a living room and two separate bedrooms, one for Joan, and one for me. As soon as we'd checked in, she unpacked. For our two-day visit she brought twenty-two dresses, which she spread out all over her room, and fourteen hats. "I don't know what I'll want to wear," she explained seriously when my eyebrows hit my hairline, "so I brought them along in case."

We were no sooner unpacked than she rang for an iron and ironing board. The iron the bellboy brought wasn't the kind she liked, so she sent him out to buy a new one. With it, she proceeded to press every one of the dresses and hang each in its cellophane wrapper in her closet.

"Would you like to see my jewels?" she asked. I nodded, speechless. She unlocked the case and—abracadabra!—it was like peering at Aladdin's treasure, half a million dollars' worth; trays and trays loaded with diamonds and emeralds and pearls, bracelets and necklaces and earrings.

"This is the most dangerous thing you've ever done," I said. "Someday you'll wake up with your throat cut."

"But I always have it guarded," she said, "and I keep it beside me on the plane."

"Why isn't it in a safety-deposit box?"

"I like to look at them," she said, as though she were talking to an idiot.

I went into my room for a minute. When I came back into the living room she had disappeared. "Where are you?" Her voice came from the bathroom: "In here." She was on her hands and knees scrubbing the floor. "It wasn't very clean," she said.

Next to the goddess in their prayers, many of the worshipers place a compulsive kind of cleanliness. Sinatra, Jerry Lewis, Doris Day—they'll shower three times a day like pilgrims in the Ganges trying to wash away their sins. But only Joan and Garbo will personally scrub the bathroom or kitchen floor to make sure there are no germs lingering there.

The mayor returned to make us his guests at a small dinner party. We both wore simple dresses because Omaha doesn't run much to evening clothes. We were back in the hotel by eleven-thirty and had Mr. Mayor and two or three others up for a drink.

As soon as they had said their good nights, Joan, who doesn't smoke, flung every window wide open and carried the ash trays out into the hall, where her night guard had dutifully stationed himself outside the door. She gathered up the glasses and washed them in the kitchenette off the living room. She then unlocked another item of her luggage that the bellboy had staggered under when we moved in.

It was a massive chest perhaps a yard long, packed with ice. It contained four bottles of hundred-proof vodka, bottles

152

of her favorite brand of champagne, and a silver chalice, which she took out for her bedtime ceremony. Into the chalice she poured a split of champagne and raised it in a simple toast, "To Al," before she put it to her lips.

"What do you want for breakfast?" she asked when the chalice was empty.

"Can't we order in the morning?"

"No, I like breakfast when I get up. I'll put our order in tonight." I settled for juice, coffee, and a boiled egg. That taken care of, we agreed that eight-thirty in the morning would suit us both as time to arise. Come the morrow, I'd bathed when at eight-thirty sharp there was a rapping at my bedroom door. In the living room stood a waiter ready to serve us. Outside the front door stood a new guard, keeping the daytime watch.

Then we spent a full, fascinating, reassuring, awe-inspiring day at SAC; saw the H-bombers take off in a practice scramble; again met General Power, who gave us dinner. I started sleeping more easily from that night on as a result of what I'd witnessed. It seemed to me to be an up-to-date necessity in a fearful world where the best rule for America's conduct was advocated by Teddy Roosevelt: Speak softly and carry a big stick. The next morning, every inch a star and clean as a hound's tooth, Joan flew on to Chicago, with her twenty-two dresses, fourteen hats, jewel case, ice chest, and silver chalice, to scrub another bathroom if she had to.

Some of our women can walk through the temple's sacrificial flames and not get as much as singed. They're so deep-down innocent they wouldn't recognize the goddess if they saw her. Ann Blyth, a devout Catholic and a darling, doesn't know that she's used as regularly as tap water by people seeking favors, charity, or a conducted tour around the studios.

Kathryn Grayson is another, so guileless that a fat, bow-legged producer with lust in his eyes used to arrive on her doorstep many a morning before she'd had breakfast and literally chase her through the house.

The most gullible of all is Mary Martin, who sees, hears, and speaks no evil and, by a miracle, lives by it and through it. Judge Preston Martin's daughter was friendly as a kitten when she drove her bright, new, yellow convertible to Hollywood in 1936 from Weatherford, Texas, which boasted a population of 5000 people at the time. She'd always been the girl who sang sweetest in church, stood out in school plays, worked the most enthusiastically in civic causes.

Her father gave her $500 as stake money on the strict understanding that as soon as that was gone, she'd come back home. He also saddled her with her five-year-old son, Larry, who resulted when Mary eloped from finishing school in Nashville, Tennessee, with a boy from Fort Worth. That marriage lasted in fact two years, was dissolved in five. "Larry's your responsibility and you've got to take him along," her father insisted, figuring this was a fair means of keeping his wide-eyed darling out of new romances and would bring her back quicker.

Around the studios they got to calling her "Audition Mary." She sang for everybody, and everybody turned thumbs down. "Nice voice, fair figure, but impossible to photograph that face," was the verdict. She sang for Oscar Hammerstein II—remember *South Pacific?*—at his house on Benedict Canyon at the end of my dead-end street. He knew she wasn't ready. Years later Mary told me he taught her how to phrase a song, how to read lines, how to move. "In fact," said she, "I learned show business from Oscar Hammerstein."

When he thought she was ready, he and Richard Rodgers adapted a play called *Green Grow the Lilacs*, and she was offered the leading role. At the same time, she had also been offered a lead in a play produced by Vinton Freedley, who'd given Mary her first Broadway chance in *Leave It to Me*.

"I was torn between the two offers. Talking to Hammerstein over the phone, I said: 'Will you give me a minute?'

I tossed a coin and Freedley won. The play was a success in Boston, but I felt certain it'd never reach Broadway—it didn't."

Green Grow the Lilacs also failed and later was rewritten for a man instead of a woman in a new version called *Oklahoma!*

When her $500 had melted away, she picked up what jobs she could find. She sang for $60 at a little night spot. She taught slew-footed stars how to get through dancing scenes. Her voice was dubbed on sound tracks for tin-cared girls who couldn't sing. Then she managed to get signed by a producer named Lawrence Schwab for a Broadway musical he had in mind.

When she got to New York, she found that plans for the show had come to nothing, but Schwab lent her to another producer, Vinton Freedley, for *Leave It to Me*. It had a song called "My Heart Belongs to Daddy," by Cole Porter, which Sophie Tucker encouraged Mary to sing with the innocence of a lamb. That was the making of Mary. Soon she was singing on radio, then back in Hollywood with a contract at Paramount. Judge Martin went to his grave believing that "My Heart Belongs to Daddy" was written especially for him.

But making movies is a cold-blooded, impersonal, highly technical business. Some performers slowly freeze inside when they work for staring cameras instead of for human beings sitting in a theater waiting to burst into applause. Mary was like that. "I beat my brains out," she says, "and I like to hear the echo." She didn't cotton to Hollywood.

Glamour and Mary were strangers in those days. The studio put her in curls and ruffles. She arrived at one dress-up affair in a sports suit. And make-up men hadn't yet acquired their present techniques, which can transform literally any girl into a beauty queen.

Mary didn't start to glow until Mainbocher took her over and made her one of America's best-dressed women. Any woman wearing a beautiful gown can peek at herself in a mirror and think: "My, how pretty you look in that!" The thought itself puts a sparkle in her eye and a smile on her lips, making her just what she fancies herself to be.

I only once saw Mainbocher cringe at the sight of his pride and joy. That was in New Orleans, when we sat together watching Mary's opening in *Kind Sir*, produced by her long-time friend and Connecticut neighbor, Josh Logan. I smelled a fiasco during her rehearsals, but I did whatever was possible to boost her morale. She poured out her gratitude in a telegram: ONCE BEFORE ANOTHER GREAT WOMAN SOPHIE TUCKER HELPED ME IN MY VERY FIRST SHOW STOP NOW YOU BY SOME MIRACLE WERE SENT TO ME GOD BLESS YOU AND THANK YOU MY LOVE ALWAYS—MARY.

But nothing helped *Kind Sir*. On opening night, when the last-act curtain fell, even the flowers that were pushed into her arms were tired. In the seat next to me, Mainbocher, who'd done her costumes, slid down almost out of sight so he wouldn't be asked to take a bow. But he took it with a smile like all the rest.

I almost made an enemy of Josh Logan by nagging him to use Mary in the movie of *South Pacific* instead of Mitzi Gaynor. "There are make-up men today who'll make Mary look like a young girl," I told him. "Mitzi's a fine entertainer, but she'll be only a carbon copy of Mary as Nellie Forbush." Josh wrote me a twelve-page letter explaining why I was wrong. *South Pacific* turned out to be only a modest success as a movie, earned around $5,000,000, but it would have done better if Mary had starred in it.

She played Nellie in London, of course, and reported rapturously, in red ink yet: "Dear Hedda: Look where we are! Exactly where you said we'd be! And—oh!—it has been just as wonderful as I had hoped and *dreamed* it would be. All of it has been unbelievably perfect."

When she came home she was bone-weary. She and her husband, Richard Halliday, had booked passage on a slow boat to South America. Then Leland Hayward told her: "I'm going to do a big TV spectacular, and I can't do it without you." She begged off and started on the cruise. When they reached Brazil, Adrian talked her into buying land near the house he and Janet Gaynor built in the middle of the jungle that he loved.

Mary had as much need for a Brazilian hideaway as for two heads, but she can't go on saying no to anybody. She and Richard, who was the only big reward she won in Hollywood, discovered that the first jungle real estate they bought was sold to them by a woman who didn't own it. The local authorities hushed that up since they couldn't afford to have the news leak back to the United States. So Mary, $40,000 poorer, sank another $50,000 into some other property, which the surrounding, giant-sized greenery constantly threatens to steal back from her.

When Leland Hayward heard about her proposed rest cure in Brazil, he flew down ahead of the Hallidays and was waiting for them as they landed. Brushing aside her pleas of fatigue, he told her: "Ethel Merman says she'll do my TV show if you will." Mary, as ever, couldn't say no. After the two of them made television history that season, she asked Ethel casually one day: "How did Leland get you to do it?"

"At first I told him to go to hell," said Ethel, "but then he said you'd do it if I would, and I couldn't refuse."

Where Joan can't stop washing, Mary can't stop working. She hasn't a clue as to the size of her bank account, and I'll guarantee she never looks inside a checkbook. She waded trustingly into ventures, often backed with her own money, where she found herself up to her ears in problems.

"But that's all ended," she declares. "Never again would I do a play that I'm not suited to and take another two and a half years out of my life."

But so long as she can go on flying, she'll be happy in the theater. As Peter Pan, which was a lifetime dream come true, she's the world's most celebrated flying grandmother. Her son, Larry, and his Swedish wife are the parents of two children.

The other member of the Halliday family, daughter Heller, "eloped" with her fiancé, Tony Weir, along with her parents, his parents and family, and the twenty-six guests. They'd planned a reception at New York's River Club. Her bridal gown by Mainbocher was made but never worn. Heller decided that instead of a big wedding, she'd rather have cash to get her household started, so Mary's big production plans went up in smoke.

This was an elopement with a difference. In two cars, one Friday morning, the wedding party made for Elkton, Maryland, without anyone remembering that the state law there requires forty-eight hours' residence before the knot is tied. That made it impossible for them to get a marriage license before Monday. Heller, Tony, and his sister Karen took one of the cars and headed south for Alexandria, Virginia, while the rest of the faltering band drove up to stay in Baltimore.

The bride and groom went through their blood tests in Alexandria. Heller had to be jabbed half a dozen times before blood could be drawn, and she finished the day with three pieces of adhesive plaster on each arm. But they still couldn't get a license; Heller, short of twenty-one, needed her parents' consent. On the following day, Saturday, the nearest license bureau open in the state of Virginia was in Leesburg. The doors there closed at noon. So the party took off bright and early, covered 150 miles in waltz time, and got to Leesburg just before the deadline.

"Our darling elopers," Mary related, "were married there in the first Methodist Church to be built in America. Both mothers cried. I sat on the wrong side of the church, the groom's. The happy pair were, oh so happy, and we are, oh so tired." Heller went to work showing off wedding gowns as a model, instead of wearing one.

Sometimes the first breath of success converts an otherwise nice, well-adjusted girl into a priestess of the cult. Sometimes it takes longer. It took eleven years, her third husband, and a turnabout in her faith to convert Doris Day, who was born to Wilhelm and Alma von Kappelhoff, a German-Catholic couple in Cincinnati, on April 3, 1924, and christened

Doris because her mother rated Doris Kenyon the greatest actress that ever breathed.

The von Kappelhoff became "Day" because band leader Barney Rapp wanted a name that would fit on the marquee of the Cincinnati night club where Doris, a puppy-fat sixteen-year-old girl, earned $25 a week singing with his orchestra. She graduated from there to sing with Les Brown and His Band of Renown, and the goddess started to breathe harder on her when Doris recorded her first hit, "Sentimental Journey" with them. She was making $500 a week when she left the band.

She was a girl who fell in love without pausing for breath. In April 1941 she up and married Al Jorden, a trombonist from Cincinnati who played for Jimmy Dorsey. On February 4, 1942, Doris gave birth to her son, Terry. A year later, she went through her first divorce, left her baby in her mother's care, and joined up again with Les Brown, the girl singer who sat primly in front of the band until her turn came to go up to the microphone.

They were playing at the old Pennsylvania Hotel, which became the Statler, on Manhattan's Seventh Avenue, when agent Al Levy first heard her. Struck by a funny feeling that this girl might go someplace, he sent her a note inviting her to join him at the table where he sat with Mannie Sachs, who was then head of Columbia Records. "Have you ever thought of going on your own?" he asked.

"Not really," she said. "I'm going to get married soon."

Eighteen months after, Les Brown was appearing at the Palladium in Los Angeles, and Doris and her new husband, George Weidler, a saxophonist in the orchestra, were living in a trailer camp on Sepulveda Boulevard out toward Long Beach. They quit Les Brown and went on living in the camp, Doris out of work, George picking up occasional weekend engagements. Terry was still with his grandmother.

Al Levy had trouble contacting Doris. The trailer was a block away from the only telephone and, if anybody called Doris, the proprietress of the camp found it easier to say

"She's not here" than go get her. But Al managed to exchange a few words: "Call me sometime if you get ambitious, and we'll talk some more."

Mannie Sachs got her one brief job—as singer on a sustaining radio show that starred Bob Sweeney, now a TV director, and Hal March, who made a Broadway hit in *Come Blow Your Horn*. She worked for thirteen weeks at $89 a week, after deductions, but then she was dropped; the network figured she had no future. So, with no money coming in, it was time to call Al Levy. "All right, let's see what can happen now," she said.

He had put $25,000 into a management agency called Century Artists, which gave him forty per cent ownership. Dick Dorso had started the business with a small stake from Lew Levy, no relation of Al's, who was manager of the Andrews Sisters and the husband of one of them, Maxine. Lew wasn't acting out of undiluted generosity—he wanted to get his brother-in-law, Marty Melcher, out from under his feet. Marty, Patti's husband, used to handle such chores as fixing the lights for the sisters' act. Marty became the second partner in Century Artists as part of Lew's deal with Dorso. The agency, which took on the sisters as clients, had its offices next to mine in the Guaranty Building on Hollywood Boulevard. Al also assisted my manager, Dema Harshbarger, in booking talent for my weekly radio show.

Al brought Doris to say hello as soon as he'd signed her. She was a scared little creature, smothered in freckles, wearing scuffed-up shoes, skirt and sweater, but not a lick of make-up. For months she wore skirts and sweaters. When I asked why she never wore a dress, she said: "I can only afford skirts and sweaters." Her first need was clothes. He found a little dressmaker in Los Angeles to make her four evening dresses on Century Artists' money.

In New York, Billy Reed was opening his Little Club on East Fifty-fifth Street, uncertain whether or not to have any entertainer work in the squeezed-in room he'd rented, which he was doing up with striped-silk walls. A friend of Billy's,

Monte Proser, thought Doris might fit there. He passed the word to Al, who persuaded Billy by telephone to try her for two weeks at $150 a week.

Al bought train tickets to New York for Doris and himself. Still deeply in love with George Weidler, she telephoned him every night. For the opening of the Little Club, Billy and Al had packed their friends in, making sure Doris got a good hand. This was going to be her springboard. If she succeeded here, it would be easier to make it in Hollywood.

The notices she received were encouraging. Billy engaged her for an extra four weeks, and Al returned to California to see what he could line up for her there. Ten days later she telephoned him in tears: "I can't handle the rest of my time at the club alone. I want to get back to George. I've had it." Al took it philosophically. "Come on back then," he said. On the way, she stopped off in Cincinnati to see her son.

Meantime, Mike Curtiz, a sentimental Lothario from Hungary at Warner Brothers moved in to succeed Hal Wallis, who started in business for himself. Mike had Jack Warner breathing down his neck to start making a musical to be called *Romance on the High Seas.* Betty Hutton was supposed to play the girl lead, but at the last minute Curtiz wouldn't hire her. He decided to look around for a lesser, cheaper name, though he was growing more panicky by the day with Warner starting to twist his arms.

Song writers Sammy Cahn and Jule Styne, who were writing the score for *Romance,* had an idea that Doris might do for the picture and suggested to Al that he ought to arrange an audition for her. He called Doris to come home. The day of her promised return to Los Angeles brought no news of her, though her audition had been fixed for the following morning. In the evening, on a hunch, Al drove out to the Sepulveda camp. In the darkness he thumped on the trailer's door until Doris put her head out the window and promised again to turn up in the morning.

When he collected her in his car, she was weeping hysterically. Her marriage was on the rocks, she said. George Weidler

161

wanted out. "I can't do the audition. You'll have to cancel."

"Look, if your marriage is breaking up, you'll sure need a job," said Al. "It'll get your mind off your trouble, and you'll have to make a living."

She accepted the logic of that and dried her tears. He sent out to buy her new stockings, since those she was wearing were laddered, then took her to meet Curtiz. In the middle of singing for him, fresh tears trickled down her cheeks at the thought that her husband was leaving. Curtiz thought this was one of the great acting performances of all time and invited Al to talk contract. They settled on $500 a week for her, and because Jack Warner regarded television as nothing more than furniture that stares back at you, Al got her TV rights. Doris wasn't in a mood to care much about anything. She was still pining for George, hoping she could bring them back together.

Moving out of the trailer, she was so lonely that her agent wanted some place for her to live where she could look out the window and see people; she had no more company than that. He put her in the Plaza Hotel across the street from the Brown Derby and stopped by every morning to take her to the studio. When the picture was finished, he came up with another idea. Why not see Sinatra, for whom Al had worked, and check whether Frank could use her on his radio "Hit Parade"?

Frank, who knows talent, liked that fine. She went with him to New York for the weekly shows, and life was starting to look rosy when the blight attacked again. The sponsors, the American Tobacco Company, decided that her singing style was too close to Frank's and they dumped her. Doris was knocked off her feet again. This time she felt sure she was finished. "I guess I can always go home to Cincinnati," she said.

Al was running into complaints from his partners. "Why do you waste your time on this dame?" they demanded. "She's not the most beautiful girl in the world; she's loaded with freckles; she's got no clothes sense; she's going nowhere." But

Al's mind revolved around the memory of Alice Faye, another girl with a voice. "People could identify themselves with Alice, and they can with Doris," he argued. "Because any girl in the audience could be Doris Day, and she could be any girl."

So when Curtiz wanted her to work for him again but was stuck for a story to do, Al promised rashly to think up a plot, which he dictated to a writer as *My Dream Is Yours*. She went into that with Jack Carson and Lee Bowman. Bob Hope was also persuaded to put her on his radio show at $1250 a week.

Doris, who nowadays shies away from appearing for charity no matter what, was more co-operative then. Hearing her sing at a benefit in the Beverly Hills Hotel, Curtiz decided she needed a vocal coach, and she went along with him for a while. By now her career was beginning to move. She was waiting for her divorce, and was going out on dates again. She also went to her lawyer and had him draft a new contract to be signed between Al and herself. It contained an escalator clause giving him up to twenty-five per cent of her earnings as they increased.

"I don't want anybody but you to take care of me," she told him.

"You're already under contract," said Al. "This new one isn't necessary, but if you really want it, then fine. I'll be happy to sign it."

His partners were still telling him: "You're spending too much time on her. You'd better get on to something new." Al disagreed. "If this girl hits like I think she will, we can make a whole business around her alone."

She decided she was secure enough now to buy a small house in San Fernando Valley, to bring out her son and mother. This was a taste of heaven for her, bringing her family under one roof. Her parents had been separated when she was twelve. In 1961, her father at the age of sixty-two married Luvenia Williams Bennett, the forty-five-year-old Negress who managed the bar he owned in Cincinnati. The telegram he sent Doris to break this bit of news went unanswered.

The last benefit Al Levy asked her to do was to be held at the Hollywood Bowl for a local disk jockey. She agreed, as usual then, but didn't show up for rehearsal with the band. Her agent telephoned to ask why.

"Marty says I don't have to do the benefit," she answered.

"What's he got to do with it? He hasn't been in the picture much so far."

"He told me you'll be traveling around a lot and getting other things. He said it will be best if he starts taking care of part of my business in case things come up when you're away."

"That makes sense," said Al. "Okay." That was the last time he had anything to do for Doris Day.

He left for Century Artists' New York office with his wife, Ruth, shortly after, to take a look at a bouncing baby called television, switching places with Dick Dorso. When the Andrews Sisters went to London for a big season at the Palladium, Marty Melcher stayed home and got to know Doris well. Later, his marriage to Patti Andrews ended in a heartbreaking divorce for her. Marty and Doris were married on April 3, 1951, her twenty-seventh birthday.

In New York on the Christmas Eve after he and Dorso had exchanged assignments, Al received a call from Melcher: "I just want to tell you that as of now you're out of Century Artists. Doris and I have decided we don't need you, and that's it."

After Christmas, Al Levy walked down the hall to his Hollywood office and found a locksmith changing the lock on the front door. Inside, Marty had his brother and sister occupying the place to prevent Al's moving back in. In his absence in New York, he had been voted out of Century Artists. He paid off the locksmith on the spot to keep the lock unchanged. He settled with Melcher and Dorso that he would retain the offices but not immediately take any big lump sum out of the agency; they would pay him off on the installment plan, sending money each month to his parents in Arizona.

Shortly before her third marriage, Doris, born a Catholic, became a Christian Scientist. Soon after the marriage Marty, born a Jew, also became a Christian Scientist.

Marty set out to do over Doris, making her an entirely different kind of woman. A long list of subjects was barred in interviews now. Questions were welcome that let the two of them concentrate on picturing her as the girl next door who never smokes, drinks, or cusses, and always minds her manners. Any queries that probed into the real past were rejected. "Doris is not a movie star," Marty told me blandly. "She's a talented girl who through circumstances has been pushed into the limelight."

That was quite an interview, telling as much in its silences as in its words. They came in to see me together, and that's how they answered, though they didn't exactly overflow with information. So they won't be misjudged, I'll quote them verbatim:

"How does being married to you affect him?" I asked.

"He couldn't live without me," she said.

"Seriously, how has this marriage affected you?"

"I've learned an awful lot."

Marty broke in: "That's pretty ambiguous."

"Let me put it this way. We're both striving to be real good people. Marriage has made a terrific change in Marty."

"In what way?" I said.

"We're very serious about our religion, but we can't discuss that."

"Why not? I think it should be discussed. Do you go to church every Sunday?"

"No, we're not churchgoers. But we're trying to be good people, and we've come a long way. It's helped me to be less impatient. I used to be so impatient. Now I'm not."

"Our religion," Marty explained in words of one syllable, "is being good. Take out one 'o' and you've got God. To do good is to prove God."

Doris hastened to explain: "For instance, we don't gossip.

We don't talk about people. We don't stand in judgment of others. We have only enough time to mind our own business."

Minding their own business has made Mr. and Mrs. Melcher into a ten-million-dollar corporation. They hold interests in a motion-picture production company, recording companies, music companies, real estate, and a merchandising firm with plans to cash in on Doris' new-found reputation as a clothes horse by peddling "Doris Day" dresses and make-up.

In spite of, or maybe because of, the dollars that come arolling in, Doris is neurotic about her health, which can cause mighty big problems for a Christian Scientist. When she was sure she had cancer—she was wrong—she put off going to a doctor in case she would be betraying her faith. Her brother Paul, who was going to be her manager on the recording side of her career, was a convert to the same faith; he died of a heart condition in his early thirties.

Both the Melchers keep a tight hold on their money. Their social life scarcely exists beyond having an occasional couple in for an early dinner—carrot juice in place of cocktails and desserts from Doris' celebrated home soda fountain. She also holds on tight to the clothes she gets from her movie roles. When Irene Sharaff, who designed her *Midnight Lace* outfits, wanted to borrow one coat to be modeled on the Academy Award night where Irene won an Oscar nomination, she had the devil of a time borrowing it—and it had to go back to Doris the next morning.

As for Al Levy, he had one more bit of business to sort out with Marty Melcher. Century Artists' client list was shrinking as Marty concentrated on Doris, and the decision was made to sell the agency to MCA, who would latch onto anything in those days that promised to increase their holdings in the industry. There was just one cloud on the legal title when the time came to close the deal—the contract Doris had once insisted that Al sign with her.

"It doesn't mean anything now," the lawyers told Al Levy.

"So just let us have a release before the first of the year."

"If it doesn't mean anything, let's forget it," he said, by this time deep with David Susskind in Talent Associates, the television production company that Al founded the day after he sent the locksmith and Marty's relations on their way.

But the lawyers insisted that something had to be done to satisfy Lew Wasserman, president of MCA, that Century Artists was in the clear. "All right," Levy told the attorneys, "I've never asked Doris Day for anything in my life. Fact of the matter is, I put more money into her than I ever took out in commissions. So you give me a check for $3000 signed by Doris—it'll buy a mink coat for my wife."

He got the check and gave it to his wife. But Ruth Levy didn't buy a coat. She put the money in their bank account.

Ten

In my business I get "genius" dished out to me as regularly as the morning mail. To believe the press agents, every dirty-shirttail boy in blue jeans who comes over the hill from Lee Strasberg's classes is the biggest thing to hit the industry since Jack Barrymore played Don Juan. Ninety-nine times out of a hundred, the gangling lad is like a dream brought on by eating Port-Salut cheese too late at night: if you wait long enough, it goes away. There's that once in a hundred, though, when the press agent is right. . . .

The chief public-relations man at Warners' was as persuasive as ever: "This one is something special. We think he's a genius, more or less. I want you to meet him." So I agreed to go over for luncheon in the commissary, and he introduced me to Jimmy Dean, brought to Hollywood to do *East of Eden* by Elia Kazan, who had been bowled over by his Broadway performance as the Arab boy in Billy Rose's production of André Gide's *The Immoralist*.

The latest genius sauntered in, dressed like a bum, and slouched down in silence at a table away from mine. He hooked another chair with his toe, dragged it close enough to put his feet up, while he watched me from the corner of his eye. Then he stood up to inspect the framed photographs of Warner stars that covered the wall by his head. He chose one of them, spat in its eye, wiped off his spittle with a handkerchief, then like a ravenous hyena, started to gulp the food that had been served him.

"Would you like to meet him?" said the studio press agent who was my escort.

"No thank you, I've seen enough. If that's your prize package, you can take him. I don't want him."

[1] At sixteen, in my first evening gown, made by loving hands—my own.

[2] My son, Bill, at age of five, relaxing against me at our home in Great Neck, Long Island. Even at that age he loved the Navy, or I did, because I selected a Navy suit for him.

[3] *(Left)* Ken Murray burping. My beloved mother, Mrs. David Furry, and her daughter Hedda. At a picture premiere. Later at Ciro's we were joined by Edgar Bergen. I introduced them. She was a bit hard of hearing and said, "Who?" I whispered in her ear, "Charlie McCarthy." She said, "Is he now?" *(Photograph copyright Vitagraph, Inc.)* [4] *(Right)* Clark Gable, who won the title of King and deserved it; he was the first I was photographed with when I started my column in 1938. And he was one of my greatest friends until the day of his death. *(MGM photo by Ed. Cronenweth)*

[5] *(Left)* Charles Laughton, Carole Lombard, and I in the good old days when pictures were fun for everyone except the producers. *(Photo by Fred Hendrickson, Copyright 1940, RKO Radio Pictures, Inc.)* [6] *(Right)* The beautiful Merle Oberon, after telling me she was divorcing Sir Alexander Korda.

[7] *(Above left)* Jane Powell and I were supposed to look alike. I was once engaged to play her mother at $5000 a week. But Louis Mayer was feuding with me at that time. Someone else got the part, but I got the money. The boy is Vic Damone. [8] *(Above right)* Ida Koverman, everybody's pet, between two of her greatest discoveries, Bob Montgomery and Clark Gable. She fought like a tigress to see they got the top roles at Metro. [9] *(Below left)* Cary Grant and Randy Scott were once young bachelors, sharing life together. *(Copyright 1935, Paramount Productions, Inc.)* [10] *(Below right)* No wonder I look sad. Errol Flynn, Marion Davies, and Cissie Patterson have all passed away. But we were a gay quartet when this picture was taken at San Simeon during one of William Randolph Hearst's birthday celebrations.

[11] At the San Simeon wedding of Mary Grace (daughter of Mrs. Grace, one of Marion's cooks) Doris Duke and Marion Davies were bridesmaids. James Cromwell, who was married at the time to Doris Duke, was a guest of honor and William Randolph Hearst was the host.

[12] *(Left)* Charlie McCarthy's Edgar Bergen and I at a fancy-dress do. Our mothers would never have known us. [13] *(Right)* I aimed for Duke Wayne, but Charles Luckman got in the way.

[14] *(Left)* Hedda and the great Hemingway in Havana. We met too late. *(Jerome Zerbe photo)* [15] *(Right)* Mario Lanza, the great. His voice is silent but you'll never forget him. He didn't sing as well as Caruso, but his voice was much sexier. When he'd sold a million copies of his first record, he received one made of gold and insisted that I present it to him. *(Photo by Earl Leaf)*

[16] *(Left)* With Moss Hart and Lady Elsie Mendl at the premiere of his *Lady in the Dark*. When Moss and I got inside, there were no seats for us. [17] *(Right)* Tony Perkins, Sophia Loren, Hedda, and George Raft. This was Sophia's first introduction to Hollywood, a party given for her by Twentieth Century-Fox. Jayne Mansfield almost stole the spotlight from her in a low-cut gown with a break-away strap—it broke.

[18] *(Left)* Designer Omar Kiam, Hedda, and Bill Hopper at the *Marie Antoinette* premiere, where Norma Shearer, the great Antoinette, wore two evening gowns— one gold, one black spangles. [19] *(Right)* Ingrid Bergman and Hedda Hopper signing autographs at Hollywood Canteen during World War II, with a member of the shore patrol looking on. This almost broke up my friendship with David Selznick. I didn't ask his permission for Ingrid's appearance at the Canteen. He called up and said: "Now you've got me into trouble with Louella." My reply: "That's your hard luck." *(Photo by Joseph Jasgur)*

[20] *(Right)* James Shigeta, Robert Merrill, Charles Durand, Luise Rainer, and Ethel Barrymore on my Hollywood radio show. I can still close my eyes and remember that lovely voice of Ethel. No one like her; no one will ever forget her. *(NBC Photo by Gerald K. Smith)*

[21] *(Left)* Stephen Boyd and Hopper when she was handed the Foreign Correspondents' Golden Globe Award by Vincent Price. *(Los Angeles Times Photo)* [22] *(Below)* Hedda, Mrs. Eisenhower, Mrs. Raymond Massey, Mrs. Charles Brackett lunching at Romanoff's during Mamie's visit to Hollywood. You may notice how young Mamie and I look. The best brush man in Hollywood worked on our faces and eliminated the lines. When I thanked him, he said, "I'm now retiring and presenting that brush to the Hollywood Museum." *(Photo by Twentieth Century-Fox)*

[23] Hedda Hopper receiving a new bonnet from Jackie Gleason, who was playing *Gigot* in Paris. (*Photo by Jean Schmidt, Paris*)

[24] *(Left)* Elizabeth Taylor and Arthur Loew, Jr., her devoted admirer, with yours truly, whose hair needed the attention of both Mr. Kenneth and George Masters for this party. *(Nate Cutler Photo)*

[25] *(Below)* Bob Hope and me on Christmas, 1958, with Southern European Task Force in Vicenza, first U. S. Army Missile Command Base in Italy.

[26] I've got Bob and Lucy just where I want them—at my feet—during a visit on their set. But don't worry, they didn't stay there long.

[27] *(Above left)* The conversation must have been dull, or was Darryl Zanuck just pretending to be asleep? I almost didn't get on the set. The picture was *Roots of Heaven,* directed by John Huston, who never cared for me after my review of *Moby Dick.* I felt sorry for the whale, and it was made of cement. [28] *(Above right)* I like to think it was a draw between Betty Furness and me where hats are concerned. But in all honesty she had an edge on me. Both of them came from Sally Victor. [29] *(Below left)* Henry Luce and I trying to impress each other. Jerome Zerbe, in the background, was the winner. He remembered everything we said, but I've forgotten. *(Photo by Walter Daran)* [30] *(Below right)* Mrs. Bob Considine, Gary Cooper, Hedda in Madrid, where the señoritas and señoras followed him as if he were the Pied Piper.

[31] Perry Como never did take me seriously, and here's a picture to prove it. *(NBC Photo by Frank Carroll)*

[32] Two of my best friends: Louella Parsons and Debbie Reynolds at a shower given for Debbie before the birth of her first child when she was Mrs. Eddie Fisher. I bribed the photographer to hold this print. I like it.

[33] *(Above)* Rudy Vallee, now one of the great hits in New York in *How to Succeed in Business Without Really Trying*, listening in on a radio rehearsal of Jack Barrymore and me.

[34] *(Left)* What a nerve I had showing my legs beside those of Marlene Dietrich.

[35] Hedda and Elvis sharing a koala.

[36] *(Above left)* Hedda and Robert Preston in Mason City, Iowa, June 19, 1962, when 121 high school bands paraded through the city. [37] *(Above right)* When-ever I see a picture of George Washington, I always try to get under it and this time I did with Dean Martin. *(MGM Photo)* [38] *(Below left)* Well, now, look how Senator Javits and Joseph Binns have sliced off my hips, at a party at the Waldorf for Orphans of Italy. *(Photo by Helen Grant)* [39] *(Below right)* Adolph Zukor, Hedda, Mel Ferrer, and Audrey Hepburn at Friars dinner honoring Gary Cooper, which was his last public appearance. Coop became a star at Paramount Studios, whose founder was Adolph Zukor. But those who arranged the dinner—and they didn't consult Cooper—didn't have sense enough to place Mr. Zukor as an honored guest on the dais. *(Photo by Jules Davis)*

[40] *(Left)* Jimmy Cagney and Hedda Hopper—all passion spent. *(Earl Theisen/Look photo)*

[41] *(Below)* Barry Goldwater and Hedda Hopper at a luncheon for crippled children in Scottsdale, Arizona.

"He doesn't always behave like this," said my companion apologetically.

"Why now?"

"I don't know. To be frank, he never acted this way before."

I went back to my office and wrote a story describing every heart-warming detail of James Dean's behavior. "They've brought out from New York another dirty-shirttail actor. If this is the kind of talent they're importing, they can send it right back so far as I'm concerned."

When an invitation came to see the preview of *East of Eden*, nobody could have dragged me there. But I heard next day from Clifton Webb, whose judgment I respect: "Last night I saw one of the most extraordinary performances of my life. Get the studio to run that movie over for you. You'll be crazy about this boy Jimmy Dean."

"I've seen him," I said coldly.

"Forget it—I read your piece. Just watch him in this picture."

Warners' cagey answer to my call was to pretend *East of Eden* had been dismantled and was already in the cutting room for further editing. I telephoned Elia Kazan: "I'm sorry I missed the preview. I hear Jimmy Dean is electrifying as Cal Trask—"

"When would you like to see it?" Kazan said instantly.

"Today."

"Name the time, and I'll have it run for you."

In the projection room I sat spellbound. I couldn't remember ever having seen a young man with such power, so many facets of expression, so much sheer invention as this actor. I telephoned Jack Warner. "I'd like to talk with your Mr. Dean. He may not want to do an interview with me. If he doesn't, I shan't hold it against him. But I'd love to have him come over to my house."

Within minutes his reaction was passed back to me: "He'll be delighted." A day or so later he rang my doorbell, spic and span in black pants and black leather jacket, though his hair was tousled and he wore a pair of heavy boots that a deep-sea diver wouldn't have sneezed at. He carried a silver St. Genesius medal that Liz Taylor had given him, holding it while we talked.

"You misbehaved terribly," I told him after he'd chosen the most uncomfortable chair in the living room.

"I know. I wanted to see if anybody in this town had guts enough to tell the truth." He stayed for two hours, sipping scotch and water, listening to symphonic music played on the hi-fi, pacing the floor.

We talked about everything from cabbages to kings. About George Stevens, who ultimately directed him in *Giant* and who was sizing him up at this time as a candidate to play Charles Lindbergh. "I had lunch today with him," said Jimmy, "and we were discussing Antoine St.-Exupéry's *Le Petit Prince*—the writer's escapist attitude, his refusal to adjust to anything earthbound. Reading Exupéry, I've got an insight into flying and into Lindbergh's feeling. I like the looks of Lindbergh. I know nothing of what he stands for politically or otherwise, but I like the way he looks."

"Do you fly?"

"I want an airplane next—don't write that. When things like that appear in print, the things you love, it makes you look like a whore."

We talked about Dietrich. Would he like to be introduced? "I don't know. She's such a figment of my imagination. I go whoop in the stomach when you just ask if I'd like to meet her. Too much woman. You look at her and think, 'I'd like to have that.'"

Grace Kelly? "To me she's the complete mother image, typifying perfect. Maybe she's the kind of person you'd like to have had for a mother."

Gable, who took up motorcycling in his middle-age? "He's a real hot shoe. When you ride, you wear a steel sole that fits over the bottom of your boot. When you round a corner, you put that foot out on the ground. When you can really ride, you're called a hot shoe. Gable rides like crazy. I've been riding since I was sixteen. I have a motorcycle now. I don't tear around on it, but intelligently motivate myself through the quagmire and entanglement of streets. I used to ride to school. I lived with my aunt and uncle in Fairmount, Indiana. I used to go out for the cows on the motorcycle. Scared the hell out of them. They'd get to running, and their udders would start swinging, and they'd lose a quart of milk."

We discussed the thin-cheeked actress who calls herself Vampira on television (and cashed in, after Jimmy died, on the publicity she got from knowing him and claimed she could talk to him "through the veil"). He said: "I had studied *The Golden Bough* and the Marquis de Sade, and I was interested in finding out if this girl was obsessed by a satanic force. She knew absolutely nothing. I found her void of any true interest except her Vampira make-up. She has no absolute."

I turned on some symphony music while he fished his official studio biography out of his pocket, glanced at it, rolled his eyes up toward heaven, and threw it away. While the record played softly, he went into Hamlet's "To be or not to be."

When it was over: "I want to do *Hamlet* soon. Only a young man can play him as he was—with the naïveté Laurence Olivier played it safe. Something is lost when the older men play him. They anticipate his answers. You don't feel that Hamlet is thinking—just declaiming.

"Sonority of voice and technique the older men have. But this kind of Hamlet isn't the stumbling, feeling, reaching, searching boy that he really was. They compensate for the lack of youth by declamation. Between their body responses and reaction on one hand and the beauty of the words on the other, there is a void."

At that point he casually dropped his cigarette onto a rug and said: "Call the cops." He went over to the mantelpiece, raised the lid of one of my green Bristol glass boxes that stand there, and, as if speaking into a microphone, said hollowly: "Send up Mr. Dean's car."

As he left I told him: "If you get into any kind of trouble, I'd like to be your friend."

"I'd like you to be," he said.

"I'll give you my telephone number, and if you want to talk at any time, day or night, you call me."

"You mean that?"

"I don't say things I don't mean."

I learned a lot about James Byron Dean, some from him, some from his friends. He acquired his middle name in honor of the poet, Lord Byron, whom his mother idolized. She was a little slip of a thing, a farmer's daughter, who spoiled Jimmy from the day he was born in Marion, Indiana. Five years later, in 1936, Winton Dean, a dental technician, took his wife, Mildred, and their only child to live in a furnished flat in Los Angeles.

"When I was four or five or six, my mother had me playing the violin; I was a goddam child prodigy," Jimmy reported. "My mother also had me tap dancing—not at the same time I played the violin, though. She died of cancer when I was eight, and the violin was buried, too. I left California—hell, this story needs violin music."

Jimmy rode aboard the same train that carried his mother's body back to Indiana, to be buried in the family plot. He was on his way to live with his aunt and uncle, Ortense and Marcus Winslow. "I was anemic. I don't know whether I went back to the farm looking for a greater source of life and expression or for blood. Anyway, I got healthy, and this can be hazardous.

"You have to assume more responsibilities when you're healthy. This was a real farm, and I worked like crazy as long as someone was watching me. Forty acres of oats made a huge stage. When the audience left, I took a nap, and nothing got plowed or harrowed. When I was in the seventh or eighth grade, they couldn't figure me out. My grades were high. I was doing like high school senior work. Then I met a friend who lived over in Marion. He taught me how to

172

wrestle and kill cats and other things boys do behind barns. And I began to live."

"How old were you then?"

"About twelve or thirteen. Betwixt and between. I found what I was really useful for—to live. My grades fell off—"

"Living without learning," I said.

"I was confused. Why did God put all these things here for us to be interested in?"

His Aunt Ortense was active in the Women's Christian Temperance Union. When he was ten, she took him along to do dramatic readings for her ladies. "I was that tall," he said, indicating half his adult height, "and instead of doing little poems about mice, I did things like 'The Terror of Death'—the goriest! This made me strange; a little harpy in short pants."

"You must have been a worse brat than I was."

He gave me a sharp look. "I don't know about that. I had to prove myself, and I had the facility to do so. I became very proficient at wielding a paintbrush and sketching. I won the state pole-vault championship. I was the bright star in basketball, baseball. My uncle was a tremendous athlete—he won the Indiana state track meet all by himself. I won the state dramatic-declamation contest doing Charles Dickens' 'The Madman.' When I got through, there were broken bones lying all over the stage. If 'Medic' had been running then, I'd have been a cinch for it. But let me say this: no one helps you. You do it yourself."

"Who would you say has helped you the most?"

He gestured toward himself in answer. "When I graduated from high school, I came out to Los Angeles and went to UCLA to take pre-law. I couldn't take the [long pause] tea-sipping, moss-walled academicians, that academic bull."

"You sure as hell cleaned that phrase up," I said.

He had two years at UCLA, keeping in touch with his father, who had married again, and establishing good terms with his stepmother, Ethel. Jimmy discovered that James Whitmore, movie and stage actor, ran a theater group that met once a week. "There's always somebody in your life who opens your eyes, makes you see your mistakes and stimulates you to the point of trying to find your way. That was James Whitmore. I met him around 1949, and he encouraged me to go to New York to join Strasberg's Actors' Studio. I did different things on television there and a couple of plays.

"When I came back to Warners, *Battle Cry* was being made, and Whitmore was on the lot. I wanted to thank him for his kindness and patience. He said: 'It's not necessary. Someone did something for me—Elia Kazan. You will do something for someone else.' I've tried to pass it on. I feel I've been of some benefit to young actors. It's the only way to repay Jimmy Whitmore. But you do it yourself."

I steered him on to another subject—New York. He had a contract with Warners calling for a total of nine pictures in six years. He would have had 1956 completely free to go back to Broadway. I had a feeling he'd be one of the few actors who would, in fact, return to the theater and, what's more, play *Hamlet*. He had the urge and push to do it.

"New York's a fertile, generous city if you can accept the violence and decadence," he said. "Acting is wonderful and immediately satisfying, but my talents lie in directing and beyond that my great fear is writing. That's the god. I can't apply the seat of my pants right now. I'm too youthful and silly. I must have much age. I'm in great awe of writing and fearful of it. But someday . . ."

"How old are you now?" I asked.

"Twenty-three."

"You've got a long and beautiful life ahead of you."

"I hope the second adjective is the more abundant," he said. He then had almost exactly nine more months to live.

He made *Rebel Without a Cause*—and made a friend of its director, Nick Ray.

Hollywood started to simmer with excitement over this new, young talent when *East of Eden* was released and Jimmy went into *Rebel*, causing no problems for anybody because Nick Ray could communicate with him; they got along like a house on fire. Then came *Giant*, which he should never have gone into. The part of Jett Rink, Texas wildcatter turned millionaire, was not right for him.

George Stevens is a martinet, a slow-moving hulk of a man who tried to force Jimmy to conform to George's interpretation of the role. Now Jimmy could be led but not driven; he'd bend like a young tree but not break. How poorly Stevens understood him showed in his remarks after Jimmy died: "He was just a regular kid trying to make good in Hollywood. He was determined to reach his goal of being a topnotch movie star at any price."

Tremendous trouble was brewing on the set. It reached boiling point when Jimmy went on strike and boycotted *Giant* for three days. The newspaper and town gossips started picking on him, pinning all the blame on his shoulders. It was high time we had another talk.

"I've been reading some bad things about you," I said. "I understand you haven't been showing up for work."

"Right, I haven't. Stevens has been horrible. I sat there for three days, made up and ready to work at nine o'clock every morning. By six o'clock I hadn't had a scene or a rehearsal. I sat there like a bump on a log watching that big, lumpy Rock Hudson making love to Liz Taylor. I knew what Stevens was trying to do to me. I'm not going to take it any more."

"I hold no brief for Stevens," I said, "but what you don't know is that there's a man on that set who put the whole deal together. Henry Ginsberg, Stevens, and Edna Ferber are partners. It took Henry two years to do it. This is the first time in Ferber's life she took no money, only an equal share of the profits as they come in. If this picture goes wrong, Stevens can walk out, and those two years of Ginsberg's life go down the drain."

"I didn't know," Jimmy said.

"Something else. Henry has a great deal of affection for you, but he can't show it or else Stevens might walk off the set."

"I'd no idea of that. I'm sorry. It won't happen again. Thanks for letting me know."

He could do anything he set his hand to. In Texas for *Giant*, he had so little to occupy him that he learned to ride and rope, until he could twirl a lariat as well as Will Rogers. He had overpowering ambition. Like John Barrymore, whom he might have equaled had he lived, Jimmy never thought of consequences. There was no risk he would not take. He was too young to know restraint, and he was marked for death.

He got even with George Stevens. I watched him play the climactic banquet scene where Jett Rink, middle-aged and defeated, is left alone to get drunk at the top table. He had some marvelous lines, but he mumbled them so you couldn't understand them. When Stevens realized what had happened, he wanted to retake the scene. Jimmy refused.

There was no time for Stevens to try again to talk him into it. On the evening of Friday, September 30, 1955, Jimmy was racing down Highway 41 in his new, 150-miles-an-hour Porsche, which he had christened "The Little Bastard." He ran into another car, and Jimmy Dean was dead.

Liz Taylor had two more days' work left on *Giant*, including a call for the next morning. She was extremely fond of Jimmy, had presented him with a Siamese cat, which he treasured. That Friday night she telephoned George Stevens: "I can't work tomorrow. I've been crying for hours. You can't photograph me."

"What's the matter with you?" said Stevens, who had heard the news just as she had.

"I loved that boy, don't you understand?"

"That's no reason. You be on that set at nine o'clock in the morning, ready to shoot."

She was there. When she started to rehearse, she went into hysterics, and an ambulance had to carry her to the hospital. She was in the hospital five days before she could finish *Giant*.

The body of Jimmy Dean was claimed by his father, who rode on the same train that took the casket back for burial in

Fairmount. The only man from the *Giant* set who went back to Indiana for the funeral was Henry Ginsberg.

Only once before had anything equaled the mail that deluged my office, and that came after Rudolph Valentino died. Letters mourning Jimmy came by the thousands week after week. They came from young and old alike, some crisply typewritten, some pencil scrawls, and they kept coming three years after. He was an extraordinary boy, and people sensed the magnetism. He stood on the threshold of manhood, the adolescent yearning to grow, trying to find himself, and millions knew that feeling.

I begged the Academy to award him a special Oscar, to stand on a plain granite shaft as a headstone to his grave. The Academy declined.

Another young actor often came to talk with me. The electricity of James Dean was missing in Robert Walker, but this gangling, shy man carried a gentle sweetness with him that touched your heart. He sat out on the patio one day and said: "Everybody expects miracles to come along and get him out of drudgery and misery. Not many people can face themselves, and the miracle, of course, rarely happens."

He had come over alone from a new house in Pacific Palisades into which he'd moved with his nurse and his two sons by Jennifer Jones, Robert, Jr., and Michael. "All we have is three beds," he said, "a dining-room table and a refrigerator. We're going to furnish it like we want it."

He was just out of the Menninger Clinic in Topeka, Kansas, from which he had been discharged after four and a half months of treatment for compulsive drinking and the sickness that drove him to it—the searing melancholy that was as much a part of him as the marrow in his bones. He wanted to tell me about the experience.

The background is important, reaching back as far as Bob at the age of six, when he was expelled from his first school. Undersized then and unattractive, he was ignored by his schoolmates, and he couldn't stand it. One day he ran amok, not knowing why, and raced screaming through the playground, yanking pigtails and kicking shins.

"From childhood," he said, "I found myself up against mental walls. The maladjustments of that age grew and branched out all over the place. I was always trying to make an escape from life."

He began running away from school when he was ten. Finally, his Aunt Hortense, who raised him, sent him to San Diego Military Academy. It was much the same old story. The young cadets didn't care for him, so he fought them. He trailed his class in everything, but he landed the job of playing the big bass drum in the school band, and he beat the daylights out of it.

It was just as a matter of course that he tried out for a part in a school play. There were several contestants, and the teacher made a little speech before she announced the winner. Ability and hard work always succeed, she said, and "that's why Bob Walker has won the role." On the strength of that, Aunt Hortense staked him to a course at the American Academy of Dramatic Arts, where he met a fellow student, a beautiful girl christened Phyllis Isley who later changed her name to Jennifer Jones.

When they began looking for jobs, nobody wanted either one of them. Then she had an offer to work on radio in Tulsa, and they persuaded the station to hire them both for a total of $25 a week. He was twenty years old when they were married.

They put together a dollar or two and tried to crash Hollywood. They failed, went back to New York, found a cheap little Greenwich Village flat, and sold their car so they could eat. A baby was on the way.

Bob and Jennifer, whom he called "Phyl" all his life, took turns in tending Bob, Jr., while the other scoured the town job hunting. They were poor as church mice, happy as larks. These struggling days were bound to leave their mark on both of them.

He broke into New York radio in time to pay the obstetrician's bills. He made a fair living in soap operas, so they had another baby. They outdid each other in looking after their two infant sons, born only a year apart.

One day Jennifer went out looking for a job, bearded David Selznick in his den, and landed herself a contract. Letting her go to Hollywood was almost a sacrificial blow to Bob, but he stayed in New York with his soap operas to hold up his end.

But lightning struck twice in the Walker household—the only miracle he ever knew. He was offered a part in *Bataan* that let him join Jennifer in California. They were wrapped up in each other's happiness until Selznick fell madly in love with her; then the Walkers separated. She divorced Bob in June 1945, after six years of marriage. David's wife, Irene—Louis B. Mayer's younger daughter—was separated from her husband two months later. She divorced David in January 1949, and David and Jennifer were married six months later.

"The breakup with Jennifer," said Bob on my patio, "gave me an excuse for amplifying my troubles. When I had a few drinks, I got to thinking about Poor Me and the broken home and all the et ceteras. Only now I can talk about it freely. I used to refuse to discuss my breakup with Phyl because I felt it was nobody's business. I talk about it now because it's part of the story that I want to get over. So far as I'm concerned, she is first and foremost the mother of my two children."

He went on working, detesting himself. "Laying oneself open to be hurt," he said, "is an agonizing way to be living." He tried another marriage—with John Ford's daughter, Barbara, after he'd known her eight weeks. That was two weeks longer than they lasted together as man and wife.

He relied chiefly on liquor for survival. It was a news picture of Bob Walker drunk in a police lockup, with fists clenched and mouth distorted, that convinced him he needed psychiatry. "I would rather have had a knife stuck in my side," he told me, "because then I should have known what was wrong. There was terrific remorse the day after. I decided that sometime soon I was going to end up dead. I tried an analyst in town, but I wasn't ready for him. My back wasn't yet up against the wall."

When Dore Schary took over Mayer's job at Metro, he had Bob in for a talk. "I think you need help," he said. "I want you to go to the Menninger Clinic."

"After I left Schary's office," Bob said, "fear hit me. I thought about a mental clinic like an insane asylum. I kept asking myself: 'Is there something about me that others can see and I can't?' "

But he promised Schary that he'd try Menninger's. With a studio publicity man as companion, he rode the plane to Kansas wearing a pair of dark glasses, with his hat pulled down over his face, hoping nobody would recognize him. "When I first hit Topeka, I couldn't bear the thought of people looking at me. It was as if the whole world had its eyes focused on me. Actually, nobody gave a damn."

Living in a hotel, he drove each day to the clinic for a week of tests. "I hated myself and blamed myself all my life for things I shouldn't have blamed myself for. I felt that everybody was against me, hated me, couldn't understand me. I couldn't even understand myself. I was only moments away from alcoholism, which is a slow form of self-destruction."

On the basis of the tests, the clinic recommended that he be admitted, warning his father and Dore Schary that Bob would require at least one year of treatment, possibly two. He returned to Hollywood and went to the desert to hide, afraid to see people, until it was time to sign himself into Menninger's.

"I got the idea that the clinic was something like a country club, so I asked for a single room and bath. First thing I noticed was that all the doors were locked. Then everything sharp, including my razor, was taken away from me—you could only shave with an attendant watching. The room I was taken to had bars on its window. When I was told: 'You're rooming with so-and-so,' I said I was leaving. That first night a patient who understood how a newcomer felt gave up his room and bath without my knowing it, so it would be easier on me."

For the first four weeks he was under observation only; no analysis. "You have to have a recreational therapist with you even on walks over the grounds."

He lived in one of several "lodges," with fifteen patients to each floor, ages varying from eighteen to sixty-five. "We didn't discuss our illness with each other. Most of the men were wonderful, because it's often the self-sacrificing, overly kind people who take all the blame on themselves and land up in such conditions." His one thought was to leave the place.

At the end of that quiet first month he was still a good enough actor to persuade a doctor that he was perfectly capable of going into Topeka alone one night. "Or perhaps the clinic was trying to convince me how sick I was. Anyway, when I went to town I got drunk, landed up taking a swing at another cop, and smashed my fist through a window. I was more determined than ever to get away because I was sure the clinic had driven me to it."

He contacted his father, begged him to come and take him away, signing to assume responsibility. It was suggested Bob should see one of Menninger's analysts. "I told them I didn't want to. Why spend more money on an analyst when he couldn't do me any good? Even then, I was making excuses to keep from facing facts."

Soon afterward, a psychoanalyst who had been assigned to him anyway, came to his room, said he knew Bob was leaving, but had just stopped by to say hello. "He stretched himself out on the bed and let me do the arguing. At the end of about an hour I thanked him for coming, but told him I was still going to leave. The next day I found some excuse to ask him to visit me again. I still argued that I was leaving. It was some time before I realized I was doing all the talking—not him. I made up my mind to stay."

He had one hour of analysis a day, six days a week. "For three weeks I spoke to nobody but this doctor, keeping myself shut up in my room, eating scarcely anything, sleeping very little, drinking cup after cup of coffee. When I started

181

to get some inside on the cure, I began to work constantly at it. Pouring out your thoughts and mind is an emotionally exhausting experience. But you could never know the thrill it was when I realized that hate was leaving my heart."

In September 1949 an announcement from the clinic said that he had completely recovered from a "nervous breakdown." "I came back here scared as hell," Bob said, "and I don't think I've got the world by the tail. I haven't worked for over a year, and I'd like to do two or three pictures in a hurry now and go back to the clinic for two months next spring."

He was in a proselytizing mood when he talked to me. "The $64 question is where the average man can go for mental help. They can't afford high-priced clinics, and they can't afford to take the time off for what I did. People are waiting to get into clinics, but there's not enough public demand for real work in this field because so many are unaware of its importance. If you have a decayed tooth, you can go to a dentist and have it removed. But if you have a mental stumbling block, you're provided with no such opportunity."

He spoke of trying to shield his sons from the truth about himself. They wanted to read the first newspaper interview he'd given. "Since it mentioned several unpleasant subjects like drinking, I hesitated. Then I decided to keep nothing back from them. The boys read it, and I explained the things they couldn't understand. At night I read to them. Right now, we're going through *Swiss Family Robinson*. About once a week we take in a show, usually a drive-in. They work two hours a day, scraping paint off a fence and a shed, and get fifty cents a day for it."

I had written up his interview with me when, two days later, he telephoned. "I'd appreciate it if you didn't run that story. I poured my heart out, but I wasn't thinking enough of my sons. I'd rather not have them read it all yet. When they're older they'll understand."

At six o'clock on the evening of August 29, 1951, Mrs. Emily Buck, who was Bob's housekeeper and nurse, called a psychiatrist who had been treating Bob for the previous eighteen months. Mr. Walker, she said, needed help in a hurry. He had been drinking, and he was losing control of himself. The doctor answered the call, and two hours later telephoned his associate to join him at the Walker house because he thought an injection would be necessary.

Two men among the group of friends who had gathered at the house held Bob down while the doctor prepared the needle. Bob was pleading: "Don't give it to me. I've been drinking. It will kill me. Please don't give me that shot."

The following day the doctors reported that as many as thirty times before they had injected sodium amytal to calm him. Seven and a half grains "is not an abnormal dose if the patient is extremely emotional," said the coroner's autopsy surgeon. Bob's breathing had begun to fail a matter of minutes after the shot entered his veins. The fire-department rescue squad was called at eight-thirty. Not until ninety minutes later did they give up hope. Bob was thirty-two years old.

Jennifer Jones is still a very beautiful woman, her face unlined by age. She is an excellent actress on her own account— not since A Farewell to Arms, in which she starred with Rock Hudson, has David Selznick made a picture with or without her. She is very nervous while acting, hating to be watched at work by anybody but the minimum necessary crew, flinching at even routine questions when she's interviewed.

The David Selznicks live beautifully. His income comes largely from selling or leasing his backlog of pictures, made in the days when David had walked out of MGM to open up as an independent producer. The backlog does not include Gone With the Wind, which makes a sure five or six millions every time it's sent on the rounds again. Under the terms of the ruthless bargain Metro drove with him before he could have Gable play Rhett Butler, every cent of income goes now to that studio, not to David.

At the second gala premiere held not long ago in Atlanta, where GWTW first opened in December 1939, he was asked: "Don't you feel dreadful that you don't receive a thin dime from all this?"

"No, I did it with my own little hatchet," he said. "I never regretted it." He has his own grandiose plans to stage a musical version of his greatest movie on Broadway, using two separate casts, producing it in two halves on successive evenings. Alfred Hitchcock once asked the unanswerable question about David's checkered career: "When you've produced a picture like *Gone With the Wind*, what can you do to top it?"

David still loves parties as he always did, but most always goes alone. Instead of going with him, Jennifer stays home and reads or applies herself to yoga, which she took up long ago. Sometimes she takes a trip to India to meditate. She went twice to Switzerland to see Carl Jung but was too late the second time. He was ill and receiving nobody. "If I had pressed it, I might have seen him," she said. "I shall always regret that I didn't try harder."

If David ever thinks about it, he must notice the contrast between Jennifer, who is very gracious and feminine, and Irene Mayer, who had a brain like a man, plus sound business sense and an instinct for the theater. She was also bossy like her father, and David rebelled against it. He would come home tired from slaving at a studio, which he did as a habit then, but she'd say: "Take those old clothes off, get into a tub and dress. We have guests arriving in fifteen minutes."

He'd grow so mad he'd toss his clothes on to the floor and stomp on them. Then: "David, pick those things up and put them away properly." Louis B. Mayer used to tell me about those scenes. "If I were married to Irene, I'd hit her," he said. "I love her, but I see all her faults."

David and Jennifer have one daughter, whom they adore. They also have the two sons she had by Robert Walker. Bob, Jr., is twenty-five now. He looks exactly like his father. He lives with his wife and their baby in a cottage on the Selznicks' estate. George Seaton, the director, tells me Bob will be as fine an actor as his father. The younger son is also following in his father's footsteps, cutting quite a swath with teen-age beauties in our town. It must be easy for Jennifer to remember and mighty hard to forget.

Eleven

Sorting out fact from fiction can be harder on the constitution than separating milk from whipped potatoes in a cupful of vichyssoise. And when you succeed, the results may taste sharper than vinegar on the tongue. Let's take the case of Marion Davies and William Randolph Hearst.

The newspaper tycoon, with a wife and five sons, and the golden-haired charmer from the Bronx shared many things in life—laughter, riches, tears, disaster; everything except his name. Mrs. William Randolph Hearst denied him the divorce he begged for, spurned his offers of millions and anything else she wanted. The legend is that W.R. found his golden-hearted girl when she was a mere sixteen, skipping around in Flo Ziegfeld's *Follies of 1917*. Truth is, it happened some years earlier.

He was fifty years old, with a long, pale face and piercing blue eyes when he sat in the Globe Theatre and saw her dancing in the chorus of *Queen of the Movies*, directed by Julian Mitchell. She was then fourteen years old. It was January 1914.

A sister of hers was another of the six chorus girls. Marion Cecilia Douras—she changed the name to Davies later—wanted to be with her sister and work beside her. Neither her father, Bernard, nor her mother, Rose, objected. Her one obstacle was the Gary Society, whose inspectors supposedly saved young girls from a fate worse than death, meaning sin and exploitation in the theater, by seeing they didn't dance in any chorus until they were at least sixteen years old.

She took her problem to a family friend, Pat Casey, who arranged it so that Marion would land the job, and he fibbed about her age. To all intent and purpose, she had reached the essential sixteenth birthday when she went into the show. On opening night Hearst was there with a companion, a judge. The next morning, from the Louis Cohen Ticket Agency, he ordered two seats in Row C for every performance of the show's run, one for himself, the other for any friend who wanted to see the show. Or if no friend was available, the vacant seat was a handy place to park his hat.

Most of the cast had a hunch he had his eyes on Marion's sister. But after a week or two he tipped his hand by sending a note to Marion inviting her to have supper with him in Delmonico's. She took the note to Casey to ask: "What should I do? What could I possibly talk about to a man like him?"

"Accept the invitation," answered Pat, "but be sure you always take a girl friend with you."

Pat had some sound advice for another cute beginner in the same chorus line. This other sixteen-year-old was Al Jolson's light of love. He had reached the point of promising to marry her when another beauty caught his eye and he married her, instead. The young dancer went to Pat with her troubles. "Keep quiet and let me handle it," he said.

He and Al had some serious talking to do. "I feel like a dog," said Jolson. "What can I do?"

Pat had the answer: "You can give her $100 a month as long as she lives, plus a home in Westchester County." Al was happy to escape so lightly. She outlived him and collected an additional keepsake of the glorious days that used to be. In Jolson's will he left her $100,000, and nobody knew who she was, except the lawyer who drew up the document.

Measured either in love or money, Marion did much better than that. To Hearst she was a golden, blue-eyed princess, and he showered her with treasure until ultimately she was worth more than $8,000,000 in her own right. When she died she owned three skyscrapers in New York City, the Desert Inn in Palm Springs, plus an estate in Beverly Hills.

From the moment he saw her, he fell under her spell. She didn't waver in the affection she gave him. Toward the end, though, she had different feelings about his family. She had a special reason for being pleased with her Manhattan sky-scrapers. "Wherever the Hearsts walk on the East Side, if they ever do," she said, "they have to pass one of my buildings—on Fifth Avenue, Park, or down Madison."

No princess in a picture book enjoyed such gifts as were heaped on her by W.R., history's most extravagant spender. In their early days he decreed that she was to be the greatest star in motion pictures. In New York she lived with her family, was surrounded with instructors in every subject under the sun that might further her career. She was cast in an inconsequential drama, *Cecilia of the Pink Roses*, for a start, and his newspapers and magazines started promoting her.

He insisted that she play only ingénue roles, though her talent was as a comedienne. If he'd let her play comedy, she could have been the real success he'd set his heart on. But she worked only to please him. "I was never crazy about making pictures," she told me. "It was all right once we got started. But to me it was wasting time. You live only once; you've got to have fun, and you can't work all the time."

Another typical bit of Hearst's fancy didn't do Marion any good. One cocktail was the rule for her at San Simeon. If she wanted an extra drink, she had to sneak it. In each of the castle's countless powder rooms she kept a bottle of champagne hidden in the tank of the toilet. Friends like Carole Lombard and Frances Marion knew the secret and shared the bubbles. I've seen Marion Davies drink a pint of champagne in half a dozen gulps and walk out singing. If W.R. had been less strict on the subject of liquor, she wouldn't have drunk so much.

After *Cecilia*, Marion had her own movie studio to reign over. Hearst bought the River Park Casino up on 127th Street in Harlem and converted it as the production center for his Cosmopolitan Pictures. There all the stops were pulled out for a hang-the-expense Tudor epic, *When Knighthood Was in Flower*, designed to put her in the front rank of the movies in a single leap. She cared no more for this sword-and-cloak stuff than for anything else about the business she'd been pushed into. "The only thing I liked about making pictures was the fun we had on the side," she said. "But there was always somebody pulling your hair, powdering your nose, and those hot lights!"

Hearst wasn't a man to listen to argument, much less admit defeat. She went on making pictures, some of them winning enough praise from critics other than his own men to justify his relentless ambitions for her. *Little Old New York* was "exquisite," according to the New York *Times*. *Janice Meredith*, another costume cutup, also came in for *Times* approval. "No more brilliant achievement in ambitious motion pictures . . . has ever been exhibited."

He failed in his movie plans for Marion and himself as he failed in many other things he attempted, except making money. He didn't become the greatest producer in the world; he missed laying hands on the governorship of New York; he never got into the White House. The biggest irony of his life was the deal he made by telephone from San Simeon to the Democratic convention in Chicago in 1932 to swing most of the California delegates behind a candidate he didn't like, Franklin Delano Roosevelt. More than any other man, the deeds of Roosevelt ruined Hearst. Then World War II made Hearst another fortune.

The Shepherd of San Simeon had a long way to go before he let Marion ease her way out of the career he had chosen for her. The arrangement he came to with Louis Mayer and the Cosmopolitan company brought Marion from New York to Culver City in such style you'd imagine it was Louis XVI transferring Marie-Antoinette from Paris to Versailles. Near the front of the lot a fourteen-room bungalow was built for her as a combined dressing room and summer home.

Later, when Marion left for Warners, it was transported lock, stock, and barrel there. When she departed from Warners, an addition was made and the whole thing moved to Benedict Canyon in Beverly Hills. Louis Mayer bought it and lived in it. Then it became the home of Kay and Arthur Cameron. But they were divorced, and Cameron lived on there alone.

San Simeon, two hundred miles from Culver City, was too far for daily travels to Metro. Hearst built a new castle for his princess on the gold coast of Santa Monica. This new ninety-room Georgian mansion, with two swimming pools, three drawing rooms, two dining rooms, and a private movie theater, was called the "beach house." It cost $7,000,000.

W.R., in his sixties now, and the gorgeous young girl, whose stutter only added to her charm, had dreamed that someday, somehow they would be man and wife. Mrs. Hearst—who was Millicent Willson, a chorine in a group called "The Merry Maidens" when she first met W.R.—thought otherwise. Her husband's hopes of marriage to Marion seemed about ready to bloom when Millicent was being escorted by Alexander Moore, once married to Lillian Russell and once United States Ambassador to Spain. As an inducement to divorce, W.R. was offering Millicent $10,000,000 together with the huge apartment house in which they used to live.

Millicent sought advice from one of the biggest men in the country, who was a good friend of Marion's, too. His reasoning prevailed with her: "Mrs. William Randolph Hearst is a very important name in America and the world. What would you gain if you gave it up?"

Marion made friends with Moore in later years when he was in California very ill. She sat by his bedside during his last days. "Before the end comes," he murmured, "will you put your arms around me and kiss me?" She didn't hesitate a moment.

She performed that same, final act of compassion for another man, her father, long after it was clear that, in spite of all Hearst did for her, he could never give her his name. Bernard Douras, like the rest of Marion's family, had shared in W.R.'s generosity. As a result of ties with "Red Mike" Hylan, mayor of New York, Douras had been appointed a city magistrate and was invariably referred to in Hearst papers as

"Judge" Douras. He had been a stanch Catholic all his life. He, too, died in Marion's arms.

She had a heart big as the Ritz Tower, which was one of the hunks of New York real estate W.R. owned in those days, after taking it over from Arthur Brisbane when he couldn't meet the payments. Socially, in Hollywood she was the queen bee for more than thirty years. Friends fallen on hard times could rely on a check from Marion to see them through. A girl who wanted to impress a producer or land a job could borrow Marion's best dresses, furs, and fabulous jewels—whatever the occasion called for.

When talking pictures arrived, Marion had problems like everybody else; she got going with *Marianne* and went on to *The Floradora Girl.* "Somebody told me I should put a pebble in my mouth to cure the stuttering. That goes back to the days of the Greeks, the pebble treatment. During a scene the first day, I swallowed the pebble, and that was the end of the cure."

She had no cause to worry that speech trouble would put an end to her career. The birth of the talkies ruined many another reputation. Two of the cruelest, most primitive punishments our town deals out to those who fall from favor are the empty mailbox and the silent telephone. But Marion was a hostess who took no notice of who was in and who out of the social swim. Her friends, rich or poor, were invited up to San Simeon. Her parties and picnics mixed the important guests with people you saw no other place. Mighty executives rubbed shoulders with has-beens still living under her protective wing. Quite a few careers were started all over again as a result.

In her bungalow she had a complete household staff, including a fine cook, Mrs. Grace, with a young daughter, Mary. When Mrs. Grace fell fatally ill, as a last favor she asked Marion to look after her Mary. The little orphan was raised like a daughter. When she reached school age, she went away to be educated, then returned to live with her foster mother.

Mary begged for a photograph of Marion autographed "To

my darling daughter." And on that deceptive bit of pseudo-evidence was built the juicy rumor that W.R. had children by Marion. Only after some years did she retrieve the picture from Mary Grace, but the damage had been done, prompting Hearst in his will to testify: "I hereby declare that the only children I have ever had are my sons . . ."

Marion did some matchmaking on Mary's behalf by introducing her to one of Hearst's band of trouble shooters, William Curley, publisher of the New York *Journal American*, who had five children of his own by a former marriage, plus grandchildren, and was old enough to be Mary's grandfather. Mary was married to William Curley at San Simeon.

Doris Duke, the tobacco heiress, was one of the bridesmaids, and her husband of the moment, Jimmy Cromwell, one of the guests. Before the ceremony Curley changed his will in Mary's favor; which later left her a rich widow. Marion was a bridesmaid on that occasion, as on many others. I knew how much she envied any bride.

I stayed in Hollywood largely because of her. When picture parts grew scarce as hen's teeth, I holed up in a three-room basement flat with my son. I was ready to quit and return to New York when Marion heard about it from Frances Marion and put me into a picture of hers, *Zander the Great*, for which Frances wrote the script. That also opened the door to San Simeon for me. It was the springboard to more jobs, and that kept me, for better or worse, in the movies.

Wealth came to mean nothing to Marion except in terms of the good it could do. "You're rich not because of money but only through what you give," she used to say. She built a children's wing on UCLA's Medical Center, with a trust fund added to maintain it. With her wry humor that remained intact to the end, she shrugged off any fancy talk about the building being her memorial: "It won't do me any good; I'll be down below where I can't see so high."

This Lady Bountiful extended her warmth to Hearst's close family and employees. She mothered John R., Jr., the Chief's twelve-year-old grandson, nicknamed "Bunkie," when he came to live at San Simeon after his parents were divorced. She interceded with the iron-willed man to save his sons—William, Jr., John, David, Randolph, and George—from their father's wrath. She supported one of the five for years after he had spent his inherited money as if it would last forever.

For thirty years she protected the boys from W.R.'s anger and disapproval; covering up their sins in his eyes; lending them money when they needed it; taking them and their friends in under San Simeon's roof and into her Santa Monica home. In return, the sons behaved as if she was one of their nearest and dearest friends. No hostility was ever shown until after W.R.'s death.

She bestowed the same kind of favors on Hearst's staff. Thanks to Marion, Louella's job was enlarged for her, with steady increases in salary. Through Marion, she got to know all the stars and greats of the world. Cobina Wright picked up her stint as society columnist by Marion's pleading on her behalf with W.R.

Hearst's staff treated Marion fondly during her protector's lifetime. Richard Berlin, the organization's strong man who emerged as president of Hearst Corporation, was one of the many who scrupulously saw to it that every birthday and similar anniversary in her life was marked by flowers and the cordial words of congratulations.

When W.R.'s fortunes crumbled and his empire faced sudden ruination, Marion came to the rescue. She lent him one million dollars. "You'll be left without a penny," said I, always the practical one, to her.

"What would you do?" she asked, "It came from him. Would you deny him when he needs it?"

In 1947 the two of them took refuge from the storms that blew increasingly around him—old age and an America entirely changed from the land he'd left his stamp on. They closed down San Simeon and moved into a Spanish stucco house on North Beverly Drive in Beverly Hills. W.R. was reluctantly facing the fact that he was no more immortal than any other man.

For Marion herself, W.R. had a special warning—against the wife of one of his sons. "Be careful of her," he said in his quavering, high-pitched voice. "She will be far more hostile than Mrs. Hearst."

The final act in Hearst's eighty-eight years began on the night of August 13, 1951, as he lay dying. Marion could sense it, though she would not put it into words. She summoned her nephew, the writer Charles Lederer, to the house. She had been drinking and was on the verge of hysteria. W.R.'s two physicians, Dr. Prinzmetal and Dr. Corday, were already in attendance. Presumably summoned by one or the other of them, Bill and David Hearst and Richard Berlin also arrived at the house.

When things got too hot to handle, Lederer persuaded Dr. Corday that Marion should be taken to her bedroom and given sedation. The wrangling continued after she had left, and in the course of the evening Lederer returned to his house, close by on North Beverly Drive.

Early next morning Lederer received a telephone call that Hearst was dead. He had died in the arms of his Catholic valet, Henry Monahan, now with Conrad Hilton, who said prayers for him. Two hours later the body was flown to San Francisco.

When Marion's nephew arrived back at the Hearst house, he was greeted by Berlin: "Where do you think you're going?"

"To see Marion."

"Make sure you go to her room and nowhere else."

"This house belongs to Marion Davies," Lederer said, "and I'll go where I please."

Marion couldn't be roused from her drugged sleep until after the body was being flown to San Francisco, escorted by Bill, David, George, and Randolph Hearst. Mrs. Hearst, Bill's wife, "Bootsie," and other members of the family flew from New York for the service. Louella was one of the hundreds of mourners who gathered in San Francisco. Marion read about the funeral arrangements in the paper. What W.R. had planned before his death was a quiet service in his home with only Marion and an Episcopal minister reading from the Bible.

The day he was buried, I sat with Marion in her dining room. We prayed silently together. "I had him while he lived," she said. "They can have him now." Though she disguised it, she was still in a state of shock at the loss of the man she had loved for nearly forty years.

When the announcement came, a few months later, that she had eloped to Las Vegas with Horace Brown, a hell-for-leather Merchant Marine captain who looked somewhat like a younger version of William Randolph, the Hearst paper in Los Angeles, the *Examiner*, reported with satisfaction: "It was Miss Davies' first marriage."

I decided one day to write a piece about what happens to a retired movie star and went to Marion to talk about it. With Horace and Dennis the Menace, a small brown dachshund, she lived in the house where W.R. died. Its long front hall retained a touch of the beach-palace days, with life-sized portraits of her in her leading roles hanging on the walls. In the library there were three more pictures. On a table stood a "Lucky Lindy" photograph of Charles Lindbergh autographed "To Marion Davies, best wishes and many thanks." On the mantel were two photographs of Bernard Shaw, one of them inscribed, "This is what is left of me—1948." Shaw, said Marion, was the only man that Gandhi, W.R.'s favorite dog, didn't try to bite. "He wanted to listen to what GBS had to say, but Gandhi took it out on me later."

She was wearing dark brown slacks, cinnamon-colored silk blouse, and flat-heeled leather shoes. The blond hair looked as though it had just been washed and set. On the coffee table in front of her she kept a compact and two lipsticks which, while we talked, she applied almost unconsciously, with perfect aim.

She said: "I don't look at motion pictures any more, most of all my own. I used to see one every night. I have prints of most of mine, but they're slowly molding in a vault downstairs. I have *Little Old New York*, but my projector goes too fast to run it off."

"Wasn't Bill Powell in that one?"

"No, he was in *When Knighthood Was in Flower*. Remember those symmetricals he wore to make his legs look pretty? When we ran that at San Simeon, Carole Lombard was with him. She never got over his symmetricals. He was a real villain in that picture."

"I saw him in Palm Springs. He said it wasn't exciting, but it's adding years to his life. Would you like to make another picture?"

"Not if they offered me Mars on a silver plate. I have other ideas along the theatrical line. Something big, like washing elephants."

"What was your favorite picture?"

"*The Big Parade*. Long time ago, but I liked it."

"How about *Gone With the Wind*?"

"I liked that, but I didn't see much of it. I went with Carole and Clark to the opening here. Raoul Walsh was with us, too. A man who pretended he was Burgess Meredith picked a fight with us. Clark was nervous and didn't want to sit through the picture, anyway. So we all went into the manager's office. The manager was off somewhere, and the phone kept ringing. We'd pick it up and say: 'Sorry, no reservations; all sold out for a year.' We thought that was funny. "Carole was a lot of fun. She liked to have a good time."

"So did you."

"It's taken its toll."

"Did you ever have any protégés?"

"I kept it all for myself. I couldn't act."

"Well, I know you helped Ray Milland, for instance."

"He played my brother in *Bachelor Father*. The director got impatient with him. It was his first picture and he was nervous. Who isn't, even on the twenty-fifth picture? So I told him to pretend that the director wasn't there."

I asked her about the plush party she gave for Johnnie Ray not long after W.R.'s death, which caught a bit of the glamour of our yesterdays, with six hundred invited and a thousand showing up.

"I was having my hair done when Charlie Morrison brought him in. He didn't know me at all. He must have been awful young. I never saw so many people I didn't know—I didn't know ninety per cent of the guests. We were in a turmoil for weeks. They put gardenias in the bushes and moved all the furniture."

What was her average day? "I have business things. Then I watch TV and read. I sleep late."

We talked again about the old days. "Gloria Swanson always liked to play games. So she cooked this one up at San Simeon one night. I played the minister, off in another room. All the men were to pick the girls they wanted to marry, then couple by couple they came into the room where I would perform the ceremony. Then I'd say, 'All right, seal it with a kiss,' and when they started to do that, Gloria would pick up a towel that she'd filled with ice and conk the guy on the head.

"Everybody laughed until it was Joe Hergesheimer's turn. The girl he picked was Aileen Pringle. He was so serious about it and so mad that when Gloria let him have it, he stormed out of the house and said, 'I'll write about this. I'm through with Hollywood.'"

Changing the subject: "Why did you keep making pictures if you didn't like it?"

"Mr. Hearst wanted me to," she said, "and contracts had something to do with it."

"Did he have any eccentricities?"

"Yes, he placed his faith in the wrong people."

Marion put on two more performances during her life. One was for the sole benefit of the Hearsts, when she sat in Joe Kennedy's box at his son's 1961 inaugural ball and rode with Joe in the parade, so that Millicent and her sons could see Marion undefeated and unconquerable. But she was a very sick girl and never recovered from that trip.

She'd earned Joe's hospitality by handing over her house to

the Kennedy clan for the Los Angeles convention of the Democrats that nominated John F., while she paid $3500 a month for a rented house in Santa Monica. Joe had extra phones put in her house, installed his own servants, and wouldn't permit Tom Kensington, who had been with Marion for fifteen years, to remain after he learned Tom was a former FBI man.

She also ousted her sister out of her own house, to make room for the Robert Kennedys, and rented another temporary home for the sister. When Joe heard how sick Marion really was, he sent off three specialists to see her. But Marion paid all the bills.

Earlier, she put on a fine performance, too, to appear on one of my television shows. By this time she was in the middle of her three-year fight with cancer. When word got out that I'd asked her, Kay Gable waxed indignant. "She can't possibly do it," said Kay. "She's not well enough."

"Why do you think I asked her?" I said. "For one reason only—to lift her morale."

"But she looks so ill."

"Take it from me, she'll look beautiful."

On the day the show was due to be filmed, I went to Marion's house wearing the make-up Gene Hibbs had already given me at my home. I brushed aside her compliments: "Wait until you see what he does for you. And George Masters is coming, too, to do your hair."

She was so weak that her nurse, Mrs. Mauser, had to help her downstairs to the dressing room where the two wizards were waiting to ply their arts. I went off to the bottom of her garden to shoot some scenes there. When I came back, the transformation had been worked. It was as if a magic wand had waved lovingly over her. She looked thirty years younger than when I'd left not more than an hour before.

She literally danced out of that dressing room and hurried upstairs to put on a blue satin gown. Her body was so thin I had to pin the dress in with safety pins all up the back to keep it from falling off. Her arms were as thin as wrists. "You need

197

a mink stole," I said, "to wear around your shoulders." When that last touch had been added, she took a long look at herself in a mirror. "You look beautiful," I said. She nodded agreement, smiling like a girl on her way to her first prom.

I got Charlie Lederer on the telephone. "Come over to Marion's right away. I want you to see something."

"What is it?" he said instantly, afraid as we all were that her illness was taking a bad turn. I refused to tell him, let him see for himself. At the first sight of Marion with her age and sickness erased, he burst into tears and left the room.

For fear of her stutter and of fatiguing her, we'd arranged to give her only one line to say: "Welcome to my house." She carried it off on the first take. "Is this all I get to do?" she demanded. "I want more."

"Don't be a greedy little girl." At five o'clock she insisted on going visiting. She went to Pickfair to show Mary how young she looked and then all over town, until it was time for bed. At midnight I received a call from her: "How do I get this stuff off my face?"

When the show was screened, she was a sensation. Thanks to Hibbs and Masters, she enjoyed a last flurry of fame and fun, including her trip to the inauguration, while I went off for a month to Europe. She had two more offers for TV.

When I came home, Marion had been taken into Cedars of Lebanon Hospital. She never came out alive. She was in a coma for five weeks. "I don't think she'll recognize you," Mrs. Mauser said. But I went anyway. I'll never forget my last picture of her. Weeks of daily cobalt treatments had colored her neck and part of her face a deep purple. It was heartbreaking, yet she was feeling no pain.

On September 23, 1961, the Los Angeles *Examiner* reported the death of Marion Davies the previous day. "The list of Miss Davies' close friends," the obituary said, "was long, impressive and diverse, reflecting her wide range of interests. They included George Bernard Shaw, William Randolph Hearst, Sir Thomas Lipton, Winston Churchill, Lloyd George, Bernard M. Baruch . . . Miss Davies' only venture into matrimony lasted until her death. She was married to former Merchant Marine Captain Horace Brown . . ."

A letter Frances Marion wrote her earlier struck some different notes: "Remember how we laughed even when we were crying? . . . How we danced the shimmy and the Charleston . . . tossed our petticoats over the windmill . . . went to the Follies to applaud *A Pretty Girl Is Like a Melody* and cheer the beautiful Miss Davies, who was Miss-Miss-Miss America!

"Then the thirties . . . those fabulous excursions to San Simeon . . . the long table in the dining room with W.R. shepherding his flock (and not all of us lambs) . . . nipping champagne in the little girls' room . . . those overnight picnics . . . Miss-Miss-Miss America on a gentle old nag but looking more scared than if a mouse had run up her riding habit . . . sleeping under the stars . . . W.R. pacing up and down as he waited for his forgotten Seidlitz powders . . . the ride back in the morning, the fields dappled with wild flowers . . . a lot of us wilder than the flowers but just as pretty . . . Bill Haines dressed as though for the North Pole wearing a hood over his head and face, and mittens on his hands . . . Errol Flynn smacked in the heart by the limbs of Lili Damita . . .

"All of this was ours to enjoy and be grateful for the rest of our lives. And none of these memories could have graced our past if it hadn't been for you and your loving kindness."

If anybody can sum up a life in nine words, Frances can. Of Marion Davies she says: "She was a butterfly with glue on her wings."

Twelve

The lure of the almighty dollar brings two categories of people to our community—those who work and those who prey. Like Hamlin before the Pied Piper, we are infested with rodents, from bookies to con men, from mobsters to panderers anxious to supply anything a paying customer calls for. Difference between us and Hamlin is that we've given up hoping for the Piper.

Extortioners have flocked to our town since the notorious reign of George Browne and Willie Bioff, the union racketeers, who, in the thirties and early forties, didn't even condescend to visit the studios—top producers had to stop by their hotel room and toss on to the bed wads of greenbacks for "protection."

Now there are only lean pickings left at most studios, and the leeches cling to individual stars. They sucker them into accepting loans to buy the new house, the new mink, the new car, in return for a permanent slice of income. They let them run up bookmakers' bills at strangulation rates of interest, collectable every payday. By offering fat fees for night-club performances, they entice them to Las Vegas, the sanctuary for birds of prey, and make sure they get back every cent of salary and more at the gambling tables.

Syndicate men have the run of Hollywood society. I don't know who charms whom more, the actor or the mobster. I understand that "Lucky" Luciano could charm a bird off a bough. Frank Sinatra, who has a weakness for such fragrant characters as Joe Rocco and Charlie Fascetti, of Chicago fame, is fond of boasting: "If I hadn't made it in show business, I'd have been a mobster myself."

Bookies used to have priority at studio switchboards when

they made their calls to Culver City. Nowadays, Las Vegas soaks up much more floating cash and credit. It's fashionable in some circles to brag about how much you lost down the drain. Phil Silvers has shed a fortune at the tables. Gordon MacRae has unloaded thousands at one go, so that ever-popular pair of night-club entertainers, Gordon and Sheila MacRae, parents of four fine children, have to smile with every evidence of delight when they find they've been booked around the country forty-three weeks out of fifty-two to make ends meet. When Ernie Kovacs departed this vale of tears, he left $600,000 of gambling debts.

The police departments, often reported to be openly cozy with mobsters, have a long record of blinking at other kinds of lawbreakers, provided a nimble press agent can get on to the case in time. Clark Gable, returning home from a party at Paulette Goddard's after downing too much of the bubbly, banged up his car in a traffic circle, but it was happily announced that a passing motorist was really to blame.

Eddie Mannix has related how it cost a total of $90,000 to keep the reputation of a celebrated MGM star intact when he was caught in the same desperate situation that sent Big Bill Tilden, the tennis ace, to prison as a homosexual.

Studio cops worked hand in glove with custodians of the law outside the studio gates. Some days the telephones of top public-relations men like Howard Strickling at Metro and Harry Brand at Fox rang like a four-alarm call in the firehouse, as police dutifully reported they had this or that star safely locked up for speeding, drinking, or mixing it up in a public brawl.

There's something heady about driving in Hollywood that got even Garbo tagged twice for speeding. One of the wildcat drivers was Luise Rainer. She had won her *Great Ziegfeld* Oscar and was going into *The Good Earth* as the sensation of the industry. For the picture's sake, the studio conspired with minions of the law to frame her. She'd be arrested, plead guilty, and the judge, primed in advance, would lift her license until *The Good Earth* was completed. So ran the plot. But a snag developed after the police trapped her; she clung to her innocence and vowed to fight the case in court. So the ticket had to be quashed, and the suppress agents had to 'fess up to Luise. She refused to speak to them for weeks.

Since we live in an age of corruption, almost like the declining days of ancient Rome, with the "interests" digging in deeper all the time, I ought not have been surprised at a campaign to build another Las Vegas right in the heart of our community. The plan was to incorporate a separate little city made up of the Sunset Strip, with its night clubs like Dino's and Jerry Lewis' new place, and stretching from Santa Monica Boulevard up into the hills. Like Beverly Hills, which is a town unto itself and an extremely well-conducted one, this new Sunset City, or whatever it was to be christened, would have written its own rules and controlled its own life.

The idea was perfectly feasible, however unattractive. The area involves a bit of no man's land, bounded by the city limits of Beverly Hills and Los Angeles, yet attached to neither of them. This is county territory. The promoters' objective, among other things, was to bring in gambling, making it as legal as Nevada. It was a choice location and could be a perfect haven for mobsters.

Among the unsuspecting citizens of the Strip, petitions were circulated to gather signatures as the first step to take the proposed "city" away from county control. Whether or not he realized the implications, one of the sponsors was Bart Lytton, whose modernistic new savings bank stands on the site of the old Garden of Allah at the hub of the territory. It was he who threw one of the biggest parties in Washington, D.C., on the night of President Kennedy's inauguration, which drew JFK and other members of the family. Even I received one of the gold-engraved invitations, though I'd never met the host.

Our local *Citizen-News*, which has since changed management, broke the story of what lay behind the apparently innocent moves to make the Strip independent. I got busy in my column and with some letter writing to throw a monkey wrench into the wheels.

I was amazed at the time that my words were allowed to appear, because some exceedingly powerful individuals stood to gain from "Sunset City." But it worked. Our community had seen too much of Murder, Inc. muscling in, of gangsters receiving the lead-poisoning treatment on the streets. The petitions died from anemia—but I am sure the backers haven't given up hope or forgiven me.

There was another time when the businessmen of the Strip weren't so slow to take up arms. In this other affray they succeeded in putting the object of their attention behind bars, but then she was a woman, or even a lady, and a local celebrity. She was a tall, dignified creature with a back straight as a ramrod, who introduced herself to me one day as we sat under neighboring dryers in a beauty parlor. I was happy to make her acquaintance, having heard a great deal about her.

She was a pioneer in her profession by allowing her patrons, including some super-sized stars, to run up bills for their pleasure, whereas cash in advance is, I gather, the almost invariable procedure elsewhere. She accumulated a load of bad bets as a reward for establishing her informal credit plan, though her establishment gained a certain distinction from the array of several Oscars which stood on her mantelpiece, gifts from satisfied customers.

She conceived the ambition of retiring from her former calling and opening an extremely proper and swank restaurant on the Strip. She had the plans drawn up, which envisaged upstairs dining accommodations for private parties, which are not unusual among caterers. She ordered some somber but becoming gowns to wear as hostess. The restaurateurs along the Strip were outraged. They shuddered at the thought that *chez elle* could well become the most popular, though innocent, port of call for natives and tourists alike. She was denied a liquor license and later arrested.

She had one stanch supporter to turn to—that friend to all womankind, Louise Fazenda, the zany, pigtailed comedienne of the Mack Sennett era. Mack enjoyed working late at his studio so he could chase pretty girls between takes. Louise found the only means of quieting an empty stomach and finding some fleeting peace was to take a sandwich and hide it, ready for supper, in the women's lavatory.

Louise married Hal Wallis in 1927 and began a new career as an angel of mercy who covered her philanthropies in secrecy. A law student concluded that he'd have to quit school because his girl-wife was pregnant; Louise took up all the bills. She would go out to UCLA Medical Center to feed young children, rock and sing them to sleep. Not all of her charges recovered; she made a special point of seeking out the hopeless, terminal cases because her heart was big and strong enough to pour out its love even when a child was doomed.

And she never lost her sense of fun. There used to be a vacant corner lot next to her small house. At night she'd wander over the ground scattering wild-flower seeds, just for the sake of hearing her neighbors exclaim in wonder that only a blooming miracle could have produced the flowers that sprang up. It was Louise's sense of humor, matched with the need to teach Hal and his friends a lesson, that brought the stately brothel keeper to the Wallis' home in the San Fernando Valley.

Hal was in the habit of asking his men friends and associates around for Sunday luncheon to sample his wife's delicious cooking. Most of his buddies seemed to think this was something too tasty to waste on their wives, so they brought along their girl friends. Finally, Louise's patience ran out. One Sunday, when the usual crowd had gathered for some home cooking, Louise entered with her own special guest. Almost all the men knew her instantly; some of their companions needed no introductions either. Not a single harsh word was spoken between Mr. and Mrs. Wallis; but from that Sunday on, the husbands started bringing their wives.

Faced with the certainty of a prison term, the madam asked for Louise's help. "I've no place to hide my jewels, my car, and my clothes," she said, "and they're all the savings I've got left. If the police get their hands on them, I may never get them back. Is there anything you can do?"

"Certainly," Louise said. "There's a special stall in my garage to which this is the only key. Drive in there tomorrow, lock the door, and keep the key until you're free." That is why, when search was made of the lady's place of business, there were some mighty mystified investigators around, for they could find nothing. All her valuables were safe in the Wallises' garage, and when Hal reads this it will be news to him.

Crooks as well as shady ladies like to mingle with celebrities. Bugsie Siegel's gaudy days and nights as a man-about-Hollywood ended on a davenport in the house at 810 Linden Drive, Beverly Hills, that his dear friend, red-haired Virginia Hill, rented at $500 a month. "Death at the hands of a person or persons unknown," said the coroner's jury after the machine-gun bullet holes in his back had been counted, fired (while the watchdogs remained peculiarly silent) through a window.

Bugsie loved to socialize. He'd turn up, dressed to the nines, to take a drink or play poker as the guest of all kinds of people. Every two weeks he came into Beverly Hills to get his hair cut by his favorite barber. Marie MacDonald used to dine in his company at Las Vegas. George Raft appeared as a witness for Bugsie when the mobster went on trial in Los Angeles. Leo Durocher was one of many who knew Bugsie well. The day before he was rubbed out he sent a check for $2500 to the Lou Costello Youth Foundation, a sports center Lou and his partner, Bud Abbott, built on East Olympic Boulevard. The day after Bugsie departed this life, the sun-blackened peddlers who sell maps of movie stars' homes to tourists along Sunset Boulevard latched onto a new sales dodge with hastily scrawled signs that said: "See Where Bugsie Met His End."

One old friend of his, Countess Dorothy Taylor di Frasso, was in Europe when she heard the news. "Bugsie, Bugsie?" she said, and eyebrows could be heard arching over the telephone. "Why, I don't know any Bugsie. Could you mean Mr.

Benjamin Siegel?" An amateur gentleman to the final curtain, he would have appreciated the formality.

"I was very fond of Mr. Siegel," the countess allowed, "but it is utterly ridiculous to say I was in love with him." A man in her life that she really cottoned to was Gary Cooper. She snaffled him up when he was worn out from too many pictures and too much Lupe Velez. She whisked him off aboard a slow boat to a safari in Africa.

She found our town an unplowed pasture for her type of worldliness, mixing titles with prize fighters and topnotch actors with show girls. At one of her parties she hid a recording machine under a sofa in the hope of picking up some spice from her unsuspecting guests. Jack Barrymore ruined it. He sat there, unknowing, and delivered a monologue of tangy reminiscences about every celebrity who entered, including his delightful hostess. Unaware of all this, the countess grabbed an opportunity to remove the record and summon her closest pals up to her bedroom to hear a playback. After it made a few revolutions on the turntable, she snatched the record off and smashed it on the floor.

Bugsie's darling, Virginia Hill, who'd given him a gold key to the house on North Linden Drive, was in Paris when she got word that he had turned his back to a window for the last time. "It looks so bad to have a thing like that happen in your house," she said when she'd dried her tears.

Some months after this I was dining at a left-bank restaurant in Paris with Lilly Daché, her husband, and Jean Daspras, a struggling young French designer who was about to open his own dress salon. After coffee he took us up to his roof-top garret to show us some of his sketches. There he told us about an American, a friend of his, who had recently arrived at the place with a tightly wrapped shoe box.

"Please don't open this," said the visitor. "Just hide it somewhere and forget it."

Six months later the same American returned for the box, which the young Frenchman had kept hidden under his bed. As a favor, he was allowed to take one look inside before the

206

caller departed. It was filled not with shoes but with jewels—hundreds of thousands of dollars' worth belonging, so the American said, to a woman named Virginia Hill; but who she was, Jean Daspras had no idea.

Bugsie had his finger in a lot of pies. He was trying to corner the bookmaking business as far east as St. Louis. In Los Angeles, Reno, and Las Vegas he was cramming his race wire, known delicately as "Trans-American News Service," down the throats of bookies. He had his own bookie joint at Guy McAfee's Golden Nugget in Las Vegas.

Siegel also had set up a milk route, as he called it, for running raw opium, which is a popular crop in Mexican fields just south of the United States, to cookers in Tijuana. There it was prepared for a further trip across the California border, for distribution and sale in Los Angeles. Rumors flew around that Luciano was sore at the competition Bugsie was giving him and had warned him to stay out of opium smuggling. Forty-eight hours after the gang had lost its boss, border patrolmen were battling smugglers near Calexico and confiscating thousands of dollars' worth of opium destined for Los Angeles.

Bugsie was a big man in Vegas. He was president of Nevada Projects Corporation which operated the Flamingo, a sprawling, hectic-hued hotel and gambling joint built spang in the middle of a scrubby desert at a cost of $5,600,000. He started in as vice president when Billy Wilkerson was president.

Billy was a dapper operator who used to run two plush Los Angeles restaurants, the Vendôme and the Trocadero, later the Mocambo and Ciro's, then opened a fancy haberdashery and barbershop. When they failed, he started as publisher and editor of the *Hollywood Reporter*. His greatest claim to fame is that he discovered Lana Turner sitting on a drugstore stool, playing hookey from Hollywood High School. He sold out his interest in the Flamingo to Bugsie and was on vacation in Paris when the machine gun opened fire outside 810 Linden Drive.

Bugsie had lost a fortune running the Flamingo and was

struggling to save it from foreclosure. One police report had it that he owed $150,000 to an eastern gangster. The police also had a shrewd idea that he was behind some mighty big jewel robberies in our town. Earl Warren, our governor at the time, made the expected statement of the obvious: "One lone gangster coming to California from another state where he was a power doesn't mean much, but when he becomes connected with narcotics, gambling, bookmaking, and jewel and fur thefts, he becomes a dangerous article."

Whoever knocked off Bugsie got away with it; his murder has never been solved.

One inevitable suspect was questioned but set free. "I don't think anybody's gunning for me," said slippery Mickey Cohen, who has more friends among the movie makers than Bugsie ever dreamed of. I accidentally found myself sitting at the table next to Mickey in the Mocambo one night. He had a party of ten that night, including Florabel Muir and her husband, Denny Morrison, plus a guard sitting at each corner with the usual bulge under his coat that denotes the presence of concealed artillery.

I called over the captain. "I refuse to sit next to gangsters." Florabel turned around. "But they're *not* gangsters," she said.

"They certainly look like gangsters to me," said I, and was given another table in double time.

Mickey, who was finally sentenced to San Quentin for income-tax evasion, wheedled his way into a friendship with Red Skelton, a sentimental, unpredictable man whom I admire very much. Red was a soft touch for Mickey; lent him money; took him into his home, together with Janet Schneider, a Cohen protégée whom Mickey eventually succeeded in getting onto a Jerry Lewis television show. He tried to sell Red the idea that he should play himself in a movie version of his incredible life story.

Red survived the depression of the thirties as a marathon dancer around Bayonne, New Jersey. He managed to stay on his feet sixty days at one time to win enough money to keep body and soul together, though not very tightly. He worked as a circus clown—his father was one, too—and he's never lost that quality in his nature, a sympathy for the underdog, an ability to picture all human frailties.

Not that he's slow with a wisecrack when the magic moment comes. Like the day I went to see him in the hospital soon after the last inauguration. We talked about how much Frank Sinatra had given of himself to stage the inauguration party for the President. "What can Kennedy do to repay Frank, the man who has everything?" I asked.

Red paused to consider that for a moment, then grinned: "He can repeal the Mann Act."

Red's an Abraham Lincoln Republican. In fact, he's one of our country's foremost experts on our greatest president, and he's got a Lincoln library that stirs your soul. During a lull in rehearsal at one of his television shows on which I was appearing, we decided to try to convert some of his crew to our brand of politics. We both made stump speeches and got a good round of applause. "I don't think we changed anybody's mind," I said.

"Maybe not," he answered, "but we gave 'em something to chew on, anyway."

He begged Gene Fowler to cross the Atlantic as his guest when he opened at the Palladium in the summer of 1951, following Danny Kaye, who was cutting it up all over London town as a buddy of Princess Margaret. Gene, an old Hearst reporter and once editor of the New York *American*, went along, principally to fend off some of the bites of the sharp-fanged British press. He wrote to me:

Dear Sweetie:
This is the old man's last long journey anywhere except perhaps to the cemetery. Every citizen should be compelled by law to take a trip abroad—all expenses paid—so as to know how to vote.

Skelton is a big hit at the Palladium notwithstanding all manner of handicaps. It is a hot June with all kinds of sports events going, *and* Danny Kaye failed to introduce him (as is the hitherto unbroken tradition) on Sir Danny's last night at the Palladium. Tell me, honey, is it possible for any man to be bigger than himself? And is momentary glory too precious to be shared with a fellow American and a fellow trouper? It is quite true that we cannot share personal grief, but we can and should share happiness or success.

Gene

P.S. It is not true that I have been knighted.

When they got back, Red bought Gene a car to say his thanks, but Gene would have none of it. He clung like a limpet to his ramshackle jalopy, growling: "I didn't go to London with you for a present, but because I'm a friend."

Gene wasn't around to help when Red and his wife, Georgia, took their son, Richard, on his last, long journey to see the world after doctors at UCLA Medical Center told them the boy was doomed with leukemia. The British press venomously accused Red of publicity seeking in taking Richard to see the Pope. The boy read the papers and realized for the first time that his illness was fatal. Wounded to the heart by the stories, Red brought his family home to Brentwood, to wait for the inevitable. Gene was one of the pallbearers at Richard's funeral. Mickey Cohen was among those at the ceremony.

I was working in a television studio next to Red's soon after that day. In the corridor he said shyly: "Do you suppose you could do something for me, Hedda?"

"Anything, Red."

"My wife is mourning, just as I am. I get home tired from working and burst into tears, and so does she. She says everybody knows how I feel but nobody thinks of her. Could you write something about her, how she's having a bad time, too?"

Four years later Red has been unable to shake off his melancholy. He sits by the hour in his garden rather than go into the house, which holds too many memories. Though he's earned enough to make him a millionaire, he has gone through so much money—diamonds for Georgia, gifts to friends—that he has been compelled to sell the $3,500,000 TV studio he bought in hopes of becoming a big producer like Desi Arnaz. His health isn't good, he sleeps poorly. Yet before the cameras or on a night-club stage, he'll work hard enough to break his heart—and put a chip or two in yours.

Mickey Cohen had another friend among the comics in Jerry Lewis, whom he tried to set up as producer of Red's movie life story. Jerry was another who lent Mickey money: $5000 with no security "because he needed help." In his Martin and Lewis incarnation, Jerry came from playing night clubs in Philadelphia, where the majority of clubs are controlled by Frank Palumbo, no stranger to the racketeers.

When Dean and Jerry first appeared at Slapsie Maxie's in Hollywood, every studio in town tried to sign them. It was Hal Wallis who succeeded. Incidentally, in their days together, Dean and Jerry had an admirer and occasional companion in the junior senator from Massachusetts. In show business language, they found John F. Kennedy was a square John who seldom caught on when they were kidding him. Jacqueline hadn't yet come into his life. The girl he was most gone on was Helen O'Connell, who delivers warm jazz with a genteel air.

Before Dean and Jerry could start work for Hal Wallis in movies, they had some more night-club dates to fill, including one in Philadelphia. They were joined in that City of Brotherly Love by the actress wives of two of our better-known Hollywood personalities, one of them a woman who had dragged her patient husband to Slapsie Maxie's night after night to ogle Dean. If you can prevent catastrophe, you're bound to give it a try. So when I found out what was going on in Philadelphia, I went to see Hal Wallis.

"Unless you nip this in the bud," I said, "you're going to start your first Martin and Lewis picture with a couple of divorces to contend with."

Hal was petrified. "What can I do?" he pleaded.

"Stop it before the news gets out."

He called his partner, Joe Hazen, in for consultation. "How would you handle the situation?" they both asked.

"Telephone the boys right now. Tell them that unless those

women get out of Philadelphia immediately, you'll cancel the contract. And tell them why."

Hal liked the idea. I sat by his desk while he made the call, and two foot-loose actresses caught the next available plane from Philadelphia to New York.

There is a New York night club with a deserved reputation for high-class entertainment called the Copacabana, formerly conducted by Jack Entratter, who became the impresario of the Las Vegas Sands, and Monte Proser, who went on to operate Broadway's Lanai. For some years the Copa has enjoyed the services of Jules Podell, who has a gravel voice and a sharp temper.

Not long after the Martin and Lewis breakup Jerry was visiting New York to do a television show, while Sinatra was appearing at the Copa, drawing such crowds that they waited outside in the winter cold for hours in lines that stretched halfway around the block.

Jerry had played the Copa with Dean some three years earlier and quarreled briefly with Podell in the course of the engagement. One day Frank came down with an occupational sore throat, and Jerry agreed to substitute at the Copa for him, though he had no formal act and hadn't played a night-club date alone since his parting from Dean. He appeared that night ad-libbing like crazy, but that was the last time the Copa ever saw him.

Jerry had a press agent who knew the Copa and Podell well. In a previous job, when he'd had his own public-relations business, the agent represented the place as one of his clients. The agent was in the bar one night watching Podell, in his overcoat, ushering in the customers to the restaurant and floor show downstairs. "You're doing fantastic business with Sinatra," the agent said admiringly.

"I need you to tell me?" snapped Podell. "Get the hell out of here."

The agent snapped right back. The two fell into a shouting match, which ended with the agent spitting at Podell and walking out the front door, back to the Hampshire House suite where Jerry was staying. There was no satisfying Jerry until he'd heard the full account of the set-to. By now it was after midnight, but Jerry picked up the telephone to get two vice presidents of MCA out of bed, with a summons to meet him at ten o'clock the following morning at the Brooklyn studios where he was rehearsing his television show.

The pair of them showed up on the dot. They knew Jerry had a contract for a future appearance at the Copa. "I want you," he ordered, "to write Mr. Podell a letter saying I will never appear, never set foot there from now on. You can say I don't give a damn what pressure they try to put on me. I told Podell years ago if he ever talked nasty to any one of my people or laid a hand on one of them, he'd see the last of me."

Over the next few days Jerry had some interesting telephone calls from all kinds of people promising to straighten things out with Podell. Jerry had a stock answer: "Not if I live to be a thousand will I talk to Podell. Nobody should look to get lucky with me. I'm not going into that place—ever."

He made that decision stick. One side of Jerry knocks himself out to have people like him. The other side includes a mind like a steel trap; when he says no, he means not bloody likely. He won't run away from a fight, but he shies away from people who frighten him intellectually because they're better educated than he is. He's the son of show-business parents who left school in the tenth grade after swatting a teacher for saying: "All Jews are stupid."

He makes $3,000,000 a year, and he can't stand it. Money is something he disdains. He is probably the one entertainer in our business who has never struck out in a movie, and he's been twenty-six times to bat. Does he have any ideas why? You bet your life he knows exactly:

"I appeal to the kids and ordinary people who spend all their lives under the thumbs of authority and dignity. And I appeal to children, who know I get paid for doing what they get slapped for. I flout dignity and authority, and there's nobody alive who doesn't want to do the same thing.

"No matter how high you go, there's some schnook up over

you. Any General Motors vice president, for example, thinks he can do a better job than the guy above him, except he's down here and his boss is up there. I'm getting even for every little guy in the world. I'm the kid who throws snowballs at dignity in a top hat."

Jerry, who'll do anything for anybody he likes, once agreed to fill in for Sammy Davis, Jr., in Las Vegas, because Sammy wanted a few days off over Christmas in Aurora, Illinois. When I got the tip, I realized the fat was in the fire. It happened that Kim Novak was also spending the holidays at her sister's house in Aurora.

Now Harry Cohn of Columbia, who made Kim everything she is today, had been getting trouble from her. Her favorite weapon was to date men that Cohn detested, either for personal reasons or because they clashed violently with the carefully fostered image of her as a sweet, friendly girl from Chicago. Sammy was a heavy date. I'm sure he occupied quite a few pages in the oversized diary which she keeps in code and carries around with her all the time.

Kim was a girl tied hand and foot by her Columbia contract: "I haven't got enough money to invest," she told me one day. "I've been under contract on a straight salary for six years. When I'm loaned out, I don't get anything extra—the salary goes to the studio. On *Man with a Golden Arm*, I was promised a percentage of the picture, but I guess they forgot somehow."

"You never got a bonus?" I asked.

"One time before *Vertigo* my agents got me a sort of bonus. They got me a special loan at seven per cent interest for a year so I could buy my house. But I was on my old salary schedule."

"Don't you collect for TV?"

"I can't do TV."

The house she bought on Tortuosa Drive in Bel Air cost her $95,000. It contains an all-blue bedroom, an all-purple study, an all-gray living room, an all-gray sleeping porch, and a pool where she swims wearing a straw hat. She gets along without a housekeeper, cooks a big pot of chile on Sundays, and dips into it for dinner three or four times a week. "I sometimes get stomach trouble," she admits, to nobody's surprise.

Sammy had been a frequent visitor at her house, but not after he returned to Las Vegas from Aurora. Harry Cohn, who collapsed with a fatal heart attack some months later, was not a man who enjoyed being thwarted. His passion for keeping his fingers on everybody's business led him once to install an intercom system at Columbia so that, by flicking a switch, he could eavesdrop on conversations all over the lot.

The rumor was that it cost him $200,000 to break things up between Kim and Sammy. Truth is that it cost him no more than a single telephone call from his office to Las Vegas, where Harry knew one of the mob with a certain reputation in the business. Cohn was a man you had to stand in line to dislike. A bitter, final jest about him alleged that two thousand people attended his funeral, wanting to make sure it was true.

Over the telephone to Vegas, he said to the man on the other end: "You take care of this for me, will you?"

"Sure," said the voice on the telephone. "I'll just say: 'You've only got one eye; want to try for none?'"

Very soon after that Sammy announced his marriage to Lorena White, a Negro show girl in Las Vegas. A few more weeks elapsed before Sammy and Lorena started proceedings for divorce. On November 13, 1960, Sammy married May Britt, who gave him a daughter the following summer, and let me tell you they're very happy, or were when I wrote this.

Two years after the Sammy incident, Kim told me: "I guess I never really adjusted to being in Hollywood." She found, she said, that her telephone hadn't been ringing for quite a while. "I'm not really anti-social. It's just that I prefer smaller parties to big ones," she said.

With the help of a house guest, a girl who went to high school with her, she was fixing up her patio, to make it all turquoise. She was also building a fallout shelter in her back yard for herself, her friend, and her dog.

Thirteen

The magic word now is "television." It used to be "Hollywood," and there was no end to the miracles it could work. It transformed plowboys into princes, peasant girls into goddesses. The stars were American royalty and revered as such by their subjects. The magic word would bring whole villages out on the street to watch a star go by. It opened palace doors, stopped trains, brought you the keys of a city or an audience with the Pope.

Hollywood set the social style for thirty years of our history, until TV came along. Clara Bow wore a cupid's-bow lipstick job; fifty million women copied her. Clark Gable shucked off his undershirt; so did fifty million men. The studios stuck to a simple rule and coined fortunes with it: "Show the stars like kings and queens in a glamorous setting, and the crowds will flock to see them." Today it's a calculated risk to put a man on the screen in evening dress in case the popcorn-munching customers decide that he's a square.

They follow television stars just as they used to emulate the motion-picture variety. My reader mail proves that. "Is Dorothy Provine a natural blonde?" "Whatever happened to Edd Byrnes?" "When did Richard Boone get married?" Ben Casey's surgical gown turns out to be a Seventh Avenue fashion hit. The children switch from coonskin hats to space helmets to Soupy Sales. Some of the biggest names in our town —Sinatra, Burt Lancaster, Tony Curtis, and all—go on to let Soupy toss a custard pie in their faces. The children love it and the networks want the child audience.

The impact on the audience—and I don't mean from the custard pies—is astounding to anybody like me who's been making pictures since World War I. One of the early ones

216

was a thing called *Virtuous Wives,* in which I sank my entire salary of $5000 on my clothes and got $25,000 worth of the loveliest outfits you ever saw from Lady Duff-Gordon, known professionally as Lucile and one of the greatest dressmakers of them all. The biggest impact I made was on a pudgy little fellow who used to lurk around the set.

When the picture was finished, he sidled up to me. I mistook his intentions. "I don't want to buy any fur coats," said I.

"You don't understand," said he. "My name's Louis Mayer. I'm the producer and this is my first picture."

Making a reputation then was slow going. Producers used to say: "Get what's-her-name who played the rich bitch in *Virtuous Wives*—she might be good for this one." But when you go on television the impact is felt overnight. The following morning a cab driver won't let you pay your fare, a workman on a construction job offers you his hard hat.

Outside Saks Fifth Avenue, after an Easter Sunday appearance on "What's My Line?", I found myself surrounded by a crowd of autograph hunters so big that a disgruntled policeman threatened to turn me in unless we all went around the corner into a side street. "You'll have to call the paddy wagon," I warned him, "and a picture of Hopper behind bars is all I need for my collection."

For another "What's My Line?" appearance I had some fun with Dorothy Kilgallen, who likes to queen it on the panel. I knew I'd have to do something exciting to knock her in the eye, so I asked Marion Davies to lend me a diamond necklace. "Which one?" asked Marion. "Or would you like them all?"

"Just one," I said. "The small one with the pear-shaped pearl. That will be showy."

I didn't allow Miss Kilgallen to see me until just before we were introduced on camera. She gulped, turning slightly enviously green: "Isn't it wonderful to see real jewels again? It's so *beautiful!*"

I didn't let on that I'd borrowed it. "It *is* rather nice," I purred. The following week she had to top me. She arrived with her hair dyed bright red. . . . We females do that to each other.

I've made a lot of friends through television and a few enemies. On the whole, I imagine that enemies are better for me. I love them, because they keep me on my toes. That's one small debt I owe "Stoneface" Ed Sullivan, the Irish Sunday supplement to the American home.

After "Toast of the Town" was launched, Billy Wilkerson made Ed an offer to come out and work for him on the *Hollywood Reporter*. Ed gave in his resignation to Captain Joseph Patterson, who ran the New York *Daily News* until he died. "I wonder if you know what you're doing," said Joe. "You'll be in a trade paper with maybe 7500 readers instead of a two-million-plus circulation."

"I think I'll make a lot of money," answered Ed. "I'll know everybody out there and be able to get them for my TV show."

"If that's what you want, go ahead; but don't ask to come back."

Billy Wilkerson, who could run a dollar to ground as fast as any man, canvassed Hollywood, collecting advertisements for a special issue of the *Reporter* welcoming Ed Sullivan to his new roost. When that issue appeared, it was thick with page after page of greetings, all proceeds going to Billy as publisher. Somewhere along the line, Ed must have realized who was going to find himself on the better end of his new deal. He went back to Joe and announced that he'd changed his mind. "Don't do that again," Joe chided him. "Another time, if you make up your mind to go, you go."

When his "Toast" was in its salad days, Ed pursued the practice of inviting Hollywood stars to appear for free. Jack Benny was nudged into appearing for him, Bob Hope went on for the same nonexistent fee five times, until he got his own show, which was programmed opposite Ed's on a different network. Ed repaid Bob's earlier courtesies by opening fire on him in his "Broadway" column.

He invited Frank Sinatra to appear for nothing except the sheer joy of it to plug *Guys and Dolls*. When Frank refused, Ed roasted him in a press statement. Sinatra promptly took a full-page in the *Reporter* to holler:

Dear Ed: You're sick. Sincerely, Frank. P.S. Sick, sick, sick!

As a newsprint neighbor, his "Broadway" often runs cheek by jowl with my "Hollywood" in the *News*, though the Chicago *Tribune* won't print him. I'd been asked several times to go on his show and be introduced from the audience. He received the standard reply: "Mr. Sullivan, when I appear on TV, I go as a guest and get paid for it." The Screen Actors' Guild ruled long ago that an interview doesn't constitute a performance, since it tends to promote the career of the player involved. The union set a minimum pay scale of $210 for interviews.

That was what I paid each of a long list of stars who agreed to appear in interview format on "Hedda Hopper's Hollywood," a Sunday television hour that Talent Associates arranged for me to do for NBC, 8 to 9 P.M., while Ed was on CBS at the same time. I took on the show to see how TV and I got along together, on the understanding that there'd be five more similar shows if I liked it. But Ed was told that I was going to do the half dozen for certain. That's what got his bowels in an uproar.

The rumble gave us a singularly un-merry Christmas. The only time we could hire the big MCA studio we needed for one hour was on Friday, December 25. Use of the sound stage there for sixty minutes cost $1000, plus double pay for the crew. I had another taping session set up for three days later, with *Ben-Hur's* Charlton Heston, who had given his promise five weeks earlier and cabled from London that he would land in Hollywood on Sunday, December 27, ready to work with me the following day.

I didn't know a blessed thing about it until I read it in the *News*, but Ed was scared I was going to steal his TV audience. He'd been busy trying to engage extra stars for his show, including Heston, who turned up that Sunday evening, the twenty-seventh, on Sullivan's soiree, reading from the Bible for a $10,000 fee.

On the Monday, three other actors from *Ben-Hur*—Stephen Boyd, Francis X. Bushman, and Ramon Novarro—sat waiting with me for Heston, all of us made up and rarin' to go. At the appointed hour of 2 P.M. a telephone call reached the studio from his agent, Johnny Dugan of MCA. "I have advised Mr. Heston," he told me, "not to come on your show."

"That is very kind of you. Might I ask why?"

He had assumed the program would be local, not network, said Johnny. "He's negotiating for two more shows with Ed Sullivan, and he's afraid this might jeopardize those two engagements."

"What about his promise, as a man, that he would appear with me? When did he arrange with Mr. Ed Sullivan to go on last Sunday?"

"I don't rightly remember," said Johnny Dugan.

"Is Mr. Heston there?"

A moment's hush fell between us. "Yes."

"Put him on," I said. There was some murmured conversation in the background, then the agent came back: "He's busy."

"Then please tell Mr. Heston to go to hell. I never would have asked if I'd known he had a conflicting job at $10,000. I'd have said 'God bless you' and certainly not have asked him to give it up."

The Hearst papers went to town with front-page headlines as Ed continued shooting. TV columnists all over the country starting playing up the feud between Sullivan and Hopper. He needed a gimmick to help him. "Heston played Moses in *The Ten Commandments*," he said. "This week he was the Moses who led all these people out of the wilderness." "All these people" were the alleged walkouts from my program. The complete list over which he raised hosannas consisted of:

Bette Davis, who was ill;

Steve McQueen, who was in Alaska;

Robert Horton, who left for an engagement at the London Palladium before we ever got started;

Joan Crawford, who was not notified in time by Talent Associates that they could not tape her segment in New York;

Tuesday Weld, with whom negotiations had not reached any conclusion;

Mickey Rooney, who could not match his schedule to ours for taping.

After the show Jack Benny asked me why I hadn't invited him on. "I don't know you as well as I do the others," I replied. "I wasn't sure you'd respond."

"I'd have loved to," said Jack. "You've no idea the pressure Ed put on me to appear with him when he started his shows."

Just for the record, these are the people, in alphabetical order, who did make their appearances on "Hedda Hopper's Hollywood": Lucille Ball, Anne Bauchens, Stephen Boyd, Francis X. Bushman, John Cassavetes, Gary Cooper, Ricardo Cortez, Robert Cummings, William Daniels, Marion Davies, Walt Disney, Janet Gaynor, Bob Hope, Hope Lange, Harold Lloyd, Jody McCrea, Lisa Minelli, Don Murray, Ramon Novarro, Anthony Perkins, Debbie Reynolds, Teddy Rooney, Venetia Stevenson, James Stewart, Gloria Swanson, King Vidor, and the four Westmore brothers.

Ed blasted me twice before I tried to fire back. He was still banging away like thirty-nine weeks of "Wagon Train." He tried another tactic. He complained to two show-business unions, the Screen Actors' Guild and the American Federation of Television and Radio Artists, that he found me guilty of "the most grievous form of payola." "Here," he said, "is a columnist using plugs in a column to get performers free."

For this, I called him a liar. I have never pressured anybody to do anything for me in my life. On the air on January 10, the Hopper show did fine. Our rating matched Ed's exactly—and we were brand-new. He didn't appear that evening on his own show. His ulcer wouldn't let him.

There was an epilogue. The United Services Organization gave a benefit luncheon at $25 a plate for Mary Martin at the Hotel Pierre in New York. I sat on the dais, due to make a speech, near Ed Sullivan, who was billed to introduce me. At least two hundred people at the other tables knew what had gone on between us, including Mary Patterson of the *News*, Joe's widow.

Ed mumbled his few opening words without looking at me. I know the whole room was hoping I'd let fly. I said: "Thank you very much, Mr. Sullivan. That is the most beautiful introduction you have ever given me." Then I went on with my speech.

"I expected fireworks," Mary Patterson told me afterward.

"I wouldn't do that to Mary Martin," said I.

If this was television, they could keep it. Never in my life had anything like the brawl with "Stoneface" happened to me. Maybe a TV camera brings out the worst in people, though some of them do all right without much prompting.

I've known Elsa Maxwell for years. I met her long before she came out to Hollywood under contract to Darryl Zanuck to stage a party for him in a picture he was producing with Linda Darnell as its star. Elsa's inspiration was to dress every male as Abraham Lincoln and have two poodles dancing on a piano. Then she booked herself a lecture at the Los Angeles Philharmonic Auditorium on her perennial theme: "How to Give a Party." For a solid hour, while the audience fidgeted, she eulogized Zanuck. After the performance she found she'd run into a roadblock. The backers of her lecture refused to pay her fee. "Go ahead and sue," they said cheerfully. "You never got around to your subject. Let Zanuck pay you."

I dutifully reported this in the column and added: "If she thinks she's going to collect any money from Zanuck, she's out of her ever-loving mind." By way of reply, she sent me a large, fragrant bunch of catnip. Another feud was on.

While she was visiting Hollywood as Evelyn Walsh McLean's guest, Elsa organized a victory party to celebrate the liberation of Paris toward the end of World War II. It was set up in the garden of the Countess di Frasso, complete with special outdoor stage, footlights, spotlights, and special effects all supplied by Mr. F. B. Nightingale, a minor celebrity of Beverly Hills, sometimes known as "the wizard of light," who was recommended to Elsa by Lady Mendl.

"Why not make it complete by inviting some GI's? You'll have a lot of vacant seats at the back," I suggested to Elsa.

"I wouldn't think of it," she said. "It isn't a party for them, it's for my friends."

Nevertheless, it was a beauty, with top stars singing and dancing in Mr. Nightingale's extravaganza. He was so proud of his job that he donated his and his assistants' labor to the cause, and charged only $200 for materials. He sent a succession of bills to Elsa. They went unanswered.

Finally, Lady Mendl called me. "This is dreadful. Mr. Nightingale needs that money."

"Oh, come on, Elsie," said I. "Let's each send him a check for $100 and forget it." She was willing, but not Mr. Nightingale. He sent Elsa a receipted bill to which he added a postscript: "Your friends Lady Mendl and Hedda Hopper took care of it."

Within forty-eight hours I had a telephone call from Elsa, and I got a $100 check from her one day after that. Elsie Mendl had to wait two weeks. But she didn't have a daily column.

Elsa has boasted: "I'm full of beans. You can't embarrass an old woman like me." Four of her friends once sat together at luncheon in the Beverly Hills Hotel. Each came from a different city, and each was well up in society. One woman steered the conversation to the subject of their common friend: "I felt desperately sorry for her when Elsa's mother died in Los Angeles. She sent me a cable from Paris, saying she hadn't a bean and would I cable $3000 so she could bury her mother. Of course, I was happy to."

The woman across the table broke in. "But I had the same kind of cable, and I sent the money. It was I who buried Elsa's mother."

The third woman could scarcely believe her ears. "But I mailed Elsa a check for the same purpose."

The fourth of them, who lived in San Francisco, said quietly: "You are all mistaken. My husband knew Elsa and her mother well. He had several cables from Elsa like that over the years. Finally, she convinced him she was telling the truth one day, but he went down to Los Angeles to make certain. Sure enough, her mother had died. My husband took care of her funeral."

Elsa and I met again in San Francisco, during the birth there of the United Nations in 1945. Ina Claire was giving a party for Averell Harriman, who was then our ambassador to Moscow. As a joke, she confided to six other guests, including Elsa and myself, that each of us was the guest of honor. Harriman told us off-the-record tales of the horrors committed by Stalin and his gang. "How can you talk like that to us," I demanded, "when you say just the opposite to the newspapers?"

"It couldn't be printed," was his only reply.

Elsa sailed away with that party, if you could believe what she wrote about it. She was Ina Claire's real guest of honor— so Elsa said. Her special brand of self-promotion demands that she has a celebrated name to play on. She built her own reputation by using other people's names, such as the Duke and Duchess of Windsor, as the drawing card. She took up Maria Callas, and with the burning-eyed prima donna beside her, Elsa could attract virtually anybody into the Maxwell circle.

I was introduced to Callas and her then husband, Giovanni Battista Meneghini, by Henry Sell, who runs *Town and Country* magazine. He gave a luncheon for the three of us at Pavillon. I did my bit, in turn, by introducing Maria to some people sitting directly across from us who were members of the board of the San Francisco Opera. "Why don't you get her to open your season?" I prompted. Later, it was arranged that she would do just that, in *Lucia di Lammermoor*, the coming September and, in October, also launch the Los Angeles season.

But before either event could take place, Callas went to Europe and met Elsa, who fell hook, line, and sinker for her. The verbal bouquets blossomed in every Maxwell column. Overnight, Maria became "my favorite friend" . . . La Prima Donna del Mondo . . . a goddess . . . a joy forever." She was out until all hours, caught up in a hectic round of parties. Preparations for *Lucia* got lost by the wayside. Only a matter of days before she was due to arrive in San Francisco, she canceled out.

Elsa couldn't forgive what I promptly wrote about her loved one, Maria: "The day of the temperamental opera star is over; has been for some time. Her rich husband, a businessman, should know you can't do business that way." San Francisco opera lovers couldn't forgive Maria.

She wrote me from Milan: "If I wouldn't always be in this nervous tension caused by these constant attacks by the papers and dishonest people and dishonest, jealous colleagues and so many other stupid things of artistic life, I would have nothing wrong with me. My nerves can stand just so much and not more. I'm sorry that I'm troubling you with these ridiculous things, but I feel you must know exactly how things are . . . If you drop me a line, I'd be grateful, and please consider me your sincere friend." She proved that in 1961 in Mallorca, when we had a jolly old time together.

Elsa couldn't let it go at that. Thanks to Jack Paar, she landed herself a new job on his "Tonight" show on NBC and announced: "I have invaded TV. The great American public loves me." Not every member of it, let it be said. Walter Winchell threatened to sue all twelve of Paar's sponsors for $2,000,000 apiece after Jack and his companion had raised questions about Walter's role as a good citizen.

Miss Maxwell decided to take it out on me, though I didn't see her crowning performance. John Royal, NBC vice president, telephoned me the following morning about it. "She went on and tried to distort you," he said. "I suggest you call your lawyer and get a transcript of what she said. More than that, make them show you a tape of the show. We tried to get her off the air once before when she talked about somebody on Broadway and made a gesture indicating the woman was crazy."

"Why don't you get her off now?"

"We can't. Paar loves her. But if she slanders you, you can get her off. Put your lawyer on to it." My New York lawyers are also the *News*' lawyers. They insisted on a transcription from NBC. Their considered opinion was that Elsa stopped just short of libel. "What she wants," they said, "is the publicity you and your circulation could give her. Our advice is 'Don't let her have it.'"

Not long ago Dave Chasen came across to the table at which I was sitting in his restaurant. In tow he had a dapper young man in a blue blazer with brass buttons. "Hedda," he said, "I'd like you to meet Jack Paar."

After we'd exchanged our how-do-you-do's, I asked: "Mr. Paar, why do you hate newspaper people? They've been very good to you. You wouldn't be where you are today but for them." I thought he was going into his tears-in-the-eye routine, but I pressed on. "I certainly should hate you for what Elsa Maxwell did to me."

"What did she say?" he asked, all innocence.

"I have a transcription in my office, though I don't carry it around in my purse. But tell me, why do you hate newspaper people?" He excused himself and went off. I thought he was going to burst out crying.

By this time Jack Paar and Elsa Maxwell, who belong to the same cradle but a generation apart, had gone their separate ways. The Paar staff told me several times: "He's very anxious to have you on his show." But I refused. The inscrutable workings of television may have made Jack a bigger name than Bob Hope or Jack Benny, but insults leave a bad taste in the mouth.

My fellow target on the Paar show, Walter Winchell, did not always see eye to eye with me. We used to suffer from a chronic case of mutual astigmatism as far as the other was concerned. The symptoms developed rapidly during the war, when he was shunted off by the United States Navy on a mission to South America. Walter raised no objections except: who was going to look after his Sunday night radio show for the Andrew Jergens Company?

The chosen candidate to replace him was Hopper. But W.W. screamed in pain at the thought. What happened next is best told in its distinctive press style by *Daily Variety* dated December 7, 1942, one year precisely after Pearl Harbor:

Hedda Hopper got caught among numerous complications last week that ended up in John Gunther, Robert St. John and Baukage taking over the Walter Winchell Jergens spot on the NBC chain last night instead of she.

Last Monday morning, Lennen-Mitchell agency handling the account made a deal with Dema Harshbarger, manager for Miss Hopper, to have the latter replace Winchell on the fifteen-minute period during his absence abroad. On Tuesday, confirmation came through from New York on the Hopper deal, and Jack Andrews, of the agency, was en route to Hollywood to start the ball rolling.

Miss Hopper in the meantime was preparing to take over the task when Thursday night she received a wire from New York informing her that due to complications the deal for her to fill the spot was off . . .

In radio circles it is understood that the Jergens outfit had changed its mind about having Miss Hopper replace Winchell after Andrews had been authorized to engage her for the December 6 broadcast. Also that the client had reversed its plan to engage her for the spot following Winchell, now occupied by the Parker family, starting January 3.

And that's how Louella Parsons got the job following Winchell and stayed on the air four years.

It was clearly the moment for me to do a little yelling of my own, with some assistance from my attorneys, Gang, Kopp and Tyre. Our disagreement with Jergens and that company's advertising agency was settled out of court. I received a check for $16,670. Walter took sly digs at me in his column as part of his own personal war effort clear through V-J day.

Then when the United Nations Charter was being framed in San Francisco, Hubbell Robinson of CBS asked me to fly up there to do two fifteen-minute broadcasts a week. I was to give the woman's angle on the birth pangs of the world's new peace baby. "I'd like to try," I said, "even if it's a long way from doing a Hollywood column. If I fall on my face, at least I shall have learned something." I already had a once-a-week show for Armour and Company.

I flew my crew and myself up, expecting that a big network like CBS would have laid on all the necessary arrangements for us, since I was working for nothing and paying all my own expenses there. Not a bit of it. For my first show, interviewing some women delegates and wives of delegates from the founding nations, I learned two minutes before we went on the air that no announcer had been provided.

I scurried into the corridor outside the studio and grabbed the first man in sight. "Can you read?" He nodded, startled. "Then come on in. Here's the script. I'll give you a nod when it's time, and you start reading where it says 'Announcer.'"

We got on and we got off without casualties. Years later, when I was interviewing that calm, cool, and collected young man, Jack Webb, he said to me: "You know, you put me on radio, where I got started in show business. I was the guy you kidnaped one day in a CBS corridor in San Francisco. I was just out of uniform and needed a job."

The first hesitant and somehow inspired sessions of the General Assembly were held in the San Francisco Opera House. Only the year before, I'd sat in a box there admiring the ladies and the glitter of a fashionable crowd listening to Puccini. Strictly as an observer of how the world was waging the peace, so I thought, I sat squeezed into one of the boxes of the Diamond Horseshoe with H. V. Kaltenborn on one side, Bill Henry on the other, and Walter Winchell to the rear with his knees digging into my back.

Walter was delivering some staccato comments into a microphone when a sound engineer tapped me on the shoulder: "You're on next," said he, "and you'll have five minutes." This was Friday.

"But I don't start until Monday," I whispered. Too late. I was on. I closed my eyes and prayed. I had no more idea than the man in the moon what I was going to say.

With my eyes closed, I thought how different it was now from the last time I'd been there. I said into the microphone: "The entire Diamond Horseshoe is now taken over by the press, cameras, radio equipment. Not one of the people who sat here a year ago is with us. They're up in the gallery, and happy to be there because we're all here for one reason, to help bring peace to a troubled world."

I went on like that for five minutes. When I'd finished, Winchell thrust out his hand and said: "I'd like to congratulate you. I couldn't have done that for the life of me." And so we made up, and we've been good friends ever since.

Fourteen

Every time I go out on the town twisting, I murmur a silent apology to Elvis Presley. I realize that I'm indulging in the same gyrations that pushed Sir Swivel Hips along the road to fame. I told him in a note not long ago: "You'll be surprised to know that I'm now doing the twist. Not as well as you, but I'm doing it. I have taken one inch off my waist and two off my *derrière*. Now I know how you keep so thin."

When I originally saw the act, I was horrified. I said so, loud and clear. He was rolling around on the stage floor of the Pan Pacific Auditorium in Hollywood with his arms and legs wrapped around the microphone as though they were bride and groom. Nine thousand teens shrieked with excitement as he wiggled, jiggled, and bumped, and six husky policemen looked the other way. At the crucial point, from my front-row seat for opening night, I saw him give his bandsmen a broad wink that spoke volumes.

The policemen's job was to keep the hands of the audience off the boy. He's been manhandled so often by his frantic fans that he's scared he'll be torn to shreds someday, suffering the same fate as his shirts and suits. "If anyone comes down the aisle," the loud-speakers announced, "Elvis will go off stage and not come back." In his gold jacket with white lapels, he twisted and writhed for an hour, belting out the whole skull-cracking repertoire, from "Heartbreak Hotel" to "Jailhouse Rock."

It was like a neighbor of ours in Altoona, who had fits, fell down, and squirmed on the sidewalk. Mother told me it was an illness and not to be upset. I hadn't heard then about epilepsy.

The next day the Los Angeles police told Elvis to clean it

up and tone it down. That night the six cops had their backs to the audience to make sure he did. I'd said my piece in the column: "Every muscle jerks as though he were a marionette. I've seen performers dragged off to jail for less. But Elvis' audience got the emotional impact of the lines and screamed their undying love for the greatest phenomenon I've seen in this century."

Time passed, but it doesn't necessarily heal all wounds. When Norman Taurog, who directed Elvis in G.I. *Blues*, came up with the idea that his star and I should get together for luncheon, I fancied Presley might be tempted to swat me. "He isn't what you expect," Norman promised, so I went along, ready to keep my guard up.

I've seldom been more mistaken about anybody. I hadn't been with Elvis five minutes when we were cozy as old pals who've been dragged apart and have a lot of talking to make up. His manners would have put Lord Chesterfield to shame. His face was firm, lean and unlined as a four-year-old's. "What did you do with sideburns and the pompadour?" I asked.

"The army barber got the sideburns, and I gave the pompadour to the Sealy company to stuff mattresses with."

"I'm one of those who felt you were a menace to young people who imitate you without realizing what they—or you —are doing."

I must have sounded defensive. He smiled. "I gathered that. You can't make everyone like you, but I try." He toyed with a container of yoghurt, a bottle of Pepsi, and a cup of black coffee—nothing more. I remember how he used to lunch on a huge mound of mashed potatoes and a bowl of gravy, meat, tomatoes, a quart of milk, with half a dozen slices of thickly buttered bread to top it off.

Two years in the Army had brought many changes. I found that out when I talked with his commanding officer in Berlin. "I'd be happy if I had ten thousand more like him," said the C.O. Sergeant Elvis, the highest-paid entertainer that ever lived, realized only $12 a month of his $145 pay because it was subject to ninety-one per cent surtax. But the trade in

Presley souvenirs—a fantastic assortment of shirts, slacks, ties, statues, masks, dog tags, records, and sheet music—brought in $3,000,000 while he was out of civilian circulation.

He's one of the few new faces in our industry who has been promoted into a living legend, and we need dream stuff like Elvis to survive. He owes his reputation to the labors of "Colonel" Tom Parker, the old-time carny and circus hand who isn't above peddling photographs and programs at his protégé's personal appearances to boost the take. He and his wife are childless; he's quick to say he loves Elvis like a son. The "colonel," with eyes like ball bearings and a mind like a bear trap, acts the part of the hick from the sticks in business dealings. "I only went to fifth grade" is his line, "so I have to go slow." Elvis' role is to create the impression of the country boy whose head is still awhirling from the bedazzling luck that's befallen him.

"Sometimes a silly tale starts a lot of repercussions," he told me. "One time I was out at the beach with some fellows throwing baseballs at milk bottles lined up in a booth. I kept on winning Teddy bears, and I gave them to the kids that gathered round. Then somebody printed a story that I owned a collection of Teddy bears. Ever since then they've been coming in from all over the world. I've got an attic full of them at my home in Graceland, Memphis. All kinds of bears, some in tuxedos, some dressed like me with guitars strapped to them. It's fantastic."

Elvis is an identical twin whose brother died at birth. His mother, who could bear no more children after that, is dead, too. That combination of circumstances may go toward explaining his built-in fear of being left alone, which keeps a hand-picked group of wiry young men, roughly his own age, constantly with him as companions, bodyguards, chauffeurs, and partners in judo and karate, two pastimes he picked up in the Army. The group includes his cousin, Gene Smith, an army buddy from Chicago, and boyhood pals from Memphis. If they're temporarily unwanted in his company, they melt away in the flick of an eye.

The "colonel," drawing on his circus experience, has seen to it that nobody has ever been hurt in any of the public melees that have a habit of building up around Elvis. But it makes for a secluded private life. When he's in the mood to roller-skate, another hobby, he escapes the crowds by hiring an entire rink for the evening. He drops in at night clubs with his little gang and their dates only after the lights have dimmed for the floor show, and he leaves in a hurry if he's recognized.

The same routine applies to his movie going—he sits in the last row and high-tails out if anybody stops by to stare. Every time he leaves his rented Bel Air home for the studio, he and his companions travel in two Cadillacs, one driven hard on the tail of the other. The same compulsion for protection from who knows what sometimes results in his being delivered to an auditorium or arena where he's singing in a moving van, lying on a couch.

He works conscientiously at a long list of charities in semi-secrecy. In twelve months he will raise as much as $118,000 for benefits; prides himself that every cent of it goes to the chosen cause with nothing subtracted off the top for expenses. "We buy our own tickets, and no free tickets are handed out to anybody. We pay every entertainer on the program. When the benefit's over, we give local newspapers a story in which every item of money is accounted for."

Sooner or later, he says, he aims at becoming a good actor. It looks as though he'll have to pick up his training in front of the cameras as Gary Cooper and many others did. He isn't depending on the gyrations any longer. "They call it the twist, but it's the same thing I've done for six years. The old wiggle is on the way out now."

Apart from sensations like Elvis, the only place a young entertainer can get training is in television. The studio schools, where promising beginners were compelled to go to classes in speech, drama, dancing, or what have you, were disbanded years ago. The studios claimed they couldn't afford them any longer. There's very little point in a raw re-

233

cruit trying to crash Hollywood today. My advice, if anybody asks for it, is: "Start in New York; get on TV; do bits on Broadway; then take a stab at movies. Otherwise, you're going to find California can be a great spot to starve in."

Elvis is lucky, too, in having an agent like the "colonel," whose itch for money hasn't outpaced his protégé's talents. A good agent doesn't allow his client to take on more than he can handle. Too many ten per centers slaver for the quick buck. They're not content to wait a week longer than necessary. So the youngsters are booked into night clubs, TV, personal appearances, fairgrounds, and every imaginable kind of fee-paying frolic. In that rat race, a greedy agent can kill a promising newcomer's career in two years flat. I've seen it happen too often. The agents don't care. Ten per cent of a boy's murdered future is zero, but there are always plenty more lambs to lead to the slaughter.

Before I met him, I had an earful of Elvis one day from Natalie Wood. She was tough, very young, starry-eyed and burningly ambitious. All the beaux were after her like a pack of hound dogs—Nicky Hilton, Lance Reventlow, Jimmy Dean, Nicky Adams, Johnny Grant, Dennis Hopper, Bob Neal, and as many more. But she was crazy for Elvis. She has every record he ever made.

She wasn't only crazy for him. She was mad for stuffed toy tigers, including one that played "Ach du Lieber Augustine." She wouldn't ride on a plane without taking aboard, to read during the flight, a wad of unopened "good luck" notes written by her friends saying how glad they were that she'd arrived safely. She also took some tigers along as talismans. She went through a phase of wearing nothing but black, clear down to all her underwear. She drove a decorator way out of his mind by ordering black drapes and black furniture for her bedroom, where rugs and walls were chalk white. At that time, she was going on eighteen years old, all but four of them spent making movies.

"My father said he didn't want his child to be an actress,"

she once told me, "but my mother took me on a train to Hollywood to see Irving Pichel, who gave me a bit in *Happy Land*, on location in Santa Rosa. In my scene I had to drop an ice-cream cone and cry."

There was no turning back after that. She used to pose in the darkness of movie theaters because her mother, youthful-looking Mrs. Maria Gurdin, an ex-ballet dancer, used to pretend the cameras that ground away in the last fade-out of the newsreel were focused on Natalie. By the time she was eight she had appeared in court, calm and collected, to squeeze a pay increase, up to $1000 a week, from her studio.

The build-up toward an earful of Elvis began at breakfast in the new Hilton hotel in Mexico City. A crowd of us had gone down for its opening, including Nicky Hilton and Bob Neal, who qualified in trumps for the phrase beloved of society gossip columnists, "a millionaire playboy." Over coffee, he came in and whispered that he'd just slashed every tire on young Hilton's automobile, "so Natalie will have to ride with me."

Limousines were to take us to catch a plane home to Los Angeles. But Nicky foxed Bob. He took another car, and Natalie, to the airport. If either of the two swains thought he'd furthered his cause, he was dead wrong. En route, we landed for twenty-five minutes to refuel, and I went with Natalie to the waiting room, where a mammoth jukebox stood waiting to be fed. Like a thirsty traveler who's reached the oasis, she pumped nickels and dimes into the maw of the thing to make it play Presley nonstop from the moment we arrived until we left.

She got as far as riding on the back of Elvis' motorcycle and staying with Elvis at his home "because I wanted a vacation and a rest—his parents were there all the time." But the passion soon faded. "Since he's in town, why don't you see him?" I asked her soon after her return.

She shrugged. "He's busy and I'm working." Did she think the vogue for him would last? She shrugged again. "That depends on how he does in his next picture." Within a matter of weeks she had married Robert Wagner.

This pair of newlyweds made lovebirds look like scorpions. This was the couple that invented "togetherness." In private or in public made no difference; they held hands, kissed, clutched each other in an altogether nauseating display of coltish affection. The fan magazines drooled over Bob and Natalie as the symbol of all young lovers. They bought a boat and painted it together. They bought a $175,000 house with marble floors and went into debt together.

When Warners suspended her for eighteen months, she sat out her time on the sets of Bob's pictures, nuzzling him between takes. The marriage lasted three years. In that time, the career of Bob Wagner, who started out as a caddie carrying clubs for Bing Crosby and Spencer Tracy at a Beverly Hills country club, slowed down considerably, while his wife's took wings. Togetherness turned into that delight of the divorce attorneys, "mutual incompatibility," and Natalie cut fan-magazine interviews out of her life completely.

As an actress, she's always been a child wonder. Orson Welles remembers her vividly in her first major part, with him in *Tomorrow Is Forever*: "She was so good she was terrifying. I guess she was born a professional." In her teens, when there was nothing better to do, she'd collect a bunch of young actors together to improvise scenes with her, which she immortalized on her tape recorder. On top of the world at twenty-three, she drew $250,000 for *West Side Story*, with more money promised from Warners.

She yearns to do more live TV, which her contract allows, as a prelude to Broadway. "The last five minutes before you start, while you're waiting for the first cue, is like being poised on a roller coaster, before it swoops down. When it's over, you feel you've really accomplished something."

Off camera, she is a ninety-eight-pound kitten who gazes adoringly upward from her 5 feet 2 inches at the current man who takes her fancy. Warren Beatty jumped into that category when they worked together in *Splendor in the Grass*, and he dumped Joan Collins after two years of going steady. Joan turned down four pictures so she could stay with her ambling heartthrob. They'd talked about a wedding.

This very sexy member of the new male generation came to me to ask: "Do you think I should marry Joan?" He received a quizzical look. "If you can put that question, you know the answer."

Warren isn't alone among young actors of any generation in having an eye for the publicity mileage to be obtained from a newsy romance. As for Natalie, she wasn't talking about marrying anybody, by her account. Like most young actresses, she can't be taken seriously on the subject. Two months before she married Bob Wagner, she was saying much the same thing.

When she was seventeen, she had one concealed admirer who lost fifty pounds in weight while the torch burned him. Raymond Burr specialized in menace roles when they worked together in *Cry in the Night*. She was the screaming heroine, he was the kidnaper who had the audience chewing its fingernails down to the knuckle wondering whether he would kill her or rape her before the final fade-out.

I had Ray literally at my feet when I met him for the first time. I used to lunch most every day with Dema Harshbarger in the garden of Ivar House, a restaurant now demolished which used to stand around the corner from my office. One day a husky fellow was laying bricks in the patio where we were sitting, and we had to keep moving our chairs to make way for him.

I finally looked down and saw a handsome face and a very large body. "You don't look to me like a bricklayer," said I.

"I'm not; I'm an actor."

"Then what are you doing this for?" If looks could kill, I wouldn't be here, he was so mad. He quit his job that night and never laid another brick.

Ray Burr enjoys food, to put it mildly. When he fell for Natalie, he made up his mind to reduce. As the pounds melted off, he progressed from heavy to hero, though he made

237

no headway with her. And that's how lean, hawk-eyed Perry Mason was born. This I learned after he'd been on the show for a year.

Most of the action in Hollywood today centers on television. In the spring of 1962, only a half dozen motion pictures were in production there, while TV studios churned out hour shows and half-hour shows literally by the hundred. MCA alone owned 403 hour and 2115 half-hour negatives. The majority of the new faces in town are television faces—like Raymond Burr; like Chuck Connors, who went from baseball bats to Winchesters; like Vincent Edwards, who describes himself as "an eleven-year overnight sensation" after serving that long a stretch in the wilderness of odd jobs.

Ten years ago, the movies treated television the way a maiden aunt treats sex—if she doesn't think about it, maybe it will disappear. But TV grew into a giant, and now it's the odds-on favorite in entertainment. It's the turn of television factories like MCA to declare, in Lew Wasserman's words: "We think the movie industry has made many mistakes in judgment. It has refused to face up to the need for progress in the entertainment industry."

David Susskind, of Talent Associates, another TV production company, can arrive in Hollywood to make a movie, remarking pleasantly: "This town is dedicated to pap. Show business here is founded on quicksand. The people are quick to take offense at criticism because they have a guilt complex. They know they're turning out commercialized junk. Basically, they are ashamed of it, and they're defensive."

Neither the television industry nor Mr. Susskind used to be quite so cocksure, and working in TV was a lot more fun before the craze to put every show on film. David got his start in our town as a junior publicity man at Universal-International. He sat for three days in an agent's waiting room, trying for an interview with the boss before he clicked and was invited to join the staff there.

"We don't pay much—we're a new business," Al Levy told

238

his new boy in those days before Marty Melcher and Dick Dorso squeezed him out of Century Artists.

"I must have $100 a week," said David. "I've got two children to support." That was what the little fellow was paid, $100 and no more, when he wet his feet as an agent's assistant. After the breakup of Century Artists over Doris Day, David aligned himself on Al Levy's side and went to New York with him in a shaky new business called Talent Associates.

After a few months of getting nowhere, the company's bank balance had sunk to ten dollars. Al felt the fair thing to do was see whether he could help David land another, more secure job elsewhere. He introduced him to Sonny Werblen of MCA, and David enlisted in the regiment of cold-eyed young men in charcoal-gray suits who are MCA's shock troops.

Over the next three and a half years Al Levy pounded a lot of sidewalks. Television was still the runt of the entertainment industry. Hollywood jeered at the little black box, with its nightly parade of women roller skaters, bicycle riders, and grunt-and-groan artists in the wrestling ring. In advertising agencies the money was in the big radio shows—Jack Benny, Fred Allen, Edgar Bergen and Charlie McCarthy. The head of the agency TV department was usually tucked away in a windowless cubicle next to the mail room. Radio had not works stretching from coast to coast, television was in the chrysalis stage, centered in a few cities such as New York, Chicago, and Los Angeles.

Talent Associates began to get lucky when it signed Janet Blair, who'd been dropped by Columbia after seven years making pictures. Levy had seen June Allyson do a movie song-and-dance number with the Blackburn Twins. He put Janet in with the twins to make up a similar act, which ultimately was booked into the Wedgwood Room of the Waldorf-Astoria. Richard Rodgers saw Janet there, signed her for the road company of *South Pacific*, which kept her going for three years.

Al's hustling meantime was paying off, though nobody was making any fortune on the prices television paid. His agency put Wally Cox, Tony Randall, Marion Lorne, and Jack Warden into the first of the situation-comedy series, "Mr. Peepers"—with a price tag of $14,500, which had to be stretched to pay for everything from script to hire of a studio. The Associates also had the "Philco Playhouse," an hour-long dramatic series for which they were paid $27,000 to cover everything but actual air time. "Playhouse" had stars like Eli Wallach, Eva Marie Saint, Grace Kelly in Scott Fitzgerald's "Rich Boy"—the finest talents in the theater. I even did a couple of shows myself.

After three and a half years soldiering for MCA, David Susskind received his marching orders. He hadn't won any medals as a salesman or contact man. He wanted to be a bigger noise than that. I suspect that David's ambitions spouted the day he was born. He talked over his problems over breakfast in a Schrafft's restaurant on Madison Avenue. As a result, he was taken back into Talent Associates on a six-month trial.

They had their offices in a six-room apartment on East Fifty-second Street, rented for $210 a month. A secretary and switchboard operator occupied the living room. The master bedroom was the main office. In bedroom number two sat the script writers, pounding out "Mr. Peepers." The back bedroom comprised the quarters of Ernie Martin and Cy Feuer, who had the space on a work-now-pay-later arrangement while they labored to produce a show that developed into the Broadway hit of the season, *Guys and Dolls*.

Ernie said to me not long ago, after he and his partner had five hits in a row, including *How to Succeed in Business Without Really Trying:* "Hedda, you made me $3,000,000."

"I don't know what you're talking about. I never did any such thing."

"You drove me out of Hollywood," he said. "I had to quit radio or get an ulcer." Then I remembered. Ernie, a CBS vice president at the age of twenty-nine, was responsible for censoring my radio scripts for my weekly show. I always popped in three or four items which I knew hadn't a hope in hell of getting on the air. I'd fight over those paragraphs until the red light glowed and I was on. That kept Ernie and his legal eagles so busy they didn't have time to argue over the items I really wanted to get off my chest.

The secretary in the living room doubled as cook in the kitchen for luncheon. Meat balls and spaghetti were ladled out to the hungry mob of writers, actors, and directors who haunted the place at mealtimes. "Do you have to smell up the place with all that cooking?" Martin and Feuer would steadily complain. But since they were on the free list until later in the matter of paying rent, spaghetti and meat balls stayed on the menu.

The business was loaded with talents, a bunch of enthusiastic young men who had tremendous fun in the brand-new medium that was just beginning to grow. There were directors who went on to earn international reputations—Delbert Mann, Arthur Penn, Robert Mulligan, Vincent Donehue. There were the writers who set the future pattern for drama on TV—Paddy Chayevsky, David Swift, Horton Foote, James Miller. There was Fred Coe as producer. And David, who developed an itch to produce.

When his six-month trial was over, he was kept on for a further six. Then Levy went into the hospital for a series of operations and stayed out of the business for a year. Al Levy, who has since died, was a good and dear man; he left a glow in every life he touched.

David, meantime, had turned from selling to producing, and he proved himself to be good at it. He helped carry the business right to the top in reputation and influence. But he wanted to make a louder noise. He took on "Open End," the TV gab fest, and fell flat on his face more than once as a would-be Socrates, most notably when Nikita Khrushchev decided to pay him a visit.

The most flabbergasted man in television when that happened was David. On a previous show he'd had a panel of

United Nations diplomats, including a Russian. "I'd like to have Mr. Khrushchev himself if he ever cares to come," David said casually, as much as to say: "If your wife's coming to town, stop by for a drink sometime."

One day his telephone rang. The Russians were happy to announce that Khrushchev would be David's guest. Within a matter of hours anti-Communist pickets were parading outside Talent Associates, David's family needed police protection, and his own life had been threatened. For the program, he armed himself with a few carefully prepared words with which to prod Mr. K. and prove that David was no red flag waver. But it was like a gadfly fighting back at the swatter. David did no good for himself or America.

He would have been wiser to stick to easier targets like Hollywood, most of whose inhabitants are personally too scared to hit back. He has taken a swing at Dick Powell, Jerry Lewis, Rock Hudson, Gina Lollobrigida, and Tony Curtis, and only Tony has ever come back fighting. "I've never met Mr. Susskind," said Tony, after David had blasted him for having "no talent and no taste." "And when I do I'm going to punch him right in the nose."

David, who is unfortunately seldom at a loss for words, had his answer ready: "If I'm not the biggest admirer of Tony Curtis' talent, I've never questioned his virility or strength. He is, in my book, a passionate amoeba."

Playing in television, which used to be more fun than a picnic, is more like a salt mine now. The latest generation of TV actors, if they click in a hit program, slave six and seven days a week to keep the series going. The new faces soon show signs of bags under the eyes and crows' feet.

"Ben Casey" is a case in point. Vincent Edwards, who plays the surly, sexy young surgeon in that hour-long, weekly series, enjoyed one day off in the first eight months of production. "We're in such a bind," he told me, "we take seven days to shoot a show to keep up the quality. And we're only four shows ahead of screening time."

He has the physique of a young bull, and he needs it. He

started building muscle as a young swimmer; won scholarships to Ohio State and the University of Hawaii on the strength of his backstroke. Proving again the old axiom that actors are healthiest when they're out of jobs, his idle years on Hollywood gave him time to go out to the Santa Monica beaches to pick up a permanent sun tan and hoist seventy-five-pound bar bells over his head.

He came in to see me wearing a dark suit, red T shirt, and red socks. His lunch came with him—a mixture of carrot, papaya, pineapple, and cocoanut juice, helped down with yoghurt and a sandwich. "TV's a marathon," he said. "I think the grind probably contributed to the death of Ward Bond on 'Wagon Train.' I arrive at the studio at seven-fifteen in the morning, and I'm there until seven-fifteen at night. By the time I'm cleaned up, it's later than that when I get away. On Friday nights it's usually ten or eleven."

He has an agent, Abby Greschler, who developed Martin and Lewis in his earlier days and who was responsible for snagging the "Ben Casey" assignment for the thirty-five-year-old giant born Vincent Edward Zoine of Brooklyn. Abby is celebrated in our town for turning away wrath whenever it arises. He interrupts any harsh words from his clients by smiling ingratiatingly and asking: "Now how're the wife and kids?"

He can't use this trick with Vince because somehow he's escaped marriage. "I've been at the starting gate a few times, but I rear up and throw my head back. My most serious romances have been with dancers."

"Why dancers?"

"They've always been so healthy, most that I've known. Julie Newmar and I used to date off and on for years. She's a health-food addict, too; makes the most exotic salads." Diet is a fetish with him. "Foods in a natural state" are the mainstay. He recently showed signs of interest in a girl, Sherry Nelson, who is a jockey's widow but addicted only to live horseflesh—they play the ponies at the track together.

Besides an agent, he also had a pile of debts when "Ben Casey" came his way. So Greschler booked him, for extra money, into things like the Dinah Shore TV show, which demanded rehearsing at night after the day's stint on "Casey." For those appearances he sings in a surprisingly good baritone voice. He once did some ballads and rock 'n' roll for Capitol Records. "Five years ago one called 'Lollipop' got up to number three on the hit list, but we'll forget that," Vince said in my office. "I'm afraid the image wouldn't hold up under it."

The "image" is an invention of himself and Abby Greschler. It's straight Madison Avenue talk, but it's the immemorial style among Hollywood agents to convince the public that every star is superhuman. Casey is supposed to be what Vince has described as a "godlike kind of man," a mixture of Gable, Brando, and Albert Schweitzer. Just to liven the picture up, Vince has got to be a maverick in his clothes, like the red T shirt, the black shirt and slacks he sported for Dinah Shore.

Greschler has a three-year plan for his protégé which calls for the two of them to form one or more corporations to produce movies with Vince as their star. At the end of the period Dr. Ben will supposedly finish up a millionaire. "If you have to make pictures, what would you like to do?" I asked him.

"Anything but a doctor. I doubt if I'll ever play one again. I'm so identified with it. I'm only going to do it for three seasons."

"You'll do it for five, they'll offer you so much money."

"As I sit in this office, I will make a vow. I will say: 'I'm sorry, I pass. My health is more important.'"

"Ben Casey" has one bit of pleasure he can count on. "I stay up and watch my own TV show. I have to have some reward for all this work."

There is one face in entertainment that's new and old simultaneously. Old because it's been around ever since Mickey Mouse starred in *Steamboat Willie*. New because the old master has been conjuring up a project—it tells American history with life-sized, animated figures of our presidents—

that's as revolutionary as sound was when Jolson sang "Sonny Boy."

Walt Disney has held on tight to the common touch and contact with everyday people. He maintains an apartment, furnished in grandmother's style, in one of the buildings overlooking Main Street at Disneyland. On many a Saturday night Walt and his wife will sit up there, tweaking back the lace curtains that cover the windows, gazing at the crowds below like children watching a Memorial Day parade. It's a real bit of Americana up to date.

He doesn't acknowledge that anything but clean, good-humored pictures exist. He has never, to the best of my knowledge, sat through a single reel of the off-color, highly seasoned imports from France, Japan, and Italy that flood our screens today. By sticking to purity and fun he makes more money than ever before—and spends it as fast as it pours in.

He once almost lost Disneyland to the bankers who had extended necessary construction loans. But he was saved by the gong. He made a new picture, which earned more money than anyone had anticipated, and the big bad wolves were foiled again. The only living soul that Walt fights with is his brother Roy, who is the professional hard guy in Disney Productions, doomed to keep on wailing: "Walt, you're spending too much money."

My own modest contribution to the bank balance consisted of badgering Walt for five years to reissue *Snow White*, since I was convinced that a new audience grew up every season for his picturing of this timeless classic. In the end, he was persuaded and showed his thanks in the heaped-up basket of presents he sent my granddaughter Joan every Christmas.

He insisted on throwing a birthday party at his studio for her, with her whole school class, their mothers and teachers invited. We all watched a special showing of some Disney cartoons, then made our way to the party, which was held in Walt's private penthouse atop the studio building. As the presents were handed out to every guest, ice cream and cookies devoured, cake cut with its miniature merry-go-round playing

"Happy Birthday," I noticed a detail that Walt had overlooked: the walls of the room had been adorned by Disney cartoonists with murals of rather handsomely equipped females without benefit of clothing.

One little fellow on the guest list wasn't paying much attention to the gifts or the goodies. His eyes were riveted on the naked girls. "I've never seen ladies like that before," he said when I went over to him. "I like *them*. I think I'll be an artist when I grow up."

I relayed the incident, with a chuckle, to Walt. His permanently raised eyebrows arched up an inch or so higher. "Oh, sure," he grinned, "I forgot all about those pictures. There was only one youngster staring at them? Well, that's all right. They won't kill him."

Fifteen

Whenever I stand up to make a speech about Hollywood, there is one question that's ninety-nine per cent certain to pop up from the audience before we're through: "Is *anybody* in the movies happily married?" The only answer I can give, of course, is another question: "Who can possibly say, except the husbands and wives?" I've been lied to many times when a marriage was crashing on the rocks and nobody would admit it. Can't say I blame them. A man and his mate have the privilege of pretending that all is well up to the bitter end, the way people do everywhere.

Three days before she filed suit to divorce Cary Grant, Barbara Hutton said to me: "If only Cary and I could have a baby someday. We both love children. We'd like to have at least three. We're praying, both of us. Maybe our dreams will come true."

Barbara, Frank Woolworth's granddaughter, was a shy, self-effacing woman who allowed Cary to play lord of the manor in their Pacific Palisades house, which had a staff of eleven servants. They moved into it with her son of a former marriage, Lance Reventlow. Cary had by far the biggest bedroom, complete with wood-burning fireplace, beautiful antiques, private entrance, and a private bathroom approximately the size of Marineland. Cary always liked his creature comforts. And if she had dinner guests he didn't care for, he didn't come down to dinner.

He asked me to kill the interview when Barbara called quits to their marriage seventy-two hours after she talked to me. I did him that favor. Then he married wife number three, Betsy Drake. Number one, Virginia Cherrill, who later found a titled husband, was the blonde in Charles Chaplin's *City*

Lights, and she lasted less than twelve months with Cary. Barbara lasted five years.

With Betsy, he took up hobbies, from yoga to hypnosis. The former Archie Leach, of Bristol, England, ex-stilts walker and chorus boy, had Betsy hypnotize him into giving up liquor and cigarettes. He subsequently gave up Betsy, who finally sued to divorce him.

When Joe Hyams wrote a series of articles quoting Cary as saying he'd been seeing a psychiatrist, Cary denied that he'd said a word to Joe. That outraged reporter promptly retaliated with a $500,000 suit for slander. It came to an unusual but amiable settlement: Cary agreed to have Hyams collaborate with him in writing his memoirs and other articles, with Joe collecting the full proceeds. Joe didn't know how lucky he was going to be. Once he got at a typewriter, Cary couldn't be pried loose, asked for no help whatever from his fellow author. So the actor did the writing, and the writer drew the pay. I should be that lucky.

If yoga can't hold a marriage together, confession sometimes can. One cowboy star talked himself out of a jam for which a less forgiving woman than his wife would have thrown him out on his ear. Talking didn't come hard to him. He was laconic on the screen, loquacious off. He had some tall explaining to do when the scandal-sniffing hound dogs on the staff of *Confidential* tracked him down on a weekend at Malibu, spent in the company of one of our bustiest blondes, and I don't mean Jayne Mansfield.

The sensation hunters had compiled a timetable, at fifteen-minute intervals; the precise time he and the girl arrived in his car; the trip to do some shopping; the swim they took in the sea—every detail of the three days, supported by the affidavits of witnesses. There could be no disputing it. He couldn't sue. Certain of that, publisher Robert Harrison already had the story on the presses.

Howard Rushmore, the lanky, sad-eyed former Communist who quit the New York *Journal-American* to edit *Confidential*, gave me the tip two weeks before the issue of the magazine was due to hit the newsstands. "I thought you'd like to know ahead of time," he said. "I know you're fond of the guy, and you might like to warn him."

"It's a horrible thing to have happen," I said, "but I appreciate your telling me."

As soon as Rushmore left, I called the delinquent husband and got him over to my house. "How could you do this, and just after you're reconciled with your wife?" I said. "If you wanted something like that weekend, why did you go in a car that anybody can recognize? Why didn't you go further afield—to Santa Barbara, Laguna, La Jolla?"

"I guess I was out of my mind."

"You must have been. You and your wife are so happy now."

"How can I tell her?"

"Tell her the truth. Ask her to say, when her dear friends come to gossip, that she knows all about it, and it happened a long time ago. If you're lucky, she'll forgive you."

I heard from him within an hour. "I told her," he said, "and she was wonderful. Now things are better than ever." And they remained that way until his death.

There's probably more temptation to the square mile in our town than anywhere else on earth. A male movie star is bait to all seven ages of women, including female movie stars. A good-looking, virile male can take his choice among literally thousands of girls when it comes to romance. Some of them go into it for thrills, some in the hope of advancing their careers. Some of them get hurt, and some do the hurting. Many sell themselves too cheaply, a few value their favors too highly.

Gable could have had his pick of half the women in Hollywood after the plane carrying Carole Lombard home from a defense-bond drive crashed on Table Rock Mountain, Nevada. He couldn't appear in public or private without starting a near riot. They flocked around him like moths around a candle—duchesses, show girls, movie stars, socialites—name them, he could have had them. He had the knack of taking just one look at a girl and flattering her to swooning point. He looked like hundred-proof romance, and was, unless you knew about his dental plates, a full upper and lower set. He hadn't a tooth of his own in his head.

As a newcomer to Hollywood, he'd faced the usual months of torment having his teeth, which were in poor shape, fixed and capped to repair the cavities and fill the gaps. There was one difference between Clark and other recruits of his age group like Jimmy Cagney, Spencer Tracy, and Pat O'Brien. Clark had a rich wife at the time in Ria Langham. On her money, he had all his teeth yanked and a false set installed so natural-looking they deceived almost everybody but a dentist.

The script of *Command Decision*, filmed long after Ria had made her exit and he'd paid her a quarter of a million dollars for the divorce, called for a slam-bang screen battle between Clark and Walter Pidgeon, to be staged near a fire that was blazing outdoors. The two of them mixed it up like heavyweights. In the middle of a wild, openmouthed swing, Clark's uppers and lowers went sailing out of his jaw straight into the flames. He collapsed on the ground, helpless with laughter. "They ought to see the King of Hollywood now," he gasped.

Clark's dentures supplied me with the news beat that he was about to join up as a private in the Air Corps; a friend of his dentist tipped me off that he was making Clark an extra set of teeth, which had to be finished before he left to enlist.

Before Clark was nabbed by Lady Sylvia Ashley, he took his fill in high society. Millicent Rogers, married three times before, considered him the one real man she'd ever known. The Standard Oil heiress' first husband was a fortune hunter, an Austrian count who revealed himself a hidden hero when he died at the Gestapo's hands in Budapest in 1944. Her second was "Lucky Arturo" Peralta-Ramos, who won two French lotteries in a row then lost her. Number three was a New York broker, who turned the tables by divorcing her.

Millicent enjoyed twelve unforgettable months with Clark before she said good-by. In his affairs he always had to do the pursuing, as any man should, but she made the mistake of pursuing him. If she hadn't revealed how much she loved him, she might have captured him. Then he might have been spared the miserable year and a half he had with Sylvia. Millicent sent him a farewell letter that put into words the feelings of every woman for a man like this:

My darling Clark:

I want to thank you, my dear, for taking care of me last year, for the happiness and pleasure of the days and hours spent with you; for the kind, sweet things you have said to me and done for me in so many ways, none of which I shall forget.

You are a perfectionist, as am I; therefore I hope you will not altogether forget me, that some part and moments of me will remain in you and come back to you now and then, bringing pleasure with them and a feeling of warmth. For myself, you will always be a measure by which I shall judge what a true man should be. As I never found such a one before you, so I believe I shall never find such a man again. Suffice that I have known him and that he lives . . .

You gave me happiness when I was with you, a happiness because of you that I only thought might exist, but which until then I never felt. Be certain that I shall remember it. The love I have for you is like a rock. It was great last year. Now it is a foundation upon which a life is being built.

I followed you last night as you took your young friend home. I am glad you kissed and that I saw you do it, because now I know that you have someone close to you and that you will have enough warmth beside you. Above all things on this earth, I want happiness for you.

I am sorry that I failed you. I hope that I have made you laugh a little now and then; that even my long skinniness has at times given you pleasure; that when you held me, I gave you all that a man can want. That was my desire, that I should be always as you wished me to be . . . Love is like birth; an agony of bringing forth. Had you so wished it, my pleasure would have been to give you my life to shape and mold to yours, not as a common gift of words but as a choice to follow you. As I shall do now, alone.

You told me once that you would never hurt me. That has been true . . . not even last night. I have failed because of my inadequacy of complete faith, engendered by my own desires, by my own selfishness, my own inability to be patient and wait like a lady. I have always found life so short, so terrifyingly uncertain.

God bless you, most darling Darling. Be gentle with yourself. Allow yourself happiness. There is no paying life in advance for what it will do to you. It asks of one's unarmored heart, and one must give it. There is no other way . . . When you find happiness, take it. Don't question it too much.

Goodbye, my Clark. I love you as I always shall.

You may wonder why I am using this. Millicent gave me a copy of this letter to read and asked if I thought she should send it to Clark. I said: "By all means." She never heard from him again, but I think it is one of the most beautiful love letters I have ever read.

Millicent Rogers found nobody else, never married again. Clark, on the other hand, got as far as proposing to another woman, Dolly O'Brien, which was rare with him. Julius Fleischmann, with his yeast fortune, stayed in love with his wife Dolly after she fell into the deep end for handsome, polo-playing Jay O'Brien. When he agreed to a divorce, he settled $6,000,000 on her. "I want you to be comfortable," he said. One year later Julius fell from his pony and died on the polo field, leaving an estate of $66,000,000, which could have been the former Mrs. Fleischmann's if she hadn't been in such a hurry.

Dolly, blond, blue-eyed, and full of fun, lived in style. She wouldn't go on a train without taking along her own bottled water, silk sheets, and bedding. She was a lot like Carole Lombard, and Clark was searching for another Carole. When Dolly met him a few years after Jay's death, he thought he'd found the woman he wanted as his wife. But Dolly turned him down. "We live in two different worlds," she told him. "You're a rich actor, I'm a rich woman. You like the outdoors, hunting and fishing, but I'm a luxury-loving baby. Your life, frankly, would bore me to death."

The aging male enjoys a far better time than the average aging female. If he's a big enough star, the producers throw him into picture after picture playing opposite girls young enough to be his daughters. Coop, Gable, Jimmy Stewart, John Wayne—they all were pitched into these June-and-December screen romances, and the public finally rebelled. But Duke Wayne was the first with sense enough to cry halt and insist on acting his age.

Too often the wives of both stars and producers haven't enough to do to keep them content and out of mischief. Their husbands go to the studio and spend their day working with beautiful girls. The girls, wanting better parts in pictures, will do virtually anything they can to please them. Reality and normal values got lost. The men live with both feet off the ground. They can have any girl they try for, as easy as plucking a peach off a tree.

When they arrive home, they often find waiting a wife who can't compare with the studio girls in looks. She may be complaining—I've heard it a thousand times—that she's been stuck at home with only the children and servants for company. "Why don't you take me out more? Why didn't you tell me there was a party last night? Why do you have to work so late so often?"

It can get irksome. I am certain one reason for the flight of movie making from Hollywood to Europe has been the pressing desire for producers, writers, directors, and top-money stars to escape from nagging wives. The wives, if they're lucky, may be given a week or so in Paris or Rome or London in the course of production. Then back they go to the house and the children while the husbands live it up for months on end. It's a pattern that has set Hollywood on its ear. And it's crowded our divorce courts.

Louis B. Mayer married his first wife, Margaret Shenberg, daughter of a Boston synagogue cantor, when he was nineteen and earning a meager living as a scrap-metal dealer. He worked like a stevedore, breaking into the entertainment business with a nickelodeon in Haverhill, Massachusetts, where Margaret served behind the wicket selling tickets.

Then he got into the production end of movies. He dealt now not in old iron but glamour. He was the boss of gorgeous girls, the kind he could only have dreamed about before. Margaret stayed home, the *Hausfrau*, unable to keep pace with him. This was a Jewish family with strong ties of faith and custom, and Louis waited a long time before he flew the coop. But the outcome was inevitable.

Once in New York, before the final break came, he asked me, since I wore smart clothes and was on his payroll, to take Margaret out and make sure she bought some decent clothes. We shopped all day, while she tried on dress after dress, always finding some fault, usually the size of the price tag. When we'd finished, she had just one package to show for our pains: a new girdle, which I insisted upon.

She tried her best to hold him, but it was a million miles from being good enough. She fell ill, and he put her into a sanitarium, but she refused to stay. "This has come on me because I dieted," she told me. "Louis likes slim girls, and it's left me like this." She took a suite in a New York hotel, with a sitting room overlooking Central Park. Her behavior there grew more and more erratic. Her memory wandered. She'd start a sentence, then break off and go on to something else.

After a year she moved back to Hollywood, into an apartment daughter Edie found for her. Louis wasn't living with her by this time. He had other social interests. One was a singer. Another was a woman with a child for whom he bought a house in Westwood. Yet another was a lovely chorus girl who hitchhiked from Texas and joined the Ziegfeld Follies.

Louis fell hard for her. His courtship coincided with her romance with a big agent, though Mayer didn't know about that at first. His suspicions were aroused shortly before he was due to leave on a trip to Europe, where she was to join

him in Paris. Before he left he put a detective on her trail.
The private eye's sealed report crossed the Atlantic ahead
of the girl, but Louis restrained himself from opening the
envelope until the next morning after she had joined him.
The battle royal that broke out then exploded Louis' plans
to marry her, so she married the agent.

Mayer's revenge was to bar the bridegroom from MGM and
persuade some of his pals at other studios to follow suit.
The bridegroom had a hard time of it for quite a few years.
Then Louis met Lorena Danker, an ex-dancer thirty years
younger than he was and the widow of an account executive
at the J. Walter Thompson advertising agency. He had already
divorced Margaret, which cleared the way for Mrs. Danker
to become the second Mrs. Louis B. Mayer. Now she's Mrs.
Michael Nidorf. After she married Mayer, he adopted the
daughter she'd borne Danny Danker; Louis left her half a
million dollars in his will.

Other producers and big shots habitually took their cue
from Louis, who carried a lot of weight in our town. He
was the emperor who set the social pattern. So long as he
stuck by Margaret Mayer, they stuck by their wives, too.
But Louis' divorce, after forty years of marriage, let them
loose. In the next few months there were more top-level
divorces than there'd been for years before.

Divorce has made sensational headlines and spicy dinner-
table gossip from the days when a former Denver bellhop
catapulted into fame with a sword in his hand and dagger
in his teeth as Douglas Fairbanks. His first wife, Beth, was
the daughter of Daniel Sully, otherwise known as the Cotton
King of Wall Street. As a wedding present, her father gave
her a beautiful string of pearls, which kept the Fairbankses
going year after year, when Doug was a struggling Broadway
actor.

When the larder was bare, she'd pawn the pearls and redeem
them again as soon as Doug got into another play. Those
pearls also paid for many a trip to Europe. The Fairbankses
lived at the Algonquin Hotel in New York, which bulged

with actors, from Jack Barrymore to John Drew. Included among the residents was Hedda Hopper with the only husband she ever had. In the lobby I used to stop to chat with a little boy with a frightened manner, kept forever under the wing of his mother or his nurse—Douglas, Jr., whom his father had determined should never get into show business.

Beth found the Hoppers their first Hollywood house when we followed the Fairbankses out to that never-never-land where it seemed that the rainbow had finally come to earth and deposited a crock of gold for everybody. Some years after that a brisk little blonde named Mary Pickford got herself a bungalow in a Beverly Hills canyon. Doug, Sr., was a gentleman caller. Beth and I used to walk past the place, but she didn't know who was inside. I did. One day my heart turned somersaults when she peered through a window. She saw nothing amiss. But after that I steered our walks in a different direction. Beth was ever unsuspecting about sex. Her own blood ran cool. She claimed Doug spent too much time practicing handsprings and jumping over barns to be an effective lover.

They argued for months over the divorce he wanted. He was willing to pay her a quarter of his earnings for life as alimony. She demanded every nickel he earned. The sad climax came in a suite in New York's Sherry-Netherland Hotel. In my presence she turned on him in a fury. "Get out, you Jew!" she said.

Doug's face was a mask. "You don't know what you're saying," I exclaimed. "You're out of your mind."

"I do, and he knows it. He's a Jew."

He said not a word and dragged himself from the room. He couldn't argue about his background. His father's name was Ulman. Doug's mother was married five times, and had children by other husbands, one of whom was named Fairbanks. Beth knew all about it. It had been a secret, wry joke to her that, through her father's contacts, she had been able to make her husband a member of New York's best men's clubs, where anti-Semitism was an article of faith. She collected her money from Doug—$650,000 in cash and securities that his brother and business manager, John Fairbanks, carried in a suitcase from Los Angeles to New York.

Young Doug adored his father, but stayed with his mother after the breakup. He didn't emerge as a man until he married Joan Crawford. An experienced woman can teach a lot to a youngster like Douglas, Jr. He learned much about women and the world from Joan, though she wasn't accepted by her in-laws until Lord and Lady Mountbatten, honeymooning at Pickfair, asked if they could meet her. The first time she set foot inside the front door was the night she was invited to a ball to meet Dickie Mountbatten and his bride.

The senior Fairbankses drifted apart after Mary Pickford made *My Best Girl* with Buddy Rogers. In London, Doug got to know Lady Sylvia Ashley very well, but he had little thought of marrying her. He made a special trip home to try to patch things up with Mary. But she insisted that he beg for a reconciliation, and he was too proud to beg for anything. He decided to sail back to England. For seven hours on the eve of his sailing Mary tried to reach him by telephone to tell him she was ready to save their marriage. But she missed him. She was too late. Sylvia was married on the rebound to Doug, who by the merest coincidence chanced to be a millionaire.

There was nobody quite like Doug. He loved everyone, and that sun-tanned charm of his made everyone love him. He would rather leap over the moon than go to the greatest party in the world, though he started drinking his way through the nonstop round of parties and night clubbing to which Sylvia introduced him. Vanity was one weakness of his. When the two daughters of his brother, John, who was born Fairbanks, wanted to go into pictures, Doug warned them: "You'll have to change your names, you know; there can only be one Fairbanks."

He had a handsome head on his shoulders, but it was no head for figures. I'm reminded of that every time I look out of my office window at a towering gas storage tank a dozen blocks away that looms over the old United Artists studio which Doug, Mary, and Charles Chaplin built in 1918. Doug or any of them could have bought it then for $50,000 and demolished it. But they saved their money—and it cost their company at least $3,000,000 over the years to shoot around it to avoid having the tank show up in every movie United Artists made. After many lawsuits the studio is now owned by Sam Goldwyn. It nets Frances and Sam a mighty juicy yearly income. The three stars who created it receive nothing.

Sylvia's best friend and next-door neighbor in Santa Monica was Norma Shearer, who decided one day to give the Fairbankses a party, inviting Doug's closest friends. At 7 P.M. that evening Sylvia telephoned Norma: "I'm terribly sorry but we can't come. Douglas was taken ill this afternoon, and he's much worse now."

Their two place cards had been removed from the table when the other guests sat down to dine at nine o'clock. During the first course her butler whispered a message to Norma. She turned pale for a moment, but the dinner went on into dancing, some party games, and all kinds of fun until things broke up at 3 A.M. By that time Douglas Fairbanks had been dead five and a half hours. Later I asked Norma: "How could you do it? Your guests were Doug's best friends."

She answered: "What could I do? I couldn't say anything. It would have spoiled the party."

Not all Doug's money was left to Sylvia. Douglas, Jr., was more than comfortably off when he married Mary Lee Young, whose father was Robert Young, the railroad tycoon. They live in old-world style in a small London town house with their three daughters. Douglas, Jr., does not stray from the hearthstone. They are extremely social, with British and European royalty and ambassadors of all nations, including one of our own, Winthrop Aldrich, who had a penchant at parties for pinching old ladies in the Latin fashion. They absolutely adored it—no one had paid them such attention for years.

258

Hollywood has all the excuses you find anywhere for divorce—boredom, egotism, emotional immaturity, and the rest. It also has some special reasons of its own—press agents who can get bigger headlines with a scandal than with a happy home life; producers who resent a husband or wife "interfering" in a star's business; managers who stop at nothing to hold onto their percentages. Elsewhere in the world, children are usually a bond that holds parents through many a squabble. But that's not always the case in the Empire of Guff, which was one of Gene Fowler's labels for us.

This is a hard, rocky place for a child to grow up in. Some of them don't know who their fathers really are because they've had so many in the family. They're brought up by nurses, cooks, and chauffeurs instead of parents because mother and father are too busy to give them any time. All the children can be spared is money, which is a stone to suck on when a child needs love.

Eddie Robinson, Jr., was spoiled. His mother, Gladys—the first Mrs. Robinson, Sr.—was never allowed by her husband to lay a hand on the boy. At thirteen he "borrowed" other people's cars without asking. He has been in one automobile accident after another. Now he has a wife and child, whom Gladys helps support. Edward G. Robinson couldn't be accused of being stingy toward his son, however, since he continued to make Junior an allowance of $1000 a month.

Dixie Lee Crosby brought up her four sons strictly but well. Bing somehow found other things he had to do, so the children didn't see a lot of their father. Dixie had problems in her pregnancies, when she virtually was forced on to brandy to survive. She had to stay home, sick, when Bing sailed off to Paris at the time Queen Elizabeth was crowned, taking Lindsay with him and having a gay old time. The boy went to London to see the coronation and stayed with the Alan Ladd family at the Dorchester. Bing was having too much fun in Paris to leave. Lindsay was the youngest and sweetest of the four sons. Like Gary, Philip, and Dennis, he started whooping it up the minute Dixie's restraint was lifted.

Henry Ginsberg for a while attempted to be a kind of foster father to the Crosby boys, inviting them to use his apartment as a second home while Bing was courting Kathy Grant. Finally Henry got tired of their drinking and other night-owl habits which brought them to his door at two and three o'clock in the morning. "I like you, but I can't put up with it any longer," he said, and the door was closed to them.

I have seen the frightening looks given to her mother, Lana Turner, by Cheryl Crane, who was found guilty of stabbing Lana's good friend, the hoodlum muscle man, Johnny Stompanato. I've argued with Joan Crawford after she told the oldest girl of her four adopted children that she had to leave home. "This at a time when she needs love and protection most?"

"She's a wild girl with no respect for anything," snapped Joan.

I know one young girl, the daughter of one of our most married stars, who fell madly in love with her mother's fourth husband and made up her mind to steal him away by hook or crook. She went to her mother and said: "He tried to make love to me."

This was a lie, but the woman believed her daughter. "Get out of my house!" she raged at her husband. "How dare you do such a vile thing?"

"Did she tell you that?" he said, appalled. "Are you willing to take her word against mine? You remember how old she is, don't you? She's fourteen."

"I believe her."

"Then I'll go. But I'll tell you this—you're going to have more sorrow through that girl than you've believed possible in this world. You'll see." He proved to be an accurate prophet.

Divorce is often an inherited affliction, passed on from mother to daughter, father to son, like hemophilia among the Hapsburgs. Marilyn Monroe, Judy Garland, Doris Day, and a dozen more came from broken homes. Their own chances of success as wives may well have been blighted. The children of Hollywood's broken marriages inherit a tradition of trouble. As an example, take a look at the Fonda family tree.

I used to wonder how Henry Fonda could so much as cut his meat when he sat at the table next to mine when we were fellow passengers aboard the boat sailing from Southampton to New York. His table mate was Mrs. Frances Seymour Brokaw, whom he'd met in London, and she was so stuck on him that I doubt she let go of his hands for more than five minutes at a time all the way across the Atlantic.

Hank had already tried marriage once, and so had she. Mr. Brokaw had been the husband of Clare Boothe before she married Henry Luce, the founder of Time and Life. Hank had been the husband for two years of Margaret Sullavan.

Frances Brokaw was the second Mrs. Fonda—the knot was tied in 1936—and the mother of two children: Jane, born in 1937; and Peter, who arrived in 1940.

There is a darker inheritance than divorce. As man and wife, the Fondas were seemingly happy for years. But Frances was increasingly possessive, and though no divorce suit ever was filed, Hank wanted his freedom to marry Susan Blanchard. In April 1950, Frances took her life in a Beacon, New York, sanitarium, after cutting Hank completely out of her $500,000 will.

The first Mrs. Fonda, Margaret Sullavan, went on to three other marriages; to director William Wyler in 1934; to producer Leland Hayward in 1936, to whom she bore three children, Brooke, Bridget, and Bill; to financier Kenneth Wagg, who had four children already. Margaret's life ended in tragedy, too. She was depressed by an ever-increasing deafness, which had crept up on her unnoticed at first. We discussed it together. I spoke about possible treatments, but she dismissed them. "I've discovered it too late," she said.

Then she was set for a New Haven opening of a play which she was tackling after a long absence from the stage and which she didn't much care for. Her death from sleeping pills was called suicide and blamed on the fact that she didn't want to open, while Equity rules insisted that she should. Cathleen Nesbitt, who had helped her in the part, could not accept that verdict. "I am as sure as I sit here," she told me later, "that it was an accident for Maggie."

But there was no doubt that the second daughter, Bridget, whom Margaret bore Leland Hayward, died of her own choice.

In December 1950, Henry Fonda took his third wife, Susan Blanchard, stepdaughter of Oscar Hammerstein II and mother of Hank's third child, Amy. The divorce came five years later. In 1957 he married for the fourth time. We see very little of his wife, the former Baroness Afdera Franchetti. She doesn't particularly care for Hollywood.

One more bit of tragedy hovers over Hank. His best part in years was in *Mr. Roberts*, whose author, Thomas Heggen, he knew and liked. Thomas Heggen decided life was not worth living, too, after the play was a great success.

What her family means to Jane Fonda, only she could tell. She saw very little of her mother, was brought up by her grandmother, whom she adored. Jane went to the Actors' Studio to study, tackled her own movie career like a she-wolf. She claimed, understandably perhaps, that marriage had no part in her plans. She could manage very well, she told me, without love in her life. When I wrote a column about her, her father telephoned. "I have no control over my daughter," he said. "But when the right fellow comes along, she'll marry him. She's a very smart girl and likes to make headlines."

One smart girl used to bring documents to me from the J. Walter Thompson agency in Los Angeles not long ago. I hadn't heard her name until she said: "I don't think you know it, but I'm John Gilbert's daughter. I didn't know my father—he died before I could remember him."

I thought to myself that I would never forget the screen's great lover, destroyed as an actor on the sound stage when the talkies came in. Jack's first talking picture, *His Glorious*

Night, was directed by Lionel Barrymore. I was in it. Jack's first words were: "I love you, I love you, I love you." In forming these words, his mouth and nose came together almost like a parrot's beak. I used to see the glee on Lionel's face as he watched Gilbert. Lionel was suffering painfully from arthritis, and by four o'clock any afternoon he could scarcely get out of his chair. If anybody tried to help him he'd knock their hands away and yell: "What's the matter with you? Do you think I'm sick?"

That picture destroyed Jack Gilbert. He was honeymooning abroad with Ina Claire when he lost all his money in the crash of '29. The day they landed in New York, the picture opened. He went to see it. With the opening sentence the audience started to laugh, and he crept out of the theater like a man condemned to the electric chair.

While he was abroad, the studio had built him a beautiful bungalow and raised his salary to $5000 a week. After his return, when executives saw him coming, they crossed to the other side of the street. They gave him miserable, inconsequential pictures which he did. But he never survived the hurt.

I said to his daughter: "Have you seen your father in any movies?" wondering if she knew that Jack had been desperately in love with Garbo, who was fond of him but would never marry him, for the love of her life was Maurice Stiller.

His daughter replied: "Not until the other day, when I went to see him in *Queen Christina* with Garbo." I asked what she thought of him. Her head lifted and her eyes glowed: "I thought he was wonderful."

He was, but we treated him badly.

Sixteen

I live in a town that sells dreams but is ruled by nightmares. Its stock in trade is illusion, which it manufactures in fear; not mere apprehension about fading profits or a decline in reputation, but stark terror of God's honest truth.

Power in the movie business fell into the clutches of men who stopped at nothing to lay their hands on it. In the process they picked up a chronic infection of guilty conscience. They couldn't afford to let the public glimpse the facts behind the fiction; they'd rather shell out a million dollars. They were always terrified of being found out.

There were—and are—so many closets bulging with skeletons. I've rattled a few of them in my time when I've been convinced the cause was good. But never was there such a rattling as I gave our one and only self-appointed monarch, Louis B. Mayer, and his temporary crown prince, Dore Schary. I'm glad to say it scared the living daylights out of them.

The cause was a worthy one: one of the few unsung heroines of our town had been pushed off the payroll in outrageous ingratitude for all she'd contributed to MGM. She badly needed her job back after a long illness, and I was determined that she should have it. One of the rattling sets of bones was labeled "Politics," another was "Greed," and a third was "Messages." I don't think Dore Schary has ever forgiven me.

Ida Koverman was the tall, stately, gray-haired queen mother who stood behind King Louis' throne. She taught the little gormandizer about table manners, how to handle a party without throwing Emily Post into strictures. Ida transformed the once inarticulate ex-peddler of scrap iron into an after-dinner orator in love with the sound of his own voice, and she rehearsed him in the speeches that rolled off his tongue.

She was the behind-the-scenes arbiter of good taste in the greatest motion-picture studio of them all. There was a day when she burst into his office when he was deep in conference with the New York investment bankers who had control of Loew's Incorporated—Metro-Goldwyn-Mayer is Loew's trade name, Loew's is the parent corporation.

Louis, who had issued strict orders that he was not to be disturbed, was furious. She brushed aside his protests in her best, no-nonsense manner. "I want you to come right now and see yesterday's rushes on *The Pirate*," she said. "You must see a dance scene Gene Kelly and Garland did together." She kept at him until he angrily excused himself and stumped out on his bandy legs with her.

In the projection room she gave the order for the film to be rerun. The scene was a hair curler. Gene and Judy had flung themselves too eagerly into the spirit of things. It looked like a torrid romance. "Burn the negative!" screamed Louis. "If that exhibition got on any screen, we'd be raided by the police." He summoned Kelly to his office next morning for an ear-blistering lecture on how to behave while dancing.

Mayer, who was his own best talent scout, met Mrs. Koverman when she first came to California to rally Republican women in support of Herbert Hoover. When he hired her away from the future President to join Metro as Louis' executive secretary and assistant, she was thought to be Jewish. But Ida Raynus—her maiden name—was a widow with Scottish blood. And her Scottish pride kept her from asking Louis for a raise. For twenty-five years, she was held at her starting salary of $250 a week.

On that comparative pittance she had more power than anybody in our town over stars earning forty times more than she did; over the whole product of Loew's, a quarter-billion-dollar empire; over Mayer himself, who pulled down a total of $15,000,000 over the years and preened his feathers every time the newspapers tagged him the world's highest-paid executive. Until they came to a parting of the ways, she was the only living soul in Hollywood he would listen to when she told him what was what and why.

In next to no time Ida was all but running the studio from her office next to his. Louis never personally made a picture in his life; didn't know how. That was left to Irving Thalberg, the slim, neurotic wonder boy who could carry the plot and production details of half a dozen pictures simultaneously in his head. The sheer strain made him a nervous wreck, with a trick of sitting in conference with a box of kitchen matches, carefully breaking every stick into tiny pieces and piling the bits in a mixing bowl on his desk.

Louis, however, was the impresario, who prided himself on knowing intimately what made the human heart tick. Nobody on the lot could outdo him at chewing scenery when the mood came on him. This thwarted thespian was a hypochondriac who could faint to order, fake a heart attack to win an argument or stave off somebody's salary increase. He would project anger, indignation, piteous pleading, or tears like a home movie show.

One of his favorite songs was "The Rosary." He would weep buckets just talking about it. He thought there was a fine picture idea in the lyrics and assigned two of his favorite writers to create a script. After nine months' hard labor they turned in their typescript. He discovered their story was set in a New Orleans whorehouse. That was the last assignment they ever got from the outraged Mr. Mayer.

As Louis concentrated increasingly on playing god, more and more responsibility fell on Ida's shoulders. She set up the talent school that trained a skyful of future stars who made millions for Loew's—Jackie Cooper, Freddie Bartholomew, Judy Garland, Mickey Rooney, Liz Taylor, Kathryn Grayson, Donna Reed. It was Ida, called "Kay" by her friends, who suggested having the elaborate sound-recording system installed which opened a whole new horizon in musicals. Stars like Nelson Eddy, Jeanette MacDonald, Grace Moore, and Law-

266

rence Tibbett were freed from the double burden of acting and singing at the same time, because their voices could now be recorded separately to the filmed movement of their lips.

Ida had the feel in her bones for talent that Mayer imagined he had. She discovered a young Adonis named Spangler Arlington Brugh fresh out of Pomona College and saw to it that he was rechristened Robert Taylor. She heard an overgrown Boy Scout sing at a Los Angeles concert, which is how Nelson Eddy arrived on the scene.

Ida and a handful of others, including Lionel Barrymore, were impressed by the movie test of a husky, beetle-browed actor from a downtown stage show—he played his scene in a cut-down sarong with a flower behind one flapping ear. "A woman knows what appeals to women," was a rule she worked by, so she had the test rerun for an audience of Metro's messenger girls and secretaries. On the strength of the raves they scribbled on their comment cards, Clark Gable was signed.

Ida devised what she called "the rule of illusion" that captured daydreams on celluloid and convinced the public that Hollywood was paradise on earth. "A star," she considered, "must have an unattainable quality." Another specification of hers: "A star may drink champagne or nectar, but not beer."

Ida was a Christian Scientist who, incredibly in the motion-picture business, clung to her job because, as she saw it, her special position of power gave her a phenomenal chance to do good. "If you can't help somebody," she used to say, "what are you put here on earth for?"

That philosophy contrasted violently with her boss's point of view. He behaved as if the earth had been invented exclusively for Louis B. Mayer. He gave and withheld his favors like Ivan the Terrible. If you crossed him, he sought vengeance. During the filming of the first version of *Ben-Hur*, its star, Francis X. Bushman, offended Mayer, who saw to it that the actor was kept off the screen for the next twenty-three years.

He tried to force his attentions on practically every actress on his payroll. Jeanette MacDonald had to invent an engagement and buy herself the ring as a desperate sort of defense against the tubby, bespectacled little tyrant. He chased me around his desk for twelve years until my contract came up for renewal. "Why don't you say yes to him for once and see what happens?" said Ida, before I was ushered into his all-white sanctum to talk a new contract.

I found Louis in good form. "Why do you always resist me?" he demanded. "If only you'd been nice to me, we could have made beautiful music together. I could have made you the greatest star in Hollywood."

"I was wrong, Mr. Mayer. There are only two questions— when and where?"

His blown-up ego exploded with a bang like a toy balloon. With a stricken look he turned on his heels and ran out the private exit of his office as fast as his legs would carry him. He just liked to talk about it. (I might add that my contract was not renewed.)

Louis owned a stableful of race horses; Ida lived simply. She once inscribed a photograph to our friend, Virginia Kellogg, who was a script writer until she married director Frank Lloyd. "I would rather have the small worries of too little," Ida wrote, "than the empty satisfaction of too much."

She lived in a rented apartment, drove a Dodge that Mayer gave her in a rare burst of generosity. In the evenings she listened to music or played her grand piano, which was one of the great joys of her life. Or she embroidered petit point bags as gifts for friends. What money she could save, she used as down payments on little houses, which she'd do over and re-sell at a small profit.

Howard Hughes wanted her with him at RKO, offered her three times the salary she was making. She refused. She had too high a regard for Howard. She knew that if she walked out on Mayer, it would set him off on a vendetta to destroy Howard Hughes, and Louis, with Hearst's friendship, had the power to do him a lot of harm.

She was more than Mayer's conscience; she was his entree

to Republican politics. Through Ida, he snuggled up close to Herbert Hoover, begged Hearst to jump on the Hoover bandwagon, got himself chosen as a delegate to the Republican National Convention in Kansas City that resulted in the Great Engineer succeeding silent Cal Coolidge in the White House.

Grateful for Mayer's support, the new President invited Louis and his faithful wife Margaret to Washington as his first informal guests after the inaugural. Hearst, who saw a lot of Louis now that Cosmopolitan Pictures was under Metro's wing, gave the visit the full treatment in his newspapers, which was oil to Louis' ego.

He thought he was really going places then, with the President in his pocket. A place in the Cabinet? An ambassadorship? When years passed and none of his pipe dreams came true, he pinned the blame on Ida. Suddenly she could do nothing right for him.

He fumed because he had to pass her next-door office and see her whenever he went out his own door. She was running the show instead of him, he raged. She was usurping the power that was his. He turned on her like a tiger. That was Mayer's way. But she had too many friends for him to reach her at that time.

Another woman and, indirectly, another President saved Ida from Mayer's fury. The woman was Mabel Walker Willebrand, a brilliant attorney. The President was Franklin Delano Roosevelt, who was now in the White House with a Congress behind him that was out for Mayer's hide. I met FDR only once, and that in his White House office. "You'd have been a great actor if you hadn't been President," I said, "but I'm never going to come and see you again."

"Why not?"

"Because I'm a Republican, and if I saw you again, you might turn me into a Democrat." He laughed so hard and tipped back in his chair so far I was scared he'd topple clean out of it.

But the Democrats weren't laughing at Louis. They were

gunning for him with a reform bill that included a provision stating that breeders of race horses could claim no depreciation and write off no losses unless the stables were their stock in trade or principal business. That pinpointed Louis. His prodigal style of living demanded some income benefit from his stables. The staggering take he enjoyed from Metro put him up in solitary splendor in the ninety per cent tax bracket when a bite that size was virtually unheard of. If the bill were voted into law, he was going to bleed.

He had two key allies when he took on Congress: an accountant, Mr. Stern, who was paid the princely sum of $100 a week for taking care of Louis' personal bookkeeping, and Mabel Willebrand, who earned as much as $75,000 a year as his attorney. Out of her Washington office she battled to stave off the new bill. In the middle of the fight she came to Culver City to confer with Louis. She found he wanted to devote the time to denouncing Ida Koverman, whose value to the studio was well known by Mabel.

He paced his thick white carpet, pausing only to stand in front of the mirror in the room to admire the effect he hoped he was making. "Kay Koverman talks too much," he raved. "I've got to get rid of her. People don't want me to, but I will."

"Mr. Mayer," cut in Mabel, "we have to work day and night to keep this tax measure from passing. I need your co-operation and Kay's too. I will tell you right now that unless I can have her help with yours and unless you keep her on the payroll, we can't possibly win."

That stopped him in his tracks, and not in front of the mirror. He wriggled like a struck fish trying to get off the hook, but Mabel wouldn't let him free. Finally, he swallowed her line of argument. "And you can have unlimited money to hire anybody else you think we need," he said, in a typical complete turnabout.

But Mabel needed nothing extra except Ida's experience and wisdom in developing her strategy. Ida had been in the habit of making half a dozen trips a year to Washington to lobby for MGM interests. In joint Senate-House committee the tax bill was beaten by just one vote. Mr. Mayer said his thank-you to Mabel, but made it clear that he couldn't really give her any credit. After all, wasn't it the magic name of Mayer that had worked the trick in Washington? She didn't enlighten him, but she made a bargain. To make sure Ida was kept in her job, Mabel Walker Willebrand waived her fee for a period of one year for what she'd achieved.

Ida went on working way into her seventies, her back still straight as a ramrod, her hair iron-gray. "I wouldn't have to do it," she used to confide, "if I'd provided for myself when I was younger." Mayer refused to put her on the studio's old-age pension scheme. It was discovered later that her entire estate, including furniture, pictures, and insurance policies, amounted to less than $20,000. After twenty-two years of it she suffered a stroke and had to go into the hospital, where it was feared she would never walk again. She was forced to sell her car to pay her medical bills. Mayer didn't lift a finger to help.

Visiting her in the hospital, I remembered a call I'd made on Louis when he didn't know a horse's head from its tail and consequently got himself pitched out of the saddle in the middle of a riding lesson. He landed with such a thump that he broke his coccyx. I found him lying in a hammock strung over the hospital bed, and roared with laughter.

"What's so funny?" he said.

"You. Everybody in town has longed to see your ass in a sling, and you finally made it."

The room looked like a gangster's funeral. There were trees of orchids and roses, forests of gardenias and camellias. Ginny Simms, whom he was squiring at the time, had contributed a full-sized cradle overflowing with roses that played "Bye, Bye, Baby Bunting" when you rocked it.

Louis proudly handed me for admiration a sheaf of get-well telegrams and letters, among them a missive from the then Archbishop Francis Spellman returning a check for $10,000—Louis didn't miss a trick in trying to win friends and influence people. The archbishop sent his thanks, "but I am sure you must have many charities of your own." I had to read that letter first, aloud.

"Isn't that beautiful?" said Mayer, his eyes ready to pour tears down his cheeks.

"Not in the least," I said. "I'm certain he expected at least $50,000 from a man of your wealth and standing."

"Haven't you any sentiment?" wailed Louis.

"None. I'm a realist and believe in calling a spade a spade."

As Ida's bills piled up and weeks stretched into months of illness, he came up with the noble thought that she ought to go into the Motion Picture Relief Home, where she could live and receive treatment free. He had Howard Strickling telephone to sound me out about the idea. "Let him do that and he'll be sorry he was ever born," I said as I slammed down the receiver.

The only alternative open to her seemed to be to sell her grand piano. Two moving men were actually inside her apartment carting off her pride and joy before her heart began to harden and she decided to fight.

We need to flash-back here to Dore Schary, necktie salesman turned press agent, screen writer turned producer, who had gone the rounds of most of the studios—Columbia, Universal, Warners, Fox, Paramount—before he went to Metro. Starting in 1941, he had a phenomenally successful year and a half, making low-budget hits like *Journey for Margaret* and *Lost Angel*. Schary considered himself an intellectual and was happy to be known as a liberal. He thought pictures should carry a social message, not exist exclusively on their merits as entertainment. "Movies," he said, "must reflect what is going on in the world." Quite a few other people working in Hollywood felt the same way.

For twenty-five years a running fight was waged in our industry over "messages" in movies. Among those who fought to keep them out, you could number John Wayne; Walt Disney; Ward Bond; Clark Gable; John Ford; Pat

O'Brien; Sam Wood, who directed *For Whom the Bell Tolls*; Gary Cooper; James McGuinness, an executive producer at Metro who literally worked himself to death in the cause; and myself. On the other side stood some equally dedicated people who were convinced they were battling fascism in the days when Hitler, Mussolini, and the Japanese war lords threatened the world. Many of these politically unsophisticated innocents were used mercilessly by another group who set out in the thirties to infiltrate Hollywood—the Communists.

They were all in favor of propaganda messages; tried to squeeze them into every possible picture. A hard core of professional conspirators baited the hook to land the big stars, to use them to glamorize, endorse, and spread the party line. The strategy paid off. So did many stars who fell for it. They were soaked for millions of dollars in contributions to the party itself and its "front" organizations, like the Hollywood Anti-Nazi League, which had four thousand dues-paying members at its peak. Leader of the Communist faction was John Howard Lawson, who organized the Screen Writers Guild. He had forty or fifty card-carrying colleagues to help him manipulate the strings that stretched throughout our town and controlled the dupes.

Lawson and his gang flourished in the thirties and during the war years. They got what they wanted by convincing the stooge writers, directors, and stars who fell for what was called the "progressive" line that they were serving humanity by turning out pictures dealing with "real life." That meant throwing patriotic themes to the winds and focusing instead on bigotry, injustice, miscegenation, hunger, and corruption. What did it matter if audiences still hankered for entertainment and stayed away from most "message" pictures in droves? The Communist answer was: "Better to make a flop with social significance than a hit for the decadent bourgeoisie."

After World War II was over, however, the decline at the box office of "message" movies finally persuaded the industry as a whole that it was poor business to persist in foisting off

273

"messages" on to the public. It was a decision that combined one per cent of patriotism with ninety-nine per cent of public relations and avidity for profits. Battling communism has never been easy in a town where Sam Goldwyn once confessed: "I'd hire the devil himself as a writer if he gave me a good story."

Dore Schary and Metro came to a parting of the ways over a "message" picture in 1943. He wanted to film a script called *Storm in the West*, which was to be a sort of Western, only the villains would be easily identifiable as Hitler and Mussolini. Metro's executive committee wouldn't swallow that, but Schary refused to yield, and Mayer released him pronto from his $2000 a week contract.

David Selznick immediately picked up Schary as a producer for David's new Vanguard company. Then when Vanguard was put on ice, he farmed Dore out to RKO, later let him join that studio as its head of production. That job lasted until Howard Hughes, who had meantime bought RKO, criticized another movie, *Battleground*, that Schary badly wanted to do. So contract number three was torn up, and Schary was at liberty again.

This was now 1948, and the anti-Communist campaign in Hollywood was out in the wide, open newspaper spaces. The town had endured a strike sparked by Communists, which saw John Howard Lawson and his "progressives" marching in picket lines around Warner Brothers studio in Burbank. After one of these "peaceful demonstrations," seven tons of broken bottles, rocks, chains, brickbats, and similar tokens of affection were cleaned up from streets in the area. Congressman J. Parnell Thomas steered his House of Representatives Un-American Activities Committee to investigate our labor troubles, check into propaganda in our pictures, and make a name for himself in the headlines.

Forty-one people from the movie industry were called to Washington to testify before the House investigators. Nineteen of them announced in advance that they weren't going to answer any questions as a matter of principle. So the Committee for the First Amendment blossomed overnight. That amendment to the Constitution, remember, guarantees freedom of religion, speech, of the press, and right of petition. The committee which was christened for it covered John Huston, Humphrey Bogart, Lauren Bacall, Evelyn Keyes, and a whole lot more.

They sashayed off to Washington the day Eric Johnston, president of the Motion Picture Association of America, was due to testify. The producers had been shouting "witch hunt." They took full-page ads alleging that the industry was being persecuted. Bogey and Betty Bacall and the rest thought they'd lend their lustrous presence in the hearing room to support Johnston.

But Parnell Thomas pulled a fast one on them. The first witness put on the stand wasn't Johnston but John Howard Lawson, who screamed abuse and yelled "Smear!" until the guards had to be called. In evidence against him there was a copy of his membership card in the Communist party. There were nine more cards on view, too, to identify the full complement of the group that came to be known as the "Hollywood Ten": Lawson, Albert Maltz, Samuel Ornitz, Herbert Biberman, Adrian Scott, Lester Cole, Ring Lardner, Jr., Dalton Trumbo, Edward Dmytryk, and Alvah Bessie.

On their sorrowful way home from Washington, Bogey, Betty, John Huston, and Evelyn Keyes limped into my living room. I poured a drink or two, and we got to talking. They'd been had, and they knew it. I wanted to know from Bogey how they could have let themselves be suckered in. When Bogey started to answer, John Huston interrupted him.

It hadn't been a good day for Bogey. He turned on John to get some of the steam out of his system. "Listen," he snarled, "the First Amendment guarantees free speech. That's how we got dragged into this thing. Now when I try to talk, you're trying to deprive me of my rights. Well, the hell with you. I'll have another drink." And he talked. In fact, they all did.

One of the witnesses before the House committee was Dore

Schary. He was called to Washington along with producer Adrian Scott and director Edward Dmytryk, who had worked for him on *Crossfire*. He made no bones about his admiration for their work. As for the "Hollywood Ten," he believed —in the words of one reporter—that they "had a right to whatever they believed and did not necessarily deserve to be thrown to the dogs if it served the best interests of the producers."

The committee's chief investigator, Robert Stripling, asked: "Now, Mr. Schary, as an executive of RKO, what is the policy of your company in regard to the employment of . . . Communists?"

Schary replied: "That policy, I imagine, will have to be determined by the president, the board, and myself. I can tell you personally what I feel. Up until the time it is proved that a Communist is a man dedicated to the overthrow of the government by force or violence, I cannot make any determination of his employment on any basis other than whether he is qualified best to do the job I want him to do."

That made him a controversial figure in some people's judgment. When Nick Schenck wanted to see Schary, he flew out in secret from New York to avoid getting involved in the probing of communism, which was still drawing blood in our town.

Nick, the soft-spoken boss of Loew's who directed the world-wide empire and its 14,000 employees from his New York office, had a monumental mission to perform. He had come to take a look at Dore Schary, whom Louis B. Mayer now wanted back at Metro as vice president in charge of all productions, as Irving Thalberg's successor, as Mayer's crown prince. And Schary was insisting that if he took the job, Louis would have to keep his hands off Dore's key decisions.

Nick Schenck approved of the plan. Schary received contract number four—seven years "in charge of production" at $6000 a week. He started in on July 1, 1948. In my July 19 column, I wrote: "It will be ironically amusing to watch some of the scenes behind the scenes now that Dore Schary is the Big Noise at Metro-Goldwyn-Moscow. He testified on the opposite side of the fence in Washington from Robert Taylor, James K. McGuinness, Louis B. Mayer, Sam Wood, and other men with whom he will work . . ."

As soon as he read that, Mayer shut the studio gate in my face. But I didn't have to go there to get news; my friends inside telephoned me every day. Two weeks later Louis telephoned: "I've got to see you."

"Impossible. How can you? You barred me from the studio."

"I mean at your house."

"Louis," I said, "fun's fun. What makes you think you can come into my home when I can't go into your studio? Turnabout is fair play."

But he badgered and bullied and begged until I agreed to see him at five o'clock that afternoon. He was standing on the doorstep as the clock struck. He came in, and we shouted at each other for an hour. "How could you do this to me, write such a column?" he kept bellowing.

"How could you do it to yourself and the studio? You fired him for putting messages in your pictures. Now you take him back as head man. You don't agree with anything he stands for. But you've given him the power to do as he likes, and he'll get you out."

"You don't know what you're talking about. Besides, who else was there?"

I'd never seen fear in his face before. I saw it then. Before he left, he invited me to breakfast the next morning at his house on Benedict Canyon. I guessed what would happen there.

We were having a second cup of coffee when the doorbell rang. Somebody came in. I didn't turn around. "Dore just arrived," Mayer said. "Will you speak to him?" Of course. Moving into the library where Schary was waiting, Louis muttered a brief hello, then left us.

"You were mighty hard on me, weren't you?" asked Schary.

"I intended to be," I said. "I think messages should be sent by Western Union. I don't believe they have any place in motion pictures. Your politics should be a thing apart from your business."

"If I promise to put no more messages in my pictures, will you be my friend?"

"Yes. But I doubt whether you can. You're too full of your own ideas."

"You have my promise. Will you shake hands on that?" We shook hands, but I gave him fair warning: "The moment you start putting messages in, I'll be on your back again." But, sure enough, the "message" pictures got into production again.

This was the time that Ida Koverman faced stark poverty through her prolonged illness. She had to have a job. I went to Schary and asked him to take her back on the payroll. He was only too willing to have her. He needed her.

Ida went back on salary for the last five years left to her. She had to walk with a cane for those years. The cane appeared the day she returned to Culver City in a black limousine, which carried her from set to set. Clutching the cane, she made her entrances to cheers, crowds, and an outpouring of affection from everyone who saw her. On her last Christmas on earth I dropped by on my way home from the office to give her a check. I asked: "What did Louis send you?"

"Go into the living room. You'll find a shoe box. Take off the lid and you'll see." It was filled with homemade cookies.

While I was at her home, a huge silver bowl containing five dozen American Beauty roses arrived from K. T. Keller, president of Chrysler Motors Corporation. When I got back to my house, I called Louis Lurie, a friend of Louis B. Mayer, told him what had happened, and asked him to mail a check to Ida immediately, so she'd have it Christmas Day. He wrote a check on the spot for $250.

She lived to see King Louis deposed from his throne. It couldn't have given her any joy, because she wasn't that kind of woman. The mammoth studio, in spite of all its stars and resources, was being driven to the wall by this thing called television, which Hollywood despised. Metro lost millions when Mayer was in charge of production in the late forties. When Schary took over the job, there were some early money-makers, but not enough to offset the other kind, which he couldn't resist making.

Time and again he crossed swords with Louis. If the dueling threatened to go against him, he was quick to appeal to Nick Schenck for support. In the end Schenck had to choose between Mayer and Schary. He chose Schary, who in turn was ousted years later and, when he left, collected a million dollars. Louis spent the rest of his life burning with hatred, trying in vain to take over MGM in legal battle he could never win. At his funeral Jeanette MacDonald appeared to sing "Ah, Sweet Mystery of Life."

The fight against communism waxed and waned; so did the newspaper headlines. It took me off on a two-year lecture tour of twenty-four cities. I found myself the second vice president —the first was Charles Coburn—of an organization called the Motion Picture Alliance for the Preservation of American Ideals. John Wayne was president. As the Congressional probing continued, the studio bosses, true to form, shoved their heads into the sands like ostriches and, to protect the millions invested in unshown movies, hoped that trouble would simply go away. People like me, who dared to mention that trouble was still hanging around, discovered that strange things happened to them. Like the subpoena from Washington that didn't exist.

Variety weighed in to report news of trouble ahead for Hopper:

HEDDA'S RED RAP
STIRS STUDIO TALK
OF FILM REPRISAL

Hedda Hopper's columnizing that she "knows" the names of many Reds in Hollywood—with a resulting subpoena by the House Un-American Activities Committee—has some publicity-advertising toppers of major companies doing a quiet canvass among themselves of what their studios' attitude should be toward the syndicated writer.

Their thought is that Miss Hopper has a perfect right to say whatever she pleases. However, she is largely dependent on studio press aid for news, and there's some question as to whether such cooperation should be continued . . .

Although the pub-ad chieftains—and presumably company heads and other execs—are sizzling at Miss Hopper for further needling the Washington probe, probability is that there will be no concerted action to cut off her news sources or otherwise penalize her. Similar thoughts have arisen in the past concerning other columnists and have never worked out.

Industry execs feel that not only Miss Hopper, but all writers whose living depends on Hollywood should take a cooperative attitude.

The truth was that no subpoena had been issued, and none ever was. Someone had planted the story on that unsuspecting publication. Of all the items about me that were printed in its columns over the months ahead, only one hurt. That was a front-page, banner-lined interview with George Sokolsky, the Hearst political commentator and an old friend. He'd wept openly on my shoulder—I top him by an inch or two in high heels—at the 1952 Republican convention in Chicago when Ike Eisenhower walked off with the nomination instead of Bob Taft.

When George arrived in Los Angeles on a lecture tour, he was nabbed by a *Variety* reporter and quoted as saying that Hopper was a political babe in arms. That stung. A year went by before I got a chance to set him straight—in an elevator descending to the lobby of the Waldorf Towers in New York. I felt better when he wrote me afterward:

I was asked a question which did not include your name and which I answered without knowing it referred to you. When the question and answer appeared in print, I was chagrined to find that it was made to apply to you personally . . . We differ slightly on methods, but that is not as important as that we agree in principle. I regard myself as a missionary trying to win back the lost souls . . . Perhaps your sterner creed is more correct than mine, and I do not want ever to quarrel with you over this particular difference. You must do it your way, and I shall have to do it mine. Please forgive me.

The pot shots loosed off in my direction from some quarters of our town didn't cost me any sleep. I was raised to believe in the stern tradition of "Sticks and stones may break your bones, but words can never hurt you." Abraham Lincoln put it a touch more graciously: "If I were to read, much less to answer, all the attacks on me, this shop might as well be closed for any other business." I believe in that, too; the quote is printed on a sign that stands on my desk.

Hollywood's top brass is used to buying things, but they couldn't buy me or my silence. Dore Schary once offered to put the Hopper name up on a big Broadway sign, but it wasn't hard to refuse that bit of coaxing. All the major producers threatened to pull their advertising out of the Los Angeles *Times* unless I sweetened up my printed opinions of their pictures. That suited Publisher Norman Chandler just fine. Advertising space was very tight, Norman told them. "I like the way Miss Hopper expresses herself, and you'll be doing me a service if you cut back on ads." They didn't cancel a line. I didn't hear about this until three years later. Everybody should have a friend like Norman Chandler.

I was flattered in a different way to learn that *Confidential* had its West Coast gumshoe toiling for six months to find something to pin on me, past or present. Howard Rushmore reported that they finally quit empty-handed. "We wasted our time," he said dolefully.

"I could have told you that before you started. I've never knuckled down to anyone in Hollywood. I'm not beholden to anybody, and I've never had romances with any one of them from the day I came out here."

It's impossible to talk about movie politics without finding John Wayne on camera hammering away with both fists. He's a rock-ribbed Republican who wears his creed like a

281

medal. It's affected his popularity no more than Frank Sinatra's been hurt by his sympathies for the other side of the
street.

Duke Wayne had no hand in politics until he smelled that
Communists were infiltrating the movie business. Then he
sat down in James McGuinness' house one night with Sam
Wood, Adolphe Menjou, writer Morris Ryskind, Ward Bond,
Leo McCarey, and Roy Brewer of the A.F. of L. That's how
the Motion Picture Alliance was born.

Duke likes to tell about a producer who warned him the
next morning: "You've got to get out of that MPA. You're
becoming a controversial figure. It will kill you at the box
office. You will hit the skids." He says: "I hit the skids all
right. When I became president of the MPA in 1948, I was
thirty-third in the ratings of box-office leaders. A year later I
skidded right up to first place."

He occasionally hankers after the days, thirty-four years and
more than 150 movies ago, when he was the easygoing ex-prop
man making his first Monogram picture on a total budget of
$11,000. "We couldn't afford more than one horse. So in the
first scene I had to knock out the heavy and steal the horse."
His political faith is simple enough. For America: "I'm for the
liberty of the individual." Overseas: "We've permitted the
world to think of us as big soft jerks who're trying to buy our
way with money."

For all the burning of midnight oil he's done as a hard-
hitting businessman producing movies like *The Alamo*, he
hasn't managed to reap great profits. "I have a pretty tough
partner in Uncle Sam. I'm not squawking, but he's taken a
little of it." *The Alamo*, on which he gambled his entire
bankroll of $1,500,000, has done well in the United States and
cleaned up overseas.

Duke's a kind of patriarch, with four children born to his
first wife, Josephine Saenz, whom he married when he was
toiling in the slave market of cowboy serials. Those children
have now supplied him with four grandchildren, and by his
third wife, Pilar Palette, he has a delightful daughter, Aissa,

and a son, John Ethan. When Aissa was in her cradle, he set the beatniks around Schwab's drugstore on their ears by striding in straight from work in full Western regalia one evening demanding: "Give me an enema nipple, small size, for a sick baby."

His middle wife was a Mexican tamale named Esperanza Baur. As a warm-up to grabbing headlines with vitriolic accusations against him, "Chata" Wayne dispatched two detectives to spy on him in her native land, where Duke was filming *Hondo*. The two not-very-private eyes unfortunately got themselves arrested and thrown into jail. It took Duke to get them out.

"One had acute appendicitis. The doctor wanted to operate. You know the reputation of Mexican doctors. If anything had happened, I'd have been blamed. So I got a plane and got them out of there, over to the American side of the border. Then there could be no reflection on me if anything happened."

Today, at fifty-five, he still stands six feet six in his Western boots ("Most comfortable things in the world if you have them made to order") and behaves like a twenty-five-year-old when the script calls for action and he's "on." For *Hatari*, shot in Africa in 1962, he was pulling stunts like lassoing rhinos, missing disaster by inches when one of them charged his open truck.

He isn't a man who goes out much, though he always comes to my parties early and stays late, talking a blue streak. "I don't think the industry is going on the rocks," he decided not long ago. "We've hit as low a point as we can go, and we can't get anything but better."

How does he explain his own popularity? "It's very simple. I never do anything that makes any guy sitting out there in the audience feel uncomfortable. So when the little woman says, 'Let's go to the show,' the guy says, 'Let's see the John Wayne picture,' because he knows I won't humiliate him. I think the guys pull the girls in."

He wanted to get into Russia to make *The Conqueror*, the

first United States picture shot there, but the deal fell through. When a certain TV celebrity received the Kremlin's permission to film a television show behind the Iron Curtain, Duke asked: "If they let you in, why not me?"

"We've never said anything about the Russians."

Duke Wayne grinned. "That's the difference. I have."

Seventeen

Maybe I look like Mother or Grandma Moses to Americans in uniform if they've been away from home long enough in far-flung places. That's the only reason I could ever find for Bob Hope's wanting to take me along on his Christmas shows overseas. The first time he invited me, I was too delirious to ask why. I haven't asked him since, and he hasn't told me. But whenever he calls: "Pack your things, Hedda, we're off," I'm always rarin' to go.

You think you know what Bob's like, but you don't until you've seen him on one of these safaris. We once had to wait six hours while the fuel was drained out of our plane and replaced. When the pilot had stepped aboard, he'd sniffed and said: "My God, they've filled it with jet fuel." Which would have blown us to hell and gone at a few thousand feet. Have you ever had black coffee and Tootsie Rolls for breakfast at 6 A.M. five days running? No complaints from Hope. When I got home, I'd drunk so much of the stuff I developed coffee poisoning and didn't recover for a month.

I've watched him put on a performance in a base hospital for patients who looked better than he did after he'd been driven half blind with fatigue by army wives who wouldn't let him rest because he helped their husbands' chances for another promotion. Bob can't say no to anybody.

He would rather entertain five hundred GI's than be handed $50,000. He's looked after the money he's earned, too, though he pays as high as $2000 a week apiece to his team of writers. They deserve it. This unpredictable character, high over the Pacific, hours out on our way to the Far East, asked two of the team, John Rapp and Onnie Whizzen: "Have you got that script about a sergeant and a private you wrote six years back

285

but we didn't use?" So help me, they fished it out of one of their bags and passed it to him.

He can joke about his money, along with religion, politics, and the Kennedys. "Since it was reported that I'm worth around $30,000,000," he told me recently, "busloads of relatives have arrived at the house. We have 'em standing in corners instead of floor lamps."

He's irreverent, but never a dirty word does he utter, nor does he take the Lord's name in vain. I've been with him days on end, and I've yet to hear a cuss word out of him. Came the night that Hollywood and America honored him at a banquet as the number-one citizen of our industry, and Jack Benny stood up to make a speech. "I hadn't seen Bob for ten months until I ran into him on the golf course," said Jack, who'd arrived an hour late for the celebration after dining at home. "He stood there and said: 'I've had the goddamndest time with this ball today . . .'" We sat there in silence, not believing it.

Bob can't stay home, can't sit still any more than Jack can. And at parties Jack's the champion floor pacer, stanchly refusing to dance. "I don't have to," he says. "I don't have to prove myself. I did that in my youth."

Dolores Hope—they were married twenty-eight years ago—and their four adopted children haven't seen Bob at home for the past eight Christmases. If there's any loneliness in her life, which I doubt, religion fills it—she's a devout Catholic, who used to preach to me. We spent an hour and a half together driving from Beverly Hills to Santa Ana during the war. My mind was on my son, Bill, who was away in the Pacific, so when she started on religion, Dolores did all the talking by default.

At the end of the ride, she apologized: "I guess I talked too long about the faith."

"Only about ninety minutes too long," said I. Now she leaves the attempts at conversion to another good friend of mine, Father Edward Murphy, but we'll come to him farther along.

I spent wonderful Christmases with Bob and his troupe. There was Thule Air Base, where our servicemen hadn't seen a woman in two years except five homely nurses. Anita Ekberg was one of our party. For stark horror, you couldn't beat the looks on those GI faces when she was told to cover up in a fur coat because her gown had a low-and-behold neckline.

Not a dry eye in the house when we sang "Auld Lang Syne." A colonel got carried away and said to me: "Do you mind if I kiss you? You remind me of my mother." He couldn't have been a day over fifty-five.

The following year it was Alaska, with Hopper wrapped up against the cold like an Eskimo. "If you want anything, just ask," they told Ginger Rogers and me, so we had breakfast in bed in rooms as hot as hell's boilerhouse. Outdoors, even cameras froze if you lingered longer than fifteen minutes.

One year we discovered that the rain in Spain fell mainly on us; that day Gina Lollobrigida and the John Lodges joined us. Another Christmas Day we spent at a missile base in Vicenze, Italy; put on a show on the deck of the aircraft carrier, U.S.S. *Forrestal*. There was a bronze bust of James Forrestal aboard. I stood and wept for our country's injustice to this fine man. One of our group asked: "Who was he?"

There was the year we covered the South Pacific. Jayne Mansfield was along, a girl it's impossible to dislike, who's kind, anxious to please, and willing to do anything but cover herself up. Mickey Hargitay came, too. In the plane I peered over at the two of them in the seat behind me. He was painting her toenails firehouse red. "She'd do the same for me," he said.

Her fan letters followed her all through the Pacific. She'd read a fresh batch before she'd eat, then gulp down a stone-cold meal perfectly happy—her fans had fed her. On Guam seven thousand GI's stood up, cheered, and took pictures of her when she walked on stage, parading her monumental shape. Then, at my suggestion, Bob introduced Mickey. I should have kept my mouth shut. All seven thousand GI's booed him to the echo.

Twelve thousand marines on Okinawa marched downhill in formation to sit on the ground in a great natural bowl and watch the show. Jayne kicked off her shoes and stood barefoot for an hour and a half because she looked cuter that way, posing with everyone who wanted a picture taken with her. She signed every autograph book, too, drawing a little heart instead of a dot over the "i" in "Mansfield."

"Who's going to pay to see it," I asked Bob, "when she gives it away?"

Years later Jayne came up with a yarn about being stranded off Nassau in allegedly shark-infested waters, which I can testify are so shallow she could have walked to the mainland. I examined her later for mosquito bites; nary a dent on her back or legs. "They're higher up, Hedda," she whispered.

I had a special reason for feeling mighty privileged to join Bob on the South Pacific tour, and I used to explain it in talking to our fellows. It made me the only woman in the world able to follow the route her son took journeying from island to island to fight the Japanese.

Bill Hopper, not a bit like his father, is a shy one. The fact that he reached his full growth and height of six feet four when he was fifteen may have something to do with it. He won't talk about the war, won't let me write in my column about playing Paul Drake on the "Perry Mason" show or the movies he makes. "If I can't make it on my own, I don't want to make it" is his theme song.

In the war he made it strictly on his own as a skin-diving member of the Navy's Team Ten, Underwater Demolition. Their job was first to sneak in under water and survey the best spots for our landing craft to put ashore on islands held by the enemy. Then their mission was to blast clear paths through the coral, swimming through the reefs with eighty pounds of dynamite apiece on their backs.

One Christmas my family and friends sent off to Bill and his buddies packages with such silly, homey things as miniature bottles of scotch and bourbon, a sniff of his wife's favorite perfume. Also included was a little bag of earth, a publicity gimmick from one of the studios, labeled "The latest dirt from Hollywood."

Bill, who doesn't lack a sense of humor, took the last item along when he and his nine teammates crept ashore on one island. He left behind the tiny sack as a kind of calling card. Team Ten chuckled for weeks imagining the face of the first invading U. S. marine who found it on the beach, asking himself: "How in the name of all that's holy did this get here among these Japs?"

The team discovered there was nothing to beat one particular latex item, government issue, for keeping sticks of dynamite good and waterproof. It was pure joy for them to figure what the Pentagon must have thought about the statistics piling up in the quartermaster general's office concerning the kind of war Team Ten was apparently fighting. Bill, as the tallest and huskiest, was the last aboard the waiting pickup boats after the charges had been set—you had to swim fast because the boat couldn't hang around waiting for you. On one excursion he happened to turn his head. He saw some loose dynamite protectors bobbing up and down in the water after him and nearly drowned laughing.

Their captain was a grandson of Joseph H. Choate, once ambassador to Britain and the godfather of DeWolf Hopper, Bill's father. Team Ten received some leave to say good-by to their families. I found out later they'd been chosen for the invasion of Japan. Thank heaven, they were in America when the war ended.

A sense of humor is one of the essentials of this life. You can be rich, powerful, famous, but without a bit of fun in your nature, you're something less than human. I'm not fond of psalm-singing, solemn piety in anybody. But match devotion with kindness and laughter, and you've company after my own heart. It's time to talk about Father Murphy.

He was born in 1892 in Salem, Massachusetts, one of an Irish laborer's eight children, and he followed an older brother into the priesthood. At one time he was a student together with Fulton Sheen, but one went on to convert the rich, the other the poor. They've both exercised their persuasions on me, their faith, I guess, bolstering their hopes for the impossible.

Any danger of conversion by the then Monsignor Sheen was limited to an elevator ride I took with him from the thirty-fifth floor of the Waldorf Towers down to the entrance level. We'd just been introduced by Clare Boothe Luce, who was a fellow passenger. The monsignor, now bishop, has hypnotic black eyes and a magnetic presence that's inescapable. I was fascinated by him and his words. Then the elevator reached our destination. "Saved by the basement!" I exclaimed. "Ten more floors and you'd have had me a Catholic." He roared with laughter.

Father Murphy, bless his heart, has tried longer. I hadn't known many Catholic priests until I met him at a party in Hollywood, when he was in our town lecturing. I fell under the spell of the soft voice and gentle spirit of this giant-spirited little man. In the Josephite Order of Missionary Priests to the Negro, he served as pastor of the St. Joan of Arc Church in New Orleans, was dean of the department of philosophy and religion at Xavier University there. He did as much for the Negro in that city as anyone alive today.

There was a young man in his parish who had gone as far as he could studying sculpture in New Orleans, though it was plain to Father Murphy that he could become an important sculptor, so funds were raised to send him to New York. Some time later the priest found himself in that city on his way to Rome by way of Paris, and he invited the young sculptor to luncheon. The student had a request to make—would the priest please serve as his eyes and report back to him every possible detail, from the chisel marks to the play of light, of how the statues looked in the Louvre and St. Peter's?

Father Murphy went straight from the luncheon to the steamship office, where he exchanged his first-class ticket for two tourist berths, with a little spending money left over. He telephoned the young Negro to join him and spent two inspiring weeks in Europe seeing the greatest art treasures of the world through his young companion's starry eyes. On the voyage home they also shared a cabin.

"Father," said the young man, "may I ask you a very personal question? I understand that to white people we Negroes have a distinctive odor. What do I smell like exactly?"

Father Murphy's eyes must have twinkled, as they do constantly. "It's a little bit like burnt chestnuts." They both laughed at that. "Now," said the priest, "we must have a special odor to you. What do I smell like?"

"Well, Father, I'd say it's—it's a little bit like an old goat."

Before he had left Hollywood, it had been arranged that a party of us would meet at the next spring's Mardi Gras and I'd bought him a suit to replace the one he was wearing, which was turning green with age. He wrote me about both items soon after he got home:

Brace yourself. This is probably your first "mash" note from a dignified, almost funereal representative of the cloth, on which you made a positively ripping impression. (Me for the ecclesiastical tailors!) Your casual conversational reference, for instance, to someone as an equine posterior (remember? even though those two words are not exactly the ones you used) left me limp with inner mirth.

Girl, I'm envious for the first time in my life. With your gift of gusto, what a ministry I'd have had! I'd have blown Negro prejudice in N'Orleans to smithereens and been an electrified Abe Lincoln to the lowly. Henceforth mouse Murphy shall assume stature and verve. In sheer defiance of incipient arthritis, he shall frisk.

Don't forget our date for Mardi Gras. It is said on the Delta that all good Americans go to N'Orleans when they die, and that all wise ones come while they are living. You are very wise, *ma chère* . . .

He signed off "Mississipiously, Edward F. Murphy, SSJ." Letters over the years carried fifty-nine varieties of sign-off greetings: "Emphaticallergically" . . . "Con amore-and-more" . . . "Your sancrosanctly devoted friend" . . . "Delta-vowedly" . . . "Turkishbathetically."

His first letter deserved a prompt reply:

Now you can brace yourself after that beginning. You've won me, hands down. Don't confuse that with the Church, however, as I'm still a Quaker. You go ahead and make your contacts for our voodoo meeting down there, even if you have to hold it in the church, because Frances Marion and I are-a-comin' . . . God bless the Irish!

He promised to "put the curse of the seven wet-nosed orphans on the weatherman if he doesn't behave himself while you're here." Somebody must have had influence, because the February weather was fabulous, and Mardi Gras turned out to be a long, nonstop ball. I didn't miss anything. We lunched with Mayor "Chep" Morrison, teaed with Frances Parkinson Keyes, nibbled chicken legs alfresco with total strangers squatting on the asphalt in the middle of Canal Street.

We had a magnificent four-hour luncheon at Brennan's restaurant, where every dish had been prepared in wine, champagne, or brandy sauces. Father Murphy religiously abstained from anything that came by the bottle but ate heartily and conscientiously spooned up every last drop of the sauces. "I'm not drinking," he observed blandly, "but there's no rule against my not *eating* these things."

At six-thirty one morning I was up and off to see King Coal, the colored monarch of Mardi Gras, land at the docks with his court off a barge and parade their way through the streets on trucks. Their first stop for a drink was at a celebrated local undertaker's parlor, which was always jammed with guests for the ceremony. One year a visiting New York newspaperman discovered to his terror how they made room for all the celebrants. In the middle of festivities he opened the door of the men's room. Three corpses, which had been stood inside upright behind the door, tottered out at him, and he fled, screaming his head off.

My faithful new N'Orleans correspondent was writing more than some of the liveliest letters I'd set eyes on. He has a long string of book credits to his name, from *Yankee Priest* to *Mary Magdalene*, which was bought years ago by David Selznick, who retitled it *The Scarlet Lily* as a vehicle for Jennifer Jones. But by the time he gets around to making it, I suspect we may all be ringing St. Peter's doorbell.

The good father, too, is a fast gun with a news item.

And how about this front-page violent calm into which you and Louella-la have flown? [he wrote during one Hollywood armistice between us.] By what female magic has yesterday's equine *derrière* become a bosom pal of today? Are you quite sure that the embrace is not an *osculation de mors* or a mutual search for the most vulnerable places in each other's anatomy? Well, whatever the mystery, the moral shines clear: *Anything can happen.* After this, I shall not flicker an eyelash if Peace descends on the human race as a certified dove—not an unmistakable bucket of bricks.

In his early days he used to serve as weekend assistant at St. Michael's in New York, where he met Eddie Dowling, and a bit of grease paint rubbed off on Father Murphy's Irish heart. He's been an avid follower of stage and screen ever since.

New Orleans was set on its ear when Elia Kazan went down for Fox to make *Outbreak*, with Paul Douglas, Barbara Bel Geddes and Richard Widmark, on location there. As supporting players, Gadge rounded up six hundred local characters, from B-girls to skid-row derelicts, from detectives to three extras whom police spotted in the crowd and dragged off to prison.

My faithful correspondent kept his eyes peeled.

Well, [Elia Kazan] went the aesthetic limit the other day, [he wrote,] using some genuine Orleanian streetwalkers. Of course, the ladies were paid for their posing and the wear and tear on their delicate constitutions. A bit later, when a policeman was about to pull them in for loitering (what a name for the world's oldest profession!) they haughtily gave him the brush-off. "We're working for Twentieth Century-Fox now," they said, swishing their skirts.

He had a new sign-off for that note: "Kazanimatedly."

When a member of the actor's union led a cavalcade of stars to New Orleans and they were tendered a banquet at Arnaud's, Father Murphy outdid himself. He gave an invocation to end all invocations. It went something like this:

O Lord God, Creator of the Cohens, the Kellys, and the Murphys;

Author of the scenario of reality, from which we all play our parts, some of us so badly that we get hell for our performance and others brilliantly enough to achieve stardom;

Director of the drama of the ages, which begins with the sublime curtain-raiser called Genesis, unfolds with the dreams, sighs, and sins of mankind, culminates with the Atonement on Calvary and ends endlessly with the unspeakable visions of the Apocalypse;

Source of the silver screen of existence, which Hollywood ingeniously reflects with a silver screen of its own on which appear the animated shadows of thespians, whose fine art makes fiction seem truth, so differently from many of us poor preachers who succeed only in making truth seem fiction;

We thank you, O Lord, for this occasion that brings some of the best representatives of Cinemaland into our midst. Help us to honor them fittingly. Bless them for shedding the gleams of their gifts into our darkening times. Save them—tonight—from Bourbon Street. Inspire the mighty industry that sponsors them. And, in fine, smile beneficently on the box offices of the land, breathe into them a second spring and let there be the financial flow that is so vital to the maintenance of an enterprise without which our daily lives would be so definitely drabber. Amen.

The one man who could hold a candle as a letter writer to Father Murphy was Gene Fowler, another friend of many years. I loved him as much as I loved Agnes, his wife of nearly half a century. Gene and I knew each other well when the urge remained, but the ability in both cases had departed. I doubt whether he put a dull word on paper, whether it was a book, a three-thousand-word letter, or a post card.

After a dinner party for Gene and Agnes, for instance, he wrote:

My dear Handsome:

It doesn't require the prompting of Emily Post or that other authority on etiquette, Polly Adler, to cause me to write a note of appreciation . . . As I dined and sat beside *two* of my beloved women, I forgot my white hair and certain other elements of my physical decline. For the moment I was once again in the saddle (figuratively of course) and Life seemed new. Upon shaving this morning, I *had* to see the realities once again, and I must confess that I abhor all mirrors.

He gave the years a run for their money, slowed down sometimes by illness but stopped only once, by a final massive heart attack.

I am in fine shape, [he concluded,] except for a faulty motor. I have led such a clean life that I can't understand it (I mean I can't understand the clean life) . . . But I still carry the torch for you. The torch, alas! is becoming an ember, but it is all I have.

Did anybody ever write such letters?

He spent an evening with Gene Buck, a true friend of ours, dating back to the days when I commuted from Long Island to play on Broadway in *Six-Cylinder Love* in the evenings and make a movie in New York with Jack Barrymore by day. A letter from the Fowlers' home in Los Angeles told about the two Genes' meeting:

He tried to get hold of me for four days, a thing that Sheriff Biscalis always does within an hour, and if it hadn't been for you, the mighty squire of Great Neck would have gone without paying his disrespects to me.

I suppose there are just as many great people now as there ever were, but it does not seem so to me. Possibly I am thinking of my own youth when I recall the wonderful troupe who were knocking down bottles during the early part of this century. Jesus Christ, Hedda! What a wonderful tribe it was!

Gene and I enumerated them all and drank a toast in milk (not toast and milk) to the many memories. I do not want to classify you as an aged alumna, for you were just a baby . . . I wish to God you had been there. We would have called you, busy as you are, but you were at some damned glamorous but uninteresting party to a movie magnate . . .

If this sounds like a love letter, make the most of it; but, note well, you will have to hurry, for Forest Lawn is sending me literature.

Gene used to say: "The important thing is to see that friends, big or little, famous or otherwise, have a sincere send-off." He wrote the send-off for Red Skelton's son Richard, for Jack Barrymore, for Fred MacMurray's first wife, Lillian, and a dozen other people. "Maybe you will do this kind of thing for me when my own time comes—and may I not keep you waiting too long at that," he told me.

After his last heart attack two years ago, I did my best, such as it was, in my column: "He was as near heaven as any mortal can get. I feel the loss more every day and will for the rest of my life."

If, nostalgically, I learned something about how to love from Gene Fowler, I got some advice on how to live from Bernard M. Baruch. I was visiting Hobcaw Barony, his South Carolina plantation, hundreds of acres of pines and live oaks, draped in Spanish moss with the King's Highway running through the middle of it. The soil's so rich you can throw a seed down one day and have a plant two inches tall the next. Only a handful of servants were left when I was there; the rest went north years ago. I urged Bernie to hand over the estate to the Negro people as a memorial, to see what they could make of it by building schools, churches, a community center. But he says no: "They'd think I was showing off." He's left it to his daughter Belle and built a small house some fifty miles away, where he spends his winters with his devoted hostess-companion and nurse, Elizabeth Navarro.

I was running up Hobcaw's great sweep of stairway when Bernie stopped me. "Let me show you how to do it," he said. "I know you're not sixteen any longer. Do what I do. Go up to the first landing, take five deep breaths. Then go up to the next landing and take five more, and so on until you're at the top."

I'd arrived bone-weary from a lecture tour. Jimmy Byrnes, former Secretary of State to Harry Truman, was there with his wife to dinner. I'm a sort of middle-class Republican, while Bernie's an intellectual Democrat. He's fond of conducting his own private polls of politics, and I'm counted on to give him an opposition point of view. So while Baruch, Byrnes, and other guests stood in a group in front of the fireplace debating the affairs of the nation, Hopper sat on a sofa, ears tuned in until my head began to nod. The next thing I knew was Bernie's tap on my shoulder. "Come now, it's time for you to retire."

"But you haven't finished your discussion," I protested.

"No, but you have."

I fell asleep hours later in a huge bedroom with four picture windows in two of its walls. Through each of them I could see and hear the breeze ruffling through the moss on the live oak in the moonlight so that it danced like a *corps de ballet*. Bernie believes in plenty of rest, including a nap between the sheets every afternoon. The next morning I had breakfast in bed, served by Bernie. He'd been up long enough to have read all the newspapers, so I got bulletins along with my coffee.

With a chauffeur and one other servant, the three of us went off on a fishing expedition in a station wagon loaded to the hubcaps with equipment. At the selected spot at the mouth of a narrow river lined with oyster beds, the two helpers set out folding chairs and steamer rugs for Bernie and me and wrapped us up like mummies. Then they baited our hooks and left us to it, while the chauffeur took himself with his line off to his own favorite fishing spot.

Bernie and I waited and waited for a nibble. At last he snagged a hard-shell crab. I followed suit. "Do you want to go on?" he asked.

"Sure, I love it," said I. Only crabs were biting that day. I went on hauling them out like sixty, but Bernie turned his back on the whole undertaking, got up, shook himself, and sat in the sun. "FDR came out to this same spot," he noted dryly, "but he managed to catch fish." So did the chauffeur perched out on the pier.

If he's in town, Bernie is the first man I call when I visit New York. I took myself one day to his house on East Sixty-sixth Street, and there hanging over the mantelpiece in his drawing room was a new portrait of him. I gave it one good, hard look, then asked: "Have you a stepladder, please? I want to take that down."

"Ah, it's not that bad," he protested.

"Have you really looked at it? Whoever painted it has made your head too small, your shoulders too narrow, and stuck you on a park bench outside the White House. Whose idea was that?"

"Well," he explained, "Clare was having her portrait done . . ." He has the greatest regard for Clare Luce; years before he arranged with a single telephone call to have her play *The Women* staged on Broadway after the script had been lying around producer Max Gordon's office for months. And this for a play that Bernie told her was "the most cynical satire on your sex ever written."

I said no more against the picture, but on my next visit a year later, the portrait had been replaced by another, by Chandor, a wonderful likeness, complete to Bernie's hearing aid. He autographed a reproduction of it for me. With pen in hand, he looked up: "How do you spell gallant—one 'l' or two?"

"Never could spell," I said. "Use a different word."

"No. Gallant is the word for you," he said, and waited until the butler found a dictionary. Bernie is a loyal friend. If our top governmental officials had listened to him, we shouldn't be in the mess we're in today.

I once worked for another Democrat, not in politics, to be sure, but making two silent pictures at the studios of the old Film Booking Offices of America, called FBO for short, before it was acquired by Howard Hughes and renamed Radio-Keith Orpheum, or RKO. Joseph P. Kennedy, father of our President, had just arrived from Boston as a sharp, up and coming businessman to see if he could make a fortune in Hollywood.

He signed up a scad of stars—Joel McCrea; Constance Bennett; Fred Thompson, the cowboy Adonis who'd been a Presbyterian pastor in the Valley until Frances Marion married him on a bet with Mary Pickford. Heading Joe Kennedy's contract list was Gloria Swanson, who was always quite a gal.

She'd been married to Wally Beery and Herbert Somborn, who started the Brown Derby restaurant chain, when producer Mickey Nielan entered her life. He rapidly hired Somborn to go off on a nationwide promotion tour plugging a movie Nielan had made. To make sure that his wooing of Gloria would not be interrupted, he had Somborn telephone him every evening at eight California time from whatever city he was in that day. When Somborn hung up, Nielan would have the operator check back to verify where the call had originated.

I met Joe's wife, Rose, at a luncheon Frances Marion gave, where Polly Moran stared at Colleen Moore's straight boyish bangs and said: "Look at her—makes $10,000 a week and has a lousy haircut." Rose adored her husband.

Gloria was Joe's number-one star. He hired Laura Hope Crews as her coach, and she practically lived day and night with Gloria, including sessions at Laura's home overlooking the beach at Santa Monica. He made some good pictures before he started *Queen Kelly*, with Gloria as star, which began as a silent, then ran into the monster called Sound. He never forgot he was a businessman. He had notes for $750,000 signed by Gloria to help finance the picture. The question was: What to do? Finish *Kelly* as a silent, scrap it, or take time off to see if Sound became important?

He suggested a trip to Europe for Gloria, accompanied by Joe and Mrs. Kennedy. It must have been a mighty trying trip for all three of them. The picture was never completed, but on their return Joe sold his FBO holdings for a $5,000,000 profit, to make the first big financial killing of a career that later sent him to London as a wartime ambassador. Mrs. Kennedy's father, the legendary "Honey Fitz," onetime mayor of Boston, had a hand in getting Joe out of Hollywood.

Joe and I saw each other occasionally over the years. If I'd taken all the advice he gave me, I'd be rich today. He was one of the first on FDR's bandwagon when Herbert Hoover was the man to beat. In the lobby of a New York theater Joe told me: "Beg, borrow, or steal all the money you can and put it on FDR, because he's going to be the next President of the United States. You don't have to vote for him, but make sure you bet on him." Did I? Not on your life.

I saw him last not long before he had his stroke. I was sitting at a table in Van Cleef & Arpels, New York, waiting for a package. He came bustling in, as spry as ever then. "Hi, Joe! Buying *me* a present?"

He paused in mid-stride. "What— Oh, it's you. I might have known."

He threw me a hard look and went on into the back room. The senior assistant in the place came up, shook my hand, and said: "I didn't think anybody in the world could do that."

"Why not? I knew him when he was a Hollywood producer and had a stableful of stars," I said. "Besides, I have a mighty retentive memory."

Eighteen

His voice was the making and the breaking of him, a blessing and a curse. He could melt your soul or shatter mirrors when he set it free. One night, all over the hearthrug in my den, there lay the chunks of broken glass to prove his point. In his fevered love affairs he was a stallion, with a body as strong as an animal's, and he called himself "The Tiger."

Mario Lanza roared upward to fortune and fantastic fame like a Fourth of July rocket, then fell back to earth, a burnt stick, lost in darkness. For a moment, while he lit the sky, he brought back to incredible life the archaic days of madness, romance, depravity, and glory. But there had never been anybody quite like Mario, and I doubt whether we shall see his like again.

It was easy to be captivated, though often hard to tell exactly why. His smile, which was as big as his voice, was matched with the habits of a tiger cub, impossible to housebreak. He was the last of the great romantic performers, born in the wrong century—maybe there could never be a right one for him. "Reality," he believed, "stinks most of the time. It's a star's duty to take people out of the world of reality into the world of illusion, and a motion picture is the ideal way to do that."

He ate too much, fought too much, drank too much, spent too much. He could no more handle success than a child can be trusted with dynamite. So many of the themes of this story met and merged in Alfred Arnold Cocozza, from Philadelphia's Little Italy, who borrowed his mother's maiden name, Maria Lanza, as a ticket to destruction.

He developed a god complex a mile wide. "I'm the humble keeper of a voice," he used to tell me in all seriousness, "which

God has entrusted to me. This is not easy. There are sacrifices you must make. I love champagne—I can't drink it. Red wine I love—I must refuse it. I must not smoke—it is bad for the voice. I am the fortunate and unfortunate guy it passes through."

He couldn't be called a liar, because he found it increasingly hard to distinguish between the facts and the fables he wove around himself. He could boast of his abstemiousness and, a few hours later, wander into a bar on Sunset Strip like The Players, a favorite haunt of his, which Preston Sturges used to run. They could hear Mario coming by the slap of laces in the handmade, elevator shoes he imported from New York to add a couple of inches to his own natural-grown five feet seven. The fancy footwear must been uncomfortable; the laces were seldom tied.

He turned up at The Players one morning fifteen minutes before the 2 A.M. curfew which California law demands, awash from the red wine he guzzled after dinner. Closing time arrived, but Mario and Sturges lingered at a table with two girls, killing more wine. Two state liquor inspectors stopped by for a friendly, after-hours drink. They were off duty and well acquainted with Sturges, but Mario hadn't been told that.

One of them walked up behind him, grabbed the bottle, and, as a joke, grunted: "Okay, you're all under arrest." That was the last thing he knew until long after dawn broke. Mario snatched the bottle from the inspector. With a fist hard as a rock, with a seventeen-inch biceps behind it, he sent him flying against a far wall, cold as a mackerel, with seven teeth knocked out of his head.

The other officer tried to tackle Mario. For his trouble, he was picked up bodily and hurled against the same wall, dead to the world, slumped on the floor beside his companion like a second sack of broken bones.

Sturges was aghast. Before he called an ambulance he shoved Mario out the front door. "Start running and get lost," he grunted. The now-terrified tenor put on so much speed he shed one of his shoes in his flight to the apartment of a friend, who lived close to the Château Marmont on Sunset Boulevard. At 4 A.M. Sturges telephoned Mario's press agent to report the massacre. "Keep that maniac away from me," he said. "He's likely to kill us all in our sleep."

The press agent made a beeline for the nearest sheriff's substation, on Fairfax Avenue at Santa Monica Boulevard. Standing in full view on the desk was Mario's shoe, as distinctively his as a fingerprint, but nobody had any idea who owned it. "Have there been any charges filed?" the agent asked. There had not. "Well, my client would like to have his shoe back." "Who's your client?" asked the desk sergeant.

"That's neither here nor there. No need to identify him until charges have been filed." After some persuasion the law accepted that viewpoint and handed over the shoe. Mario got it back the following morning, along with a lecture from his agent.

Lanza was contrite and, as always, willing to pay. The inspector with the missing teeth received a $4000 job of expert dentistry. Both he and his colleague were given $200 cashmere suits by the agent as balm to their wounds. To this day they don't know what hit them—or who.

Mario may have been on to something with his claim that his voice was a gift of God; he certainly didn't owe a thing to formal training. He simply taught himself by listening to his father's collection of opera records, including one Caruso disk that he once played twenty-seven times in succession, matching his voice to the great Enrico's. He was a blubbery fat boy, an only child, spoiled rotten by his mother, who was the only working member of the Cocozza family. She was up at five-thirty every morning, to sew uniforms in an army quartermaster depot as the sole support of Mario and his father, a pensioned veteran of World War I.

The studios later had a hard time inventing jobs that Mario was supposed to have held down as a young man. The handouts pretended he'd been a piano mover or a truck driver. But he used to sprawl in bed until lunch time, hadn't done a lick of real work until he was drafted in the Army.

He had one other hobby in his Philadelphia era besides singing, and that was girls. "I can't help it if I was born in heat," was the way he put it. "I am always the lover—I never stopped. I spend ninety-nine and ninety-nine one hundredths of my time in a romantic mood. That accounts for my high notes."

Women mobbed him every step of his career. Wherever he showed his face in public, they ripped at his clothes, grabbed him, hugged him, smothered him in lipstick from the top of his curly head down. It was impossible for him to escape them. They followed him to his home, rang his doorbell in the middle of the night, and some of them were the biggest stars in our business.

As an army private, Mario got to Los Angeles on furlough. A lot happened to him there. A fellow soldier in the same outfit, Bert Hicks from Chicago, introduced him to his sister Betty, who became the one and only Mrs. Lanza after Mario was discharged. They were married in Beverly Hills Municipal Court, with neither of their families knowing anything about it. At a Frances Marion party loaded to the doors with stars, with Father Murphy up from New Orleans, and myself, Mario sang clear through from eleven o'clock one night until the birds started giving him competition at seven the next morning. At another party, Frank Sinatra heard him and invited him to stay at his home.

After I'd heard Mario sing, I asked him over to my house. There was a big, gilt-framed mirror over the fireplace in the den. "I could break that with the power of a single high note," he boasted. Like a fool, I told him: "I'd like to see you try." Like a little boy, he had to prove it. When he had gone, the house seemed oddly quiet. I was sweeping up bits of glass for days.

Walter Pidgeon and I both became Lanza boosters, but it was Ida Koverman, true to form, who took him to Louis B. Mayer. Mario had been cutting some tests for RCA-Victor to see whether his voice would be right for commercial recording. Ida, who was a board member of the Hollywood Bowl, laid hold of some of those disks to play for her boss.

To Louis, that tenor sounded like a symphony orchestrated for cash registers. Mario was presented with a seven-year contract, starting at $750 a week, with a bonus of $10,000 payable on signature. I begged him not to sign, because his voice wasn't ready to be exploited the way Metro was sure to exploit it. But he was beating his chest so loudly he couldn't hear me. He was twenty-six years old. He had twelve more years left to him.

Metro had a sad history with its tenors and baritones. There'd been Lawrence Tibbett, a baritone of large frame and a big voice, who was hauled out of the Metropolitan Opera to do *The Rogue Song*, music by Franz Lehar, screen play by Frances Marion. He did *New Moon* with Grace Moore, then faded like the morning dew.

Igor Gorin was hustled out to Culver City, too, under Mayer's strategy of always keeping an understudy in the wings to prevent any star from getting too big-headed. Gorin was kept hanging around doing nothing in particular for two years, though Louis admitted he had a better voice than Nelson Eddy, who was piling up the profits for the studio as a team with Jeanette MacDonald.

But Louis grew tired of Nelson, so he was handed the Impossible Script treatment—given stories so remote from his abilities that he was bound to turn them down. This continued until he cracked and announced: "I'm through." That was the day his bosses had been banking on and waiting for.

Food was always a delight to Mario right from the teen-age days when his invalid father used to serve him breakfast in bed. He swore by "Puccini and pizza—greatest combination since Samson and Delilah." Also by spaghetti, ravioli, meat balls, a steak and six eggs for breakfast; thirty and forty pieces of fried chicken at a sitting, rounded off with a whole apple pie and a quart of eggnog.

His studio bosses watched his weight go up and down like the stock market. There were times when they put him in a drug-induced coma for days on end; he would have to lose twenty pounds before he was allowed out of bed. They peeled him down to 169 pounds for his first picture, *That Midnight Kiss*, and kept scales on the set to weigh him every morning like a prize bull readied for market.

He hadn't started picture number two, *The Toast of New Orleans*, before he took to the bottle as enthusiastically as to the knife and fork. He recognized no authority, no discipline, no frontiers except his own gigantic appetites for food and drink and women. One afternoon on the set he fell into a brief, blazing argument with Joe Pasternak, the producer. But he resumed work in the scene, a lavishly decorated New Orleans restaurant, replete with crystal chandeliers, velvet draperies, snow-white tablecloths adorned with glass and silver.

In the middle of one take, he spotted a friend who had come onto the set, so he stopped cold, still raging from his quarrel with Pasternak, to take the visitor to his portable dressing room. Inside, Mario launched into a tirade against the producer, the studio, and the lousy picture he was making. From the little clothes closet he pulled out a fifth of Old Granddad and yanked out the cork. In two gargantuan gulps he emptied the bottle.

Suddenly he was calm as a lake. "I think I'm making too much of little things," he said, and, steady as a rock, walked back before the cameras. There were two steps leading down to the restaurant floor. He negotiated the first without difficulty, but on the second the bourbon hit him. He gave a thundering roar, then burst on the set like a bomb. Tables collapsed as he crashed into them, chandeliers shattered into fragments, curtains were torn to rags, while above the chaos sounded the screams of his co-star, Ann Blyth. He made his way across the set leaving havoc in his wake, then subsided to the floor, unconscious.

The Toast of New Orleans presented a special problem to Mario, who had been introduced to the pleasures of coffee and brandy by J. Carroll Naish. Starting before breakfast,

Mario was taking thirty cups of coffee a day, with disastrous effect on his kidneys. The picture was being shot on the old lot back of Culver City, a long block away from the nearest washrooms. He spent the better part of his working day in transit, until production had slowed to a crawl. He made poor time walking, anyway—he had broken his foot, which was in a cast, and he was forced to limp along with a cane.

His director, Norman Taurog, and Joe Pasternak appealed for help to Dore Schary, who, with Mayer on his way out, was now in charge of production. Schary luxuriated in an impeccable office furnished in old-English fashion, with a mahogany desk that reeked of class and the antique show-room. The first time Mario was summoned, he sat nursing his cane in patient silence. "We can't have the picture held up by your bladder trouble," said Schary. "We must find a solution."

"Okay," said Mario. "Leave it to me."

His solution was simplicity itself. By now, shooting was concentrated on a New Orleans quay, bright with fishing nets and boats at anchor. Mario didn't bother hobbling to the washroom. The water in the quay was more convenient. So was a bucket half filled with a still photographer's used flash bulbs.

The whole company was in an uproar, most notably David Niven, whose voice was raised in indignation on behalf of Ann Blyth and other women in the cast. Mario was called again to Schary's office. But now his temper had changed. He shouted down every word that Schary tried to utter, until the producer cowered in fright behind his beautiful desk, watching Mario pound it to a battered wreck with his cane. But Schary wasn't one to nurse grudges. After the first preview of *The Great Caruso* he showered Mario with hampers of fruit, bouquets of flowers, and cases of champagne.

When I first heard his mighty voice, I wrote: "If Lanza can act, he's the man to play Caruso." I still have Caruso records, along with a framed caricature he drew of DeWolf Hopper to celebrate the birth of our son. Caruso's eloquent title for his sketch of Wolfie, scribbled on the back of a Lambs Club banquet menu, was *The Bachelor!!!!!!!*

Nick Schenck was opposed to *The Great Caruso*, whose chances of box-office success he rated at zero. Mayer, prompted by Ida, pushed it along toward production. It was completed in thirty-one days of shooting; it ran for ten weeks and earned $1,500,000 at New York's Radio City Music Hall alone; around the world it piled up $19,000,000 the first twelve months after release. Mario's pay check was $100,000.

His finances were already tangled like knitting wool tossed into a cage full of tigers. On the face of it, he was earning from movies and records about $1,000,000 a year. But there were complications. The greatest singing attraction in the world was a monumental spendthrift. After *Caruso* he bought two dozen gold watches, had them engraved "With love from Mario," and handed them out like lollipops. He insisted on having 14-karat gold fittings on his brand-new Cadillac, which was upholstered in tiger skin. He ran up delicatessen bills so huge he was leery about showing his face in the shop.

And there was Sam Weiler, who collected a cut of everything Mario made. Weiler was a nondescript little man who owned a boys' summer camp in Pennsylvania and yearned to be a singer. Soon after the Lanzas went to New York to spend their honeymoon in the Park Central Hotel, he heard Mario singing at the studio of a voice teacher, Polly Robertson, and decided on the spot that managing this talent was a much better bet than trying to make it to glory on his own larynx.

When he offered to pay off Mario's debts—$11,000 or so, by Weiler's account—and subsidize his career, Betty and her new husband calculated they could get along on $70 a week living expenses. In return, Weiler was to collect five per cent of all Lanza's earnings for the next fifteen years. Eighteen months later the manager's share was increased to ten per cent. A third contract pushed up his cut to twenty per cent, and when Mario signed for a radio show later, Weiler was in on the ground floor at $500 a week. According to his protégé's reckoning, Weiler advanced $70 a week for seven months and drew a subsequent total of more than $350,000 in commissions.

Cash money and Mario were almost strangers. He never saw the tens of thousands of dollars he made every week. Nobody actually put cash into his hands until he was in the middle of a man-killing concert tour that took him and two or three followers clear across the nation, singing his heart out at every performance.

His life had come down to a deadly dull routine: sing every night, come off stage and drink a case of beer, sleep, drive on to the next town. Even his thick-skinned followers felt sorry for him. "Why not give him something for himself?" they asked each other. "Let him have the money from the programs." Those souvenirs of the concert sold at one dollar apiece, cost no more than twelve or so cents to produce. So while the tour was bringing in $30,000 a week in Oregon, which is silver-dollar territory, Mario was permitted to store up five hundred of those dollars, which he squirreled away in a canvas bag.

Only this bull of a man would have the muscle to tote around that sack of silver like a change purse, but he took it everywhere with him, day and night. In the car, he set it down on the floor between his legs and occasionally, subconsciously, gave it a reassuring chink. At night, he slept with the bag under his bed.

The biggest money came in, unseen by him, from his records. He sold more than 110,000 albums from *Caruso* before the picture was shown to any public audience. Then he topped this by selling a million copies in less than a year of a single record, "Be My Love." No classical artist in RCA history had ever equaled that mark. The record was cut in one flawless attempt while he was muzzy with wine and soaking wet from head to foot. When he was awarded his first golden record for selling a million copies of it, he would have nobody but Hedda Hopper present it to him. The studio was furious. They wanted one of their stars to perform that service so all the glory could be kept in the family.

He had gone through a normal rambunctious day at Culver City, drinking steadily but staying out of trouble. At seven-thirty that evening he had an appointment at Republic Studios, where one particular sound stage came so close to acoustic perfection that RCA consistently hired it for cutting its classical-label records, Red Seal. A sixty-five-piece orchestra had been engaged to work with him through the night in a four-hour session, to make an armful of master recordings.

On his way home from the studio Mario thought he'd stop by for another drink or two at the home of a good friend of his, a free-lance writer. The tempestuous tenor was distinctly the worse for wear when he arrived, and his condition did not improve. Phyllis Kirk, a young actress who lived in an upstairs apartment, was invited down to have a drink with Mario. Before he collapsed into alcoholic slumber, he had tried to rip the dress off her shoulders.

Lanza's long-suffering press agent was eating dinner when he had a call from an RCA representative waiting at Republic: where was Mario? Within minutes another telephone call provided the answer, from the free-lance correspondent: "Will you kindly come over and get your degenerate, unprincipled client out of my apartment?"

The agent had a favor to ask first: "Can the three of you drag him into a cold shower, prop him up, and keep him there? If he drowns, he drowns, but will you please try it for me?" Be happy to, the writer said. When the agent got to the apartment, Mario was fully clad, three-quarters conscious, and half drowned. The idea that he had work to do had somehow penetrated his curly head. But he had a bargain to make first.

"I'll go out to Republic if you come with me," he told the agent. "I'll do one number, then we go and have a bottle of wine together." Agreed.

The orchestra, impeccably dressed, had been waiting nearly two hours when Mario staggered in, splashing water wherever he stood. He frowned at the conductor, then turned on the musicians. "—— all of you," he said to introduce himself. "I don't want any bull. We're going through this thing once, and it had better be right."

And that's how it was done. Half an hour later Mario was sitting with his press agent in a bar in Coldwater Canyon quaffing Ruffino by the quart. A year and a half later the same agent was handed a check for Mario representing his take from nine months' sale of "Be My Love"—$405,000. The one record earned over $2,000,000. In 1961, Mario Lanza records were still collecting royalties of $275,000. Mario wasn't around to share in as much as a nickel, but the percentage merchants still had contracts which continued to give them their cut.

"Be My Love" was selling like hot cakes, especially in Philadelphia, when a fan magazine appeared on the newsstands quoting Mario's reminiscences of his old neighborhood. These memoirs had been concocted between the singer and a writer in the course of another battle of the bottles that began at five-thirty one afternoon in Mama Weiss's Hungarian restaurant and ended at seven-thirty the next morning when Mario got home to Betty. His imagination had run wild through the night with lurid tales of gang wars in Little Italy and bullets whistling past his ears when he lived on "Murderers' Row."

Publication of these highly colored tales so enraged some of his former neighbors that they invaded local stores and smashed every Lanza record they could seize. Rocks were hurled through the windows of his relatives. The mayor was forced to telephone Hollywood: "Please bring Mr. Lanza to Philadelphia for a personal appearance, or I'm afraid we may have a major riot here."

Mario was always officially on a diet. "I've never been fat," he bragged, "only seductively buxom." But he was a compulsive eater who ballooned up to three hundred pounds between pictures. Schary was forever plagued with the problem of paring down Mario, who was pure gold at the box

311

office; his four pictures for Metro brought in $40,000,000, a phenomenal figure. He had so many temptations to eat and drink in Hollywood that Schary decided his prize tenor would have to be hidden away somewhere for the poundage to be lost.

Ginger Rogers had a secluded ranch on the Rogue River in Oregon. She would be happy to let Mario use the place for reducing. He couldn't ride in planes because of a punctured eardrum, so he was driven up there with Betty, his press agent and wife, and a colored butler. Mario wasn't short of will power when the occasion demanded it. For six weeks he held himself down to eating three tomatoes and six eggs a day. Every morning he puffed half a mile each way up and down the road, sweltering in a specially made latex suit. He had to work out alone. The agent sat on the porch of the ranch house with a .22 rifle. Whenever Mario slowed down, a shot would come singing into the roadway by his feet to speed him up again.

He had one more great record, "The Loveliest Night of the Year," and one more miserable movie, *Because You're Mine*, to make before his feud with Metro took on the proportions of nightmare. Much of the blame has to be loaded onto his wife's shoulders. She loved her husband in her own shrill fashion, but she no more knew the greatness in him than she could sing *Aïda*.

She loved the money he made, the house it bought with butler, cook, maids, gardener, chauffeur. She loved the $20,000 mink he bought her, but she couldn't spare the time to listen to his new recordings when he burst into the house with them like an excited schoolboy.

He was wonderful with his own children and every other child. I've seen him romp around his living-room floor by the hour with his family—who are a family of orphans now. He tried to keep one little child alive and failed through no fault of his. Raphaela Fasona of New Jersey was a ten-year-old fan, one of the army of them throughout the Western world whose letters kept Mario's mother, father, and a staff

312

of three others busy answering them. Ray was in the hospital, a victim of Hodgkin's disease. Mario had great compassion for the sick, sent out hundreds of his albums to them. He talked to Ray in person or by telephone every week, sang to her, told her fairy tales.

He brought her with her mother to Beverly Hills one Christmas, gave her a party with stars and their children as guests—Kathryn Grayson, the Ricardo Montalbans, Joe Pasternak, David May, Mrs. Norman Taurog among them. The children chuckled over a puppet show and a magician, and I watched Ray's great luminous brown eyes fill with wonder. When her illness came to its inevitable end, Mario planned a concert in her memory, donating the proceeds for cancer research.

Betty Lanza was a cheerleader in the bleachers that were filled with the stooges who lived off Mario. "You don't have to go to the studio," she used to tell him. "You're too big a name for that now. Make them come to you."

The studio did come to him once more, to make *The Student Prince*, though the bosses were panicky about his weight, which had puffed him out to look more hippopotamus than tiger. I went to his house to get his side of the donnybrook that broke out and kept his name in headlines for months. "I was treated cheap while I was Tiffany. Box-office Tiffany. They gave me the little-boy routine, and I'm not a little boy. They took my advice before. Then when I became a big star, they said: 'We'll take the reins in on this sonofabitch.' "

I could hear all kinds of people talking through his lips as he spoke: his wife, his sycophants, whole generations of stars and the relatives of stars dating back to the days when Hollywood first made dreams of fame and greed come true.

Eddie Mannix, MGM vice president, was a target for Mario's fury. "I told him I'd kill him. He said: 'You wouldn't hit an old man.' I said: 'I'll tie my hands behind my back and fight you with my head.' "

In the middle of the battle Mario took a look into the

books of Marsam Enterprises which agent Sam Weiler had set up with his wife, Selma, as partner to handle Lanza's business affairs. The ledgers showed he had little left. Weiler promptly quit, and Mario subsequently filed suit against him. His memory was kept green in Mario's private gymnasium, a boxing ring under a tent in his garden. Painted on the punching bag was a portrait of Weiler. "I can keep in trim the rest of my life," Mario boasted, "because every time I work out I can beat the daylights out of the sonofagun."

The studio had allotted twelve weeks to cut the recordings for *The Student Prince*. Mario finished the job in two. When he played them over for me, he sat a million miles away, saturated in the music, until the last notes had died. "A critic wrote about me once: 'He sings every note as though it's his last on earth.'" Mario said softly: "It's true. I do. I can't help myself."

The sound track was all he made of *The Student Prince*. He refused to work on the picture after that. He was suspended, then sued for the potential profit on that and future pictures. The figures mentioned in the legal documents were a gargantuan jest to him. "They asked $13,500,000 plus $855,-066.73. Now what I want to know is, what's the seventy-three cents for? I guess Eddie Mannix had his drawers laundered."

He could joke about it in daylight, but darkness brought about a Jekyll and Hyde change. He kept to his house during the day; at night, with his chauffeur-trainer for company, he roved through the streets of Beverly Hills seeking out his enemies. He drove to Joe Pasternak's house to smash the entrance gates off their hinges. Another night he used the Cadillac to batter down Joe's mailbox. And some mornings the men on Mario's black list found he had ridden up to their doorsteps and defecated there.

The rocket had exploded, and the charred stick was tumbling down. A letter from Eddie Mannix, on behalf of Loew's Incorporated, came to Mario: "For good and sufficient reasons your employment under the contract between us is hereby terminated. We shall hold you fully accountable for all damage and loss suffered by us as a result of your actions and conduct; and we expressly reserve all rights of every kind and character acquired by us under said contract." Mario promptly had a banner made to hang in his house: "The Lion is Dead," it proclaimed, "Long Live The Tiger."

I was one of the friends who begged Mario to commit himself to the Menninger Clinic. Once again he tried to strike a bargain with Jack Keller, another friend: if Jack would go with him, Mario would take treatment. But he made the mistake of letting Betty know too soon.

"He's no crazier than you are," she raged at Jack.

"But it's for your happiness as much as his." It was known by now that the Lanzas were on drink and drugs together. Their domestic battles often stopped short of murder only by a hair's breadth. But Betty set her foot down; no trip to Topeka for her husband.

In theory he could still make records, but he was in no shape for singing. He tried and failed repeatedly, his throat shut tight by tension. The Lanzas owed money to everybody, from Goldblatt's delicatessen to Uncle Sam. A psychiatrist familiar with his case had an explanation: "Lanza has lost all touch with reality. He no longer knows who he really is or the personality he wants to be."

His first job after two years of seclusion was a television show, "Shower of Stars," for the Chrysler Corporation. It ended in a furor when he simply mouthed the words to old recordings as they were played off camera. The sponsors had invited reporters from all over the country to come out for the occasion, with supper afterward at the Beverly Hills Hotel.

Mario went straight home after his performance. I went to the party to hear what the reporters had to say. Most of them thought Mario was through. He hadn't even been able to synchronize his lip movements to his recorded voice.

At 12:30 A.M. I drove to his house. He sat in the drawing room with his wife and the Hubbell Robinsons, drinking pink champagne. I'd always been rough with him because I loved him. "What do you think you're doing?" I asked. "Celebrating a wake?"

He leaped to his feet in a white heat of anger. "What do you mean?"

"That's what it was—a wake. I stayed at the party long enough to hear what the reporters had to say."

Suddenly he became a little boy. "What can I do to redeem myself?"

"There's only one answer. Nobody thinks you can sing. Can you?"

"Of course, I can."

"Then tomorrow afternoon you'll invite the reporters here to your house and sing for them. You've got to if you want to save your reputation."

"Will you come? Will you sit where I can sing to you?" I reluctantly said I would. They came, and he sang as only he could when he knew it was a question of success or failure. He saved what was left of his career.

He was booked by his agents, MCA, to appear at the opening of the New Frontier Hotel, Las Vegas, at $50,000 a week. In preparation he forced himself once more on to a heroic diet, worked out religiously with bar bells and exercise machines, submitted to hours of pounding on the massage table, then took off for Vegas with Betty, their children, and his trainer, Terry Robinson, in a total entourage of twelve. The staff at the New Frontier had strict instructions not to let Mario start drinking, come what may. The town's gamblers anticipated trouble; the wise money was eight to five against.

On the afternoon of the opening Louella Parsons went looking for him. Ben Hecht, who was writing a new picture for him, also sought him out. He found Mario in his suite, pale with nerves but dry as a bone. Ben felt like a drink, and a waiter arrived with champagne.

I tried to reach Mario that afternoon but couldn't get near him. I went to his suite and knocked and knocked. I could hear voices inside, but nobody let me in. "I did all the drinking," Ben said later. "When he left me at six o'clock he was O.K. to walk out on any stage and do handsprings. Whether he had desert dust or goofy dust in his throat, I don't know."

He added: "I've never seen a guy suffer so because of what he was doing, whatever that was. Does he always have those soul agonies, or doesn't he give a damn?" And then: "I've listened to his story—some of it funny, most sad. I've heard this same story in this town for thirty years. The minute a guy gets big, people start sitting on his head. I still have complete confidence in the guy."

After he left Ben Hecht in the hotel, Mario disappeared. Half an hour before the show, he staggered back to the New Frontier. There were panicky efforts to revive him. But he passed out cold. A star-flecked audience, including Sonja Henie, Ann Miller, Jack Benny, George Burns, Robert Young, and 150 newsmen, waited for him in vain. The management canceled his contract and sued him for $125,000.

The rest was all exclusively downhill. Beatrice, the Lanzas' colored housekeeper, paid some of the bills out of her salary to hold things together. He desperately tried for work at other studios, but nobody would take a chance on him. So he took up a deal to make a picture in Rome, to give concerts there and elsewhere in Europe, taking his family along. In Rome he rented the fabulous Villa Badaglio, where crystal chandeliers gleamed on statuary and marble floors and old masters decorated the walls.

In London he failed to appear at the Albert Hall concert that had been arranged for him; same thing in Hamburg, where crowds jeered his name. He died in Rome, aged thirty-eight, suffering from phlebitis and a blood clot in a coronary artery. His enormous bulk created some macabre problems for the undertakers. Not long after, when Betty Lanza had brought her children back to Beverly Hills, her mother tried to get her committed for psychiatric care. Betty would listen to no one, any more than she'd listened when Mario's sanity was at stake. There were five more months left before drugs took Betty's life. Love for the man she'd lost? Desperation? The verdict simply said: cause unknown.

All of us, within ourselves, carry the seed of our own destruction. But in some there is an inner core beyond our powers to destroy. Jack Barrymore was one of these. I watched him try to pull himself down. He was a man embittered, disillusioned, broken in health and finances, burlesquing his own genius with a devil's grin. He saw the same public that idolized him in *The Jest, Richard III, Hamlet* shriek with sadistic laughter over his antics on and off the camera.

During a lull on the set one afternoon, some jokester said to him: "Come on, Jack, give us one of your old tear jerkers." He agreed, with a shrug; started hamming Mark Antony's lines from *Julius Caesar*. "Friends, Romans, countrymen . . . My heart is in the coffin there with Caesar, and I must pause till it comes back to me."

After the first few lines something had happened. As the voice steadied and deepened the set grew quiet. Grips, carpenters, electricians, extras approached, soft-footed. When Mark Antony finished, Hamlet took his place. The years fell away and there, on the cluttered sound stage, stood the young Hamlet, the greatest any theater ever knew.

In complete silence Barrymore walked to his dressing room. Then such a storm of applause broke out that the whole stage shook with it. More faces than one were streaked with tears. We knew we had seen an indestructible human spirit fighting its way clear of the dross of a reckless and ill-spent life.

Nineteen

We used to go riding in the moonlight, raising the dust down roads shadowed by palm trees, walking the horses through citrus groves and fields of barley, up into the trackless red hills, where we'd turn to catch a glimpse of the Pacific gleaming like pewter under the night sky. Now cowboys have to learn how to climb into a saddle before they can gallop away into the sunset for another TV horse opera. There are none of the genuine, Bill Hart variety left.

When I first saw Hollywood, Sam Goldwyn was still Goldfish, and a grain store stood on Sunset Boulevard at the corner of Cahuenga. Cecil B. De Mille, looking for some place to produce *The Squaw Man*, had rented a livery stable at Selma and Vine, founding the motion-picture capital, the wonderland that clothed dreams in flesh for millions of the world's inhabitants. Bill Farnum reigned in splendor in a suite at the Hollywood Hotel; I made my movie debut with him, played his leading lady for $100 a week, which was a fortune to me then.

Life was simple, exciting, and, most of all, fun. We worked hard and loved it. People were neighborly, kind, and didn't know the meaning of class distinction—that came later when the big money rolled in and changed everything. We used to borrow sugar, bake cakes for the folks next door, stop by each other's houses to gossip about the wonders of this bouncing new baby, the movie business, and the climate, and the everlasting sunshine. Where is it now? Hidden by fog and smog.

Now the dirty-post-card boys have moved in, churning out pictures reeking of violence, prostitution, perversion, and decay. Anybody can produce a movie—it takes no great talent. Everybody can try to make a quick killing in hard times and the devil with the consequences. Of course, we always knew there were such things as sewers, but never before have audiences had their noses pushed over so many gratings.

A different odor used to hang over our town—the smell of fresh money. It poured from the four corners of the earth like the tide coming in. That's the scent that drew the founders of our industry, a bunch of shrewd dishwashers, nickelodeon proprietors, glove salesmen, dress manufacturers, junk dealers. They knew a good thing when they saw it, and who should worry about tomorrow?

They were freebooters at heart, most of them, set on carving out empires and ruling them like despots. They started by despoiling the land when they lopped down the trees to make room for the shabby warehouses and barns we call studios. My office desk is placed nowadays so that I can turn my back on Hollywood. If I faced the window, the sun would be in my eyes, and I like the sun on my back.

They despoiled the actors and actresses, too, whose names became better known than those of presidents and kings. Money ruined many of the stars, washed over them in a deluge, then left them high and dry when their few working years were over. Lionel Barrymore, for instance, earned a gigantic reputation as director and star, with enough talent left over to make him more than competent in other arts—a water color and two etchings hang in my den, and he was a fine composer, too. But he left very little property behind, and that was seized by federal agents a few hours after his funeral, to be auctioned to pay his income tax.

He lies beside his wife, Irene Fenwick; Jack Barrymore was buried on her other side by Lionel's order. Years before, Jack had been in love with her, but his big brother broke up the romance and later tried to commit suicide. Then Lionel fell in love with her, and to marry her, he left his wife and two sons, both of whom died in their early teens. Few people knew he had children.

320

Studio heads dangled the carrots at contract-signing time and cracked the whip once the ink on the paper was dry. Not so long ago David Selznick was reminiscing about those tightly disciplined days with me: "I've called Jack Barrymore into my office for not knowing his lines; he was contrite and apologetic. I had to speak to Leslie Howard, who was embarrassing Vivien Leigh by not being prepared for the scene. But you never had to speak a second time. They recognized their fault and corrected it."

Garbo was never late. She appeared on the set at 9 A.M. sharp, made up and ready to work and no nonsense. But she was patience itself if an older member of the company had trouble remembering lines. She was considered demanding when she wanted to know who would produce, who co-star, who direct. Once she turned down a story Metro wanted her to make, David remembered, "and they cast her opposite Tim McCoy in a Western as punishment. When Lionel Barrymore heard it, he said: 'That's like cutting Tolstoy's beard so he wouldn't write any revolutionary novels.'"

Now we have Elizabeth Taylor picking up more than $2,000,000 for Cleopatra, jeopardizing the whole future of Twentieth Century-Fox by her behavior, and getting herself proposed for a seat on the board of directors by a disgruntled stockholder. We have Mr. Brando collecting more than a million from Mutiny on the Bounty, plus overtime for every day's delay his antics caused. Selznick calls such ventures "movies of desperation."

"The men who make movies have been digging their own graves," he says. "They'll put up with anything for a transient advantage." They have no long-term concern because they're busy getting dollars for the next statement, watching the effect that statement will have on the company's stock." I second that.

What went wrong with Hollywood? Well, something like this . . .

The founding fathers didn't know what competition was. They had it all their own, undisputed way so long. They hit on something, motion pictures, that the world took to like babies take to candy. The handful of families that ran the big studios made a cozy little clique by intermarriage, bringing in their relatives, sticking together like mustard plasters.

The same men owned the studios, the distributing companies, and many of the biggest movie theaters. Right down the line, they controlled what audiences saw and how much they paid to see it. An independent theater owner in any town at home or abroad either was deprived of the pictures he wanted or else had to accept block booking. To lay hold of, say, a sure-fire Humphrey Bogart picture from Warners, he had to take three others that he'd have to take a chance on.

But a picture had to be a real turkey not to pay its way, at least. If people wanted an evening out, in most cases, they had no place to go except the movies. There's never been a monopoly that brought such sweet rewards to the men who ran it. Radio proved to be no kind of competition. If I paid them enough—and some big stars demanded $5000 to stand up and read a script—I could get virtually anybody I wanted, including Dore Schary, on my weekly show when I crashed into broadcasting. A loud-speaker was no substitute for the screen, where a kind of earthy paradise was on view. Illusion had to be put into pictures, not just into words.

The film factories were organized like an automobile assembly line. They had to be. The demand for movies was insatiable. Our town turned out four, five hundred pictures a year, with close to a thousand actors and actresses under contract. Every year the bosses prepared lavish promotion programs to light a gleam in the exhibitors' eyes, listing the four colossal musicals, the half dozen scintillating comedies, the seven searing dramas, and so forth which the particular studio would deliver in the months ahead. Many times these promises were pure blue sky. They'd invent a title, pencil in the stars, then a team of contract writers would knock out a story. Today no production head can promise what next year will bring because the system's out of his control and he just doesn't know about tomorrow.

On top of the heap sat the Mayers, Schencks, Warners, Goldwyn, most of them ruling like pharaohs, unapproachable by underlings except by invitation. At the next level down, among the producers and directors, came the real pros who kept the wheels aturning. A man like Byrnie Foy, the "Keeper of the B's" at Warners, could look at a script for a Western, rip out a page after a single glance, and order: "Don't have them cross a bridge, or you'll have to build it. Have them cross a gulch and save $20,000."

That's a far cry from *Something's Got to Give*, where Fox watched $2,000,000 disappear down the gutter and all they got for it was some footage of Marilyn Monroe slipping into a swimming pool naked. Most of the old-time professional producers are dead. Our town needs the likes of them the way a burning house needs firemen.

We had directors whom actors and actresses gave their eyeteeth to work for; it was the cracker-jack directors who made the stars. Beginners in grease paint slogged their way up through bit parts in "B" pictures until they'd picked up enough experience for bigger things and better contracts. Sometimes the lightning would strike an actor like Bob Mitchum, glimpsed by Bill Wellman as he strode down Hollywood Boulevard. Bill had G.I. *Joe* to make, didn't fancy Gary Cooper for it because he needed a man with a look of sweat on his skin and the devil inside him. Bill tapped Bob Mitchum for stardom on the spot. Bob, after more than his share of headlines, ranks now as one of our more solid citizens.

Like a ride on a roller coaster, Hollywood reached peak prosperity just before the final dive began. World War II brought in profits that overflowed the tills and burst the bank vaults. It also brought on the first of the catastrophic decisions that wrecked the industry.

A soldier with a precious pass or an off-duty hour to spare, a war worker on the swing shift—the whole world flocked to the movies to escape reality for a few moments. You couldn't produce a picture, any picture, without it turning a handsome profit. So we promptly made the worst claptrap and flung it on the screens.

By way of gratitude toward the men who fought the war, our town let them wander by the thousands around the streets when they drifted in on leave, craning their necks to see a famous face or ready to settle for a pretty one. Aside from limited efforts like the much-publicized Hollywood Canteen, our hospitality was mostly private. Many towns put cots down for GI's to sleep on in town halls and firehouses if they were caught without accommodations for the night. Not us. I campaigned for vacant sound stages to be converted into temporary quarters for our visitors in uniform. For all I achieved, I was talking to myself.

The catastrophe that the studios invited was the death of glamour, which had filled the air we breathed. The stars were asked to stop wearing the golden glow of gods and goddesses and look like plain folks, as homey as apple pie and lawn mowers. You couldn't pick up a magazine without coming across publicity shots of Betty Grable out marketing, Bette Davis washing dishes, or Alice Faye changing diapers. Nobody had ever seen a picture of Dietrich hanging out wet wash or Jack Barrymore in a life-with-father layout. We were busy bringing stars down out of the sky, lousing up the act, cutting our own throats.

Realism strangled the dream stuff, and it's slowly slaughtering Hollywood. I see very little hope unless glamour is given its rightful place again. I believe that audiences wanted it then and want it now. More and more people share that point of view. Jerry Lewis is one of them.

"It wasn't good to take the soft lights off the tinsel," said Jerry. "The days of the stars must return. There's been too much haphazard mingling with the public by the stars. It killed a beautiful illusion, the illusion that helped make Hollywood and picture stars important to the public."

When the GI's came back from the war, the lean years set in for our industry. They'd seen strange sights and found new dreams. They were a restless generation, looking for fresh excitements. They turned to bowling alleys, night baseball, the race tracks. Suddenly there were a whole lot of other things to do besides going to the movies. The money that went for new pastimes used to go into movie-house tills.

They reacted by bumping up admission prices. It didn't help. Instead of a couple being able to see a double feature, cartoons, and a newsreel at thirty-five cents a head, for a first-run picture the tab leaped up to $1.50 and more apiece. Coincidentally, another great American invention had come along in the postwar years, the baby sitter.

Only a handful of households could afford living-in servants after the maids and cooks and butlers had enjoyed a taste of wartime wages on factory assembly lines. It was no longer the thing to do to ask a neighbor to mind the baby while Dad took Mother to the movies. They had to hire a baby sitter at accelerating hourly rates. If Dad stood Mother dinner out somewhere first, a couple of hours watching Luise Rainer knocked the family budget for ten or fifteen dollars. It just wasn't worth that much. The tide on the sea of gold was ebbing fast.

Then the government started huffing and puffing, and the big empires were gone with the wind. What happened was that the independent theater owners, who'd been pushed around for years, finally nudged the Justice Department into declaring that it was illegal under the anti-trust laws for the same organization to make movies, distribute them, and screen them in its own picture palaces.

This was like the Ford Motor Company waking up one morning to find it had lost all its showrooms. Or Fanny Farmer discovering she could cook up her candy but not run the stores she sold it in. The movie makers, who had never smelled real competition up to date, suddenly realized they were in a tougher grind than the cloak-and-suit business ever was.

There was a moment when they could have had another gilt-edged guarantee of money by the billions if they'd had the sense to see it. The early runners of the television industry came on their knees to Hollywood and begged the movie men to help them. "You've got the factories to make the product, we'll get the outlets to show it," they said. "Let's co-operate, and we'll all grow rich."

Oh, but the studio heads were too smart for that! They could have held television in the palms of their hands. Instead they jeered: "Who's going to stay home and watch a little box?" They sneered: "What have you got—women wrestlers and bike races? It's a fad like Yo-yo. It can't last. Movies are better than ever."

Only Paramount sensed the potential in the little boxes when there were no more than half a million of them, with post-card-sized screens, in the country. That studio joined hands with Dr. Allen Du Mont, the pioneer TV scientist, hoping to build a network of Channel Fives. But he was an inventor, not an executive who could put together the necessary hours of daily programming. The idea failed, the network amounted to nothing, and all that Y. Frank Freeman, head of Paramount, could do was watch NBC and CBS forge ahead, while he speculated on what might have been.

The bankers moved deeper and deeper into the faltering movie industry. They had to. They were the people with money to keep it going. They didn't know a thing about it, but they knew a star when they saw one. To a banker, a star looked like the safest bet in a business beset with more hazards than a steeplechase. The studios found out you could always raise the financing if you showed Mr. Moneybags a big enough star and a script the star liked. Independent producers learned the same lesson and flocked around, waving contracts. Directors, cameramen, every other key employee necessary to make good movies—the banks didn't want to hear about them.

The ever-loving agents grabbed hold hard. If the industry lived or died on names like Gable, Brando, Hepburn, and Taylor, then, by crikey, their clients were going to grab the steering wheel from the professional producers and studio heads. The only way the stars could be guaranteed enough money to tempt them to work was to give them a slice of the picture's potential profits on top of salary. The slice grew bigger and bigger and bigger.

In the old days we used to wait impatiently for the studio gates to open at 9 A.M. I couldn't get there soon enough. Nowhere else did you have such fun. You had companions of your own kind to work with, many of them the finest talents in the worlds of the theater, concert platform, fashion salon. On Saturdays and Sundays we'd hurry back to the studios to hear the orchestras record sound tracks with stars of the musicals, or maybe listen to four hundred Negroes sing spirituals for a Lawrence Tibbett picture.

When George Cukor was preparing *The Women*, I was so eager to play in it that I called him on the quiet after Dema Harshbarger had set a price on my head of $1000 minimum, whether for a day's work or a week's. "Confidentially, I'd work for nothing," I told him. A contract was drawn at a cut-down figure and sent to Dema.

She asked me into her office, next to mine. "I'd like to give you a farewell luncheon at some smart place," she said, her dark eyes gleaming bright. "We won't have any unpleasantness, and we'll stay friends, but I don't want any business dealings with you unless you let me set a value on you." I got the point—and a revised contract.

At least two once powerful studios, Fox and MGM, were driven into a corner from which they may never emerge, thanks to the present, overpriced star system. Rome and Madrid today are the temporary movie capitals of the world. Tokyo, London, Paris—all compete for the title. Soaring costs at home push more and more production overseas. The peccadilloes of foot-loose stars and producers who hanker for far-off places favor foreign production. Some countries freeze profits from the screening of American movies, so the money must be used to stake new pictures inside those countries' frontiers. Then, too, the big screen demands the real locations; you can no longer paint a mountain on a piece of glass and make it look like the Rockies.

So pictures like *Lawrence of Arabia* and *Ben-Hur* are made anywhere except in Hollywood. William Holden won't come home from Switzerland for reasons of taxes—and his pictures get picketed by our town's movie unions. Even Tom and Jerry are refugees now. They were made at Culver City before the animation studios were shut five years ago. Now Tom and Jerry are drawn in Italy, Popeye is a Yugoslav sometimes, and Bullwinkle comes to life on drawing boards in Mexico. Walt Disney remains one of the all-Americans.

MGM prayed it would be helped out of its *Mutiny* hole by the oil well that started to flow on the back lot at Culver City at about the time that Brando was stumbling through the final scenes of the picture in Hollywood.

Twentieth Century-Fox went in for sterner stuff, very late in the day. They tried to hurry *Cleopatra* production to a conclusion by cutting off the salary in Rome of Walter Wanger. They fired Marilyn Monroe and sued her for $500,000 for absenteeism from the set of *Something's Got to Give* after she had given five days of performance in seven weeks of shooting.

The Fox counterrevolution against stars found her colleague, Dean Martin, in the line of fire next. He'd promptly announced after Marilyn was dismissed that so far as he was concerned it was Monroe or nobody. He walked out; the picture was shut down. Equally promptly the studio threw a record-breaking suit for $5,678,000 at his head, claiming breach of contract, and Dean's attorneys filed countercharges.

He was no hero to the unions, though they sat back and did nothing. An official said to me: "He's putting people out of work at a time when we're all faced with unemployment due to runaway production. He's certainly demonstrating his unconcern for his co-workers."

When a star got out of line, the crew used to have a peculiar way of handling the situation. Jack Barrymore would be performing his heart out when out of the blue a crystal chandelier came crashing down, missing his head by inches. If his behavior didn't improve, the next one fell even closer.

If the handful of stars still left to us disappears, who will replace them? Who's in sight to give Hollywood the color and excitement that it needs to live? Where are the newcomers to be discovered and how can they be trained? The answers, so far as the eye can see, are Nobody and Nowhere. Opera has been stirred by new names in the past decade—Joan Sutherland, Birgit Nilsson, Maria Callas. The concert stage has its Van Cliburns. Politics has its Kennedys and Nixons. The movies have virtually nothing at the top except the same names that were shining in lights ten years ago—Bob Hope, Burt Lancaster, Cary Grant, John Wayne, Jimmy Stewart and the rest politely called "middle aged."

Television's no better off. The surge of talent there was mostly in writers and directors—Rod Serling, Delbert Mann, and others—who subsequently migrated to Hollywood. But the surge is about over. The TV networks pretend to foster young talents. But do they?

They got going on their own account when Hollywood turned them down as partners, then was compelled to sell its old movies to them to raise cash to keep the studios open. The young, untried talents who came out of the war swarmed like flies into TV. They couldn't find a place in the movie industry or in the Broadway theater. Early television was like early movie making all over again, a great adventure filled with fun but not much money; a wonderful place for experiment and experience, because everybody could afford to make mistakes.

The networks needed that mysterious thing called programming, meaning a dependable timetable of big hits and steady features, spectaculars blended with *Lassie*. Without programming, they couldn't get TV sets sold, and a network like NBC, owned by RCA, was primarily in business not to entertain its audiences but to sell sets.

NBC programming was in the hands of Pat Weaver, a farsighted pioneer at his business with a special, rare ability to spend other people's money without being frightened by the cost. Before he departed network headquarters in Rockefeller

Center, he had brought in "Wide, Wide World," Groucho Marx, Milton Berle, Sid Caesar.

CBS had an executive, too, in Hubbell Robinson, who also ran a good store. ABC had its problems as the little brother fighting to break into a situation where its rivals divided most of the country between themselves. But along came men like Bob Kintner, Oliver Treyze, Tom Moore, and Dan Melnick. They took a backward look at what Warner Brothers had done when they had to crack open a similar situation in the movies and the big studios closed ranks against them.

Jack and Harry Warner, with stars like Bogart and Cagney on the payroll, broke in with action pictures, with gang bullets flying and fists swinging in every reel. ABC copied a leaf from that book. Never had such a volley of blank bullets resounded over the land before. Critics threw up their hands in horror, but ABC arrived with a bang and stayed there.

It's a tragedy of the entertainment industry that the networks were as blind to the future needs of their business as the movie makers had been to theirs. Like Pharaoh, the television tycoons let the people go; the big talents left when the money wasn't put up to keep them together. The tycoons thought *they* made television, not the writers, directors, and producers. They wouldn't dream of setting up a studio system, a great pool of brains that could have made NBC or CBS or ABC the biggest creator there ever was of entertainment and the lively arts. They put no funds aside for research, as General Motors, Westinghouse, Du Pont and the others do.

Now TV by and large has become a dime-store business so far as creativity and talent are concerned. The half-hour and sixty-minute series rattle off the production lines like cans of beans, with an occasional dab of ham inside. If the finished film doesn't make sense, no matter. If the kid with the six-shooter can't act to save his mother's life, who cares?

The idea is that if enough people are watching, some of the advertisers' message will rub off on them to make the series worth while. But if enough people stop watching the stuff that's put on their screens, then commercial television faces a similar fate to the movies, in spite of color sets or tomorrow's gimmicks such as giant screens to hang on your living-room wall.

I believe the only possible solution for television and movies alike is a recognition of the eternal values of real talent, excitement, and glamour. Audiences are starved for all three. Entertainment must be a satisfying emotional experience, a stirring of the heart. We need all kinds of young men and women. Those people with an artist's eye and an executive's brain that we term directors. Those wrestlers with their souls and typewriters known as authors. The beggars on horseback called actors and actresses.

Hollywood is my home, and most of my friends live there. I like to travel sometimes, but I find scenery as a diet doesn't nourish me. So I intend to stick around and watch what happens, remembering a few more words from the plaque that stands on my desk:

I do the very best I know how—the very best I can; and I mean to keep doing so until the end. If the end brings me out all right, what is said against me won't amount to anything. If the end brings me out wrong, ten angels swearing I was right would make no difference.